Shooter's Bible
GUIDE TO
PLANTING
FOOD PLOTS

Shooter's Bible
GUIDE TO
PLANTING
FOOD PLOTS

A Comprehensive Handbook on Summer, Fall, and Winter Crops to Attract Deer to Your Property

PETER FIDUCCIA

SKYHORSE PUBLISHING

Skyhorse Publishing books may be purchased in bulk at special discounts for sales promotion, corporate gifts, fund-raising, or educational purposes. Special editions can also be created to specifications. For details, contact the Special Sales Department, Skyhorse Publishing, 307 West 36th Street, 11th Floor, New York, NY 10018 or info@skyhorsepublishing.com.

Skyhorse® and Skyhorse Publishing® are registered trademarks of Skyhorse Publishing, Inc.®, a Delaware corporation.

www.skyhorsepublishing.com

10 9

Library of Congress Cataloging-in-Publication Data

Fiduccia, Peter.
  Shooter's bible guide to planting food plots : a comprehensive handbook on summer, fall, and winter crops to attract deer to your property / Peter Fiduccia.
       pages cm
  ISBN 978-1-62087-090-7 (alk. paper)
  1. Deer--Food. 2. Planting design. 3. Backyards. 4. Deer hunting. I. Title.
  QL737.U55F52 2013
  639.97'965--dc23

                                  2013001092

ISBN: 978-1-62087-090-7

Printed in China

To Kate and Cody, my treasured hunting partners, valued land and wildlife stewards, and best friends. I cherish the time we spend together playing in the dirt on our farm.

CONTENTS

Introduction

I wrote this book for deer hunters who aspire to plant more productive food plots, wildlife managers and land stewards. This book is not targeted to professional biologists or experienced land or ranch managers. Rather, it is meant to help the *typical* deer hunter improve his or her deer sightings, hunting opportunities, and other wildlife management skills, goals, and experiences.

The book doesn't contain hard-to-decipher information. Instead, it is a basic, practical guide written as most of my books are: in a common-sense way that provides solid information that is both easy to understand and apply. Within its pages I share wide-ranging advice with readers about what it *actually* requires to plant food plots successfully and improve their deer herd and deer hunting.

I would guess that many of you purchased this book because your *primary* goal is to see more deer and to harvest bucks with bigger antlers on the lands you hunt. Along with those elements, many of you have a secondary objective and that is to become better food plot planters and wildlife managers.

Professional and experienced wildlife and food plot managers are extremely knowledgeable about the "how-to" aspects of achieving management objectives. The average hunter is hungry for sound, easy-to-understand advice and ideas and therefore they will tend to benefit most from the information shared in this book. I'm confident this book will help you to grow consistently successful plantings that will provide nutritional value to deer and other wildlife. Equally important, I trust it will provide you with more deer sightings on each hunt and better buck and doe hunting opportunities for many deer seasons to come.

Peter Fiduccia
New Berlin, New York
December 17, 2012

1. Introduction to Food Plots

As I mentioned in the Introduction, this book is meant to provide time-tested advice and guidelines to help deer hunters develop a sound deer management program on lands they own or lease. Through a combined management program, deer managers ensure themselves a healthier deer herd, better fawn survival, an older age class of bucks with larger antlers, a noticeable increase in rut activity and deer sign, more daily deer sightings, and better harvest success of deer and other game.

The planting of a variety of quality food plots has unquestionably become *the* most sought after information by hunters. Over the last decade, magazines and many television programs have carried articles or programming on the subject. Not long ago, planting food plots for deer was nearly unheard of. Today, that is definitely not the case. The subject is of primary interest to hunters across North America. It is regularly discussed in a wide variety of forums including the Internet, local sport shops, hunting clubs, sport shows, and at deer camps. It is almost virtually impossible to find an outdoorsman who doesn't know about the benefits of planting food plots.

I planted my first clover food plot in 1988 in a small quarter-acre field long before planting food plots became the popular strategy it is today. Back then I had no idea that in order for clovers and other legumes to grow healthy and produce a high yield, they needed to be inoculated with the proper live bacteria culture before planting. Without such inoculation, these plants could never reach their full growing and nutritional potential.

There weren't very many sources a novice could refer to in the mid-'80s when it came to planting food plots for wildlife. Texts that were available were much too difficult to understand and were scientifically written and hard to make much sense of by anyone other than a botanist or a biologist. Those days are long over. Today, anyone can learn how to plant successful food plots. They key is to understand all aspects about the subject prior to planting the first seeds.

As most hunters realize, deer have been attracted to farm crops since the earliest Native Americans planted and grew fields of maize (corn). From that time on, deer and other wildlife have enjoyed dining on all types of agricultural crops from alfalfa to zucchini planted by farmers throughout North America. Today, hunters plant a wide variety of food plots in tens of thousands of acres across North America, specifically for deer, turkey, and other wildlife. This once-unheard-of practice now takes substantial overgrazing pressure off farm crops from the state of Florida to the province of British Columbia.

Rise of an Industry

Deer managers and hunters caught on so fast to the benefits of planting food plots that an entire industry took hold. Today there are *countless* companies in the outdoor industry and outside of it that produce a mind-boggling variety of seeds and related food plot-type products. They offer an almost unimaginable assortment of seeds, fruit, mast and other trees, minerals, vitamins, flavored attractants, trail cameras, ATV planting equipment, consulting services, lime, fertilizers, soil analyses, testing equipment, inoculants, plot deterrents, tractors and planting implements, hand-held spreaders, soil testers and kits, herbicides, books, DVDs, and the list goes on.

Once a tiny segment of the outdoor industry, the manufacturing of products related to wildlife seeds and similar products has grown exponentially over the last two decades. All of which were thankfully the genesis of better deer management and deer hunting opportunities from Alabama to the southern edges of the Yukon.

▲ Over the last decade, clover food plots (like the one in which this doe is standing) have become a major part of many deer hunters' strategies. Photo courtesy: Ted Rose.

▲ This 3-acre cornfield on our farm regularly attracts deer from late September through October.

QDMA

At this point I would be completely negligent if I didn't mention and pay tribute to the organization and company that brought forward the genesis of the most important and profound philosophies of deer management and wildgame food plot revelation to the forefront of hunters throughout North America. They relentlessly lead the way with unwavering resolve in making deer management and the commercialization of the food plot seed industry common ideas among millions of deer hunters. The two men responsible are Ray Scott, founder and president of the Whitetail Institute of North America (Vice Presidents Steve and Wilson Scott currently carry out all aspects of the day-to-day operations), and Joe Hamilton, the founder of the Quality Deer Management Association (QDMA), which CEO Brian Murphy now heads.

Through their innovative management, leadership, and marketing and their entire staffs of professionals, they made deer management and planting wildlife seeds into an industry. I strongly suggest that any-

▲ Whitetail Institute Founder and President Ray Scott checks a planting. Photo courtesy: Whitetail Institute.

one dedicated to becoming better land stewards and wildlife managers through the proper enhancement of improving the land become a member of QDMA. Visit their website for more information at www.QDMA.com. And for those who are interested in gleaning top-notch information on everything about planting a variety of nutritious food plots to benefit the overall health of deer and other wildlife, I suggest visiting www.whitetailinstitute.com. It is a wise move that will pay big dividends from the information you will pick up.

Reality Check

Before going any further, it is time for a reality check. Anyone who believes they can *simply* throw some clover on the ground and it will provide better deer and more successful hunting, particularly for bucks with larger antlers, are fooling themselves right out of the starting gate. To be successful at managing deer and planting wildlife seeds, one needs to develop a *well-organized management and food plot plan* that includes several balanced elements within the program. It should also include *all* aspects of improving the health of a deer herd. When planned correctly, such a program will ultimately end in a healthier deer herd, a significant increase in daily deer sightings afield, and opportunities to bag more mature bucks sporting larger antlers. Those who plan carefully and strive for such goals eventually become more knowledgeable about all aspects of deer biology, behavior, ecology, and hunting strategies. Inevitably, they evolve into seasoned land and wildlife stewards and consistently successful deer hunters.

2. Planning a Food Plot Program

*I*t doesn't matter if you own, lease, or even hunt public land; there are ways to improve the food sources for your deer, turkey, bear, waterfowl, and other wildlife. It doesn't require a lot of brains or brawn, but it does require other commitments. All you need to start is a good foundation of deer and land management knowledge. It is also very important to begin with a realistic understanding of your investment in time, money, and willingness to work. Planting food plots and enhancing natural vegetation will improve the overall health, weight, antler growth, fawning, deer sightings, and, most importantly for most deer managers, the harvest rate of deer on your land.

There are many benefits to creating a management program on huge tracts of leased or owned lands that

▲ Photo courtesy: Ted Rose.

are 1,000 acres or more. There is no denying that large parcels of property are more conducive to developing a more pronounced long-term, year-round food plot program. Big parcels are certainly much easier to attract and are prone to keep deer on lands of enormous acreage. Very large parcels also protect immature bucks from being shot too early and therefore yield an older age class of buck more quickly than smaller managed parcels do.

However, the reality is that an overwhelming number of hunters who want to develop a deer management program that includes food plots on their leased or owned lands have property that is more likely to be between 50 and a few hundred acres than 1,000 acres or more. The fact is a wildlife management plan can be very successful on smaller properties. Recent research confirms that most hunters who have undertaken such a program own an *average* of about 135 acres.

On properties of average size, it is easy to see that the neighbor's lands heavily influence your deer movement and harvest rates, as the deer's home range (which is about 640 acres) will also include land owned particularly by neighbors who border your property. That is a fact you must accept and contend with. But that doesn't mean you can't attract and keep deer from the neighbor's lands by creating a sound planting program, particularly one that utilizes traditional food plots as well as a variety of fruit and nut trees that none of the neighbors or hunting clubs grow. However, it is helpful and important that you try to enlist the cooperation of neighbors that border your land as well as those neighbors who have property close to your land to also become seriously involved in a wildlife management and food plot program.

Weigh All Contemplations

As I mentioned earlier, developing a successful food plot program on large or small tracts of land entails a well-thought-out plan. A wildlife management program is an agenda that combines crucial elements including improving habitat; protecting yearling bucks; managing the numbers of female deer; strict harvesting guidelines; creating a sanctuary; careful monitoring of all aspects of your program; and planting the right food plots to attract deer to your land when you want them there. All of this and more will help you to improve the overall health and nutrition of your fawns, yearling,

▲ Improving natural vegetation along with planting food plots helps produce healthier deer like this dandy buck. Photo courtesy: Ted Rose.

desire to plant seeds that will provide deer nutrition year-round? Or do you want to develop a program that is more designed to attract deer mostly during deer season? Not surprisingly, most hunters tell me they want to plant food plots so they can improve their hunting opportunities during the deer season.

Food Plots

Large plots function better as feeding plots. They are not as susceptible to heavy grazing by deer as the smaller plots are. Some plantings in small plots are often overgrazed before they can mature. For instance, when we first bought our farm, we planted *3 acres* of soybeans in one large food plot. The deer ate the entire planting long before the soybeans had time to mature. We had the same problem with other plantings including lab-lab, cowpeas, and burgundy bean. It became apparent to us that the 45 agricultural acres of fields on our 192 acres was not sufficient enough to grow several plots of these types of plantings. To avoid the deer eating them to the ground before they would get enough time to grow to maturity, the plots would have to be no less than four to five acres each.

We decided to plant our food plots with different types of plantings that didn't require that much acreage in order to allow the plants to grow to their fullest potential. Our larger plots now average a half acre in size—however, a majority of our plots are about a quarter-acre, with many smaller than that. Through trial and error, we discovered by including more late maturing plants (like a variety of brassicas and late-planted small grains), the deer left them alone long enough for the plants to reach maturity and be viable from fall into winter. One of the more successful food plots we have is sugar beets. Each year we plant a field that is 1 acre of sugar beets. The deer ignore them until much later in the year.

and adult deer—and it will significantly increase your hunting opportunities. It also improves the quality of your land.

Decide What Your Goals Are

Before you start to plant, you must first decide what your *main* purpose is in growing wildlife food plots. Do you have the time, equipment, money, and

◄ We planted this 3-acre field of sunflowers to provide summer nutrition for turkeys and other wildlife, and fawning cover for deer.

▲ I have found BuckLunch to provide affordable sugar beet seeds that grow dependably when used as directed. Photo courtesy: BuckLunch.

Hunting Plots

Our hunting plots, however, are specifically designed to be smaller in size and shape and are more secluded or at least less visible than our food plots. The hunting plots we plant range in size from less than a quarter acre to about one-half acre. In these plots, we mostly plant crops that are considered to be cool-season fall to winter hardy plants. They are perused by deer from October through January. Some types of plants that will attract deer during the season include forage rape, kale, groundhog radish, turnips, sugar beets, Swede (rutabaga), winter wheat, white and red clovers, chicory, and other cold season or winter-hardy plantings.

Fall plantings include seeds that can be planted from early spring to late summer. These types of plants assure managers that deer will be using the plots when they want them there most—during the hunting season. So it is easy to see and understand why I mentioned above that the first step in planning food plots is to decide if they will be used as general feeding plots year-round or food plots that will provide needed forage from November to January when deer need the nutrition most and when it will help improve

▲ This brassica was planted in a 1/4–acre food plot that attracted deer through the late-December season.

your hunting opportunities. The astute manager plans for his plots to be at least 1 to 10 percent of the overall acreage he owns. This is crucial if your intent is to keep deer around during hunting season or at least using your property year-round.

Where to Place Feeding and Hunting Food Plots

In this case, one of the more crucial aspects of planting food plots—particularly your hunting food plots—is to determine exactly where they should be planted to provide maximum sightings of deer. As with most hunting, the prevailing wind direction is always a key factor in hunting success. No matter what type of terrain your land encompasses, it will have a "usual" or prevailing direction from which the wind is blowing.

Keep in mind, however, that a prevailing wind can be affected by topography, causing it to blow in odd and even entirely different directions than normal. Therefore, planting a food plot close to a significant topographic change can affect a prevailing wind direction. Wind directions also change according to the time of the year, so the savvy food plot planter should test his potential food plot locations in the fall *prior* to planting the plots to accurately determine how the wind will blow that time of year.

Once you establish the prevailing winds, your next concern will be to find where the deer will enter each

▲ This 1/2-acre plot of clovers and brassicas was planted in a field with a prevailing northwest wind. Deer are commonly seen in it. Photo courtesy: Ted Rose.

plot you plant from other points on your land. This may be a path along a fence row or an edge line or from a swamp, thicket, or open woods. Once you determine each deer entry point to a particular plot design, make sure it takes full advantage of a favorable wind direction of your hunting stand to help maximize your hunting success.

3. Soil, Lime, and Fertilizer

Soil Fertility

Acidity of soil is one of the most important factors behind high-quality soil fertility. It affects all soil properties including the chemistry, biological activity, and structure. Correcting soil acidity or alkalinity will improve your wild game food plots dramatically. To become a more informed food plot manager, one must understand the basic fundamentals of soil fertility and what soil elements provide to all types of vegetation. All plants need thirteen different elements to grow heartily. The elements are divided into two groups: *macronutrients* and *micronutrients*. Each group contains particular elements in either greater or lesser amounts.

Most nutrients come from weathered rocks that have become "parent material" and eventually particles. Organic matter supplies many of the same nutrients plus nitrogen, which hardly ever occurs in mineral form. Organic matter develops from the remains of plants and animals that hold many different chemical elements in their cells. As the organic matter is broken down by microorganisms, the elements are returned to the soil. Nutrients can also be commonly applied to the soil as fertilizer and limestone. Nutrients must dissolve in the soil water before plant roots can absorb them.

The macronutrient group requires the *most* amount of elements including Nitrogen (N), Phosphorus (P), Potassium (K), Calcium (Ca), Magnesium (Mg), and Sulfur (S).

The micronutrient group includes *small* or *trace* amounts of elements that are also important to healthy plant growth. They include Iron (Fe), Manganese (Mn), Copper (Cu), Zinc (Zn), Boron (B), Molybdenum (Mo), and Chlorine (Cl).

All plant growth requires these elements in various degrees in the soil to grow well.

A Tip to Help Remember the Elements

An easy way to recall all the *essential* elements needed for healthy plant growth and development is to remember the phrase "See Hopkins café managed by mein cousins Moe and Clyde Nico."

The nutrients included in the mnemonic phrase are:

C carbon
H hydrogen
O oxygen
P phosphorus
K potassium
N nitrogen
S sulfur
Ca calcium
Fe iron
Mg magnesium
B boron
Mn manganese
Cu copper
Zn zinc
Mo molybdenum
Cl chlorine
Ni nickel
Co cobalt

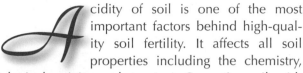

◄ Rocks eventually weather over long periods of time and ultimately provide much-needed nutrients found in soil.

Soil pH

The pH of soil has a big effect on soil chemistry. Either acidity or alkalinity can quickly bind nutrients at once. Improper pH is the most common cause for nutrients present in the soil to be absent in soil solution. Once that occurs, the nutrients are basically out of reach of the plant's root systems. Acidic soil is often referred to as "sour soil" because matter that is acidic often tastes sour. Alkaline soils are commonly called "sweet soil" because it is the opposite of acidic soils, but it does not taste sweet. The ideal pH range is 6.5 to 7.0. Depending on the plant's sensitivity to the pH, even a small drop from 7.0 to 6.5 can alter the soil conditions from perfect to sufficient.

Soil Acidity and Alkalinity (pH)

A pH level is an appraisal of the amount of hydrogen (H+) ions present in soil that can react to other elements. The term pH is defined as the "power of Hydrogen." Soil pH is the measure of the *acidity* or *alkalinity* in the ground. The soil pH scale has a common range from 0 to 14. A pH of 7.0 is considered neutral. Since the pH levels of soil are not fixed, they can be altered. If a soil pH needs to be *raised,* lime must be applied. If it needs to be *lowered,* commercial fertilizers must be applied.

The pH is a measurement of soil acidity that positively or negatively affects plant growth. A soil's pH level directly affects a plant's *nutrient* intake. Lime is used to *neutralize* acidic soil along with depositing nutrients like calcium and magnesium into the soil. The speed at which lime works to neutralize the acidity in soil is dependent relative to the condition of the elements in the lime used and, more particularly, to exactly how acidic the soil is. The smaller the particles are in the lime, the faster it will be absorbed into the soil. It is best not to apply lime without first taking a soil sample; applying too much lime to a plot may be as bad as adding too little.

The exact amount of lime required can only be accurately determined by having a soil test analyzed by a reliable soil testing laboratory. Most county extension offices offer this service. I send my soil samples to Cornell Cooperative Extension office. They charge

▲ If your budget doesn't allow for several soil samples to be professionally analyzed, use a quality soil tester like this.

▲ Building Whitetailed Paradise™ provides a quick and reliable soil test analysis for a minimal fee.

a fee per sample and I have total confidence in their analysis. However, there are countless other reliable labs around the country. A county extension agent in any area can provide a list of the labs farmers and landowners use most in a particular region.

Number of Soil Samples

Many people are surprised to discover soil samples may differ considerably from one location to another. In fact, there can be a change in a pH reading from one sample taken in a plot to another that is less than fifty yards away. To get the most accurate reading from each food plot, take a few soil samples from each plot. In the event that the soil analysis demonstrates a *low* pH level, lime and certain fertilizer blends are a "must-do" to grow a successful food plot. But remember, lime takes months to get the pH (Phosphorus, Potassium, Calcium, Magnesium) levels higher. Fertilizers take much less time to be absorbed into the ground.

Lime is available in many forms, including crushed limestone, powder, and pellets. Although each food plot manager will have a preference as to the type of lime he likes to use, I use pellets. They are more expensive to purchase, but they are much quicker and easier to apply into the soil. Powered lime will adjust the pH levels the fastest, however. For those managers who have to eliminate acidic soils, powdered lime may be the correct choice.

▲ My son, Cody, and wife, Kate, take a third sample from a 1/2-acre food plot. Taking a few samples from one plot provides a more reliable soil analysis.

When using powdered lime, remember to try to apply it to the plots on *windless* days. If it is applied on windy days, some of the lime will be blown away—wasting time and money. Powdered lime also gets all over clothing, machinery, and, worse—it may get into your lungs. For best results when applying lime, spread it as evenly as possible throughout the plot on the surface of the soil. You can also lightly disk it one-half inch under the soil.

Commercial Test Kits

Commercial test kits are available in most feed and grain stores and other farm outlet stores. They are not as accurate as pH tests done in a certified lab, but if your budget doesn't allow for you to send several samples to be analyzed at a lab, home kits can be helpful in evaluating pH levels.

Soil Conclusion

Getting soil tested before you plant is a *crucial* element to food plot success. Many novice food plot planters ignore taking soil readings because they either believe it is hard to do, is an annoyance, or too costly. As noted above, it is none of these. Taking soil samples is a quick and easy procedure, and getting the samples analyzed is well worth the money spent..

Gathering soil samples can take some time and planning, however, particularly if you're taking samples from many different food plots. *Plan accordingly* by allowing enough time to collect samples as early in the spring as possible. Be sure to send them out for analysis in a timely manner. By following this advice, you will have enough time to get the pH and other results back from the laboratory *before* you plant your plots.

Tools Needed

*   narrow spade
*   small bucket
*   small garden hand spade
*   old teaspoon
*   indelible black felt pen
*   several small Ziploc bags

To take an accurate soil sample, one needs to take a few samples of soil from each plot to be planted. Use a thin spade to dig about a few inches into the soil, deep enough to get a sample of where the root zone will exist. Place the soil sample in a small bucket and break it up until it is mixed thoroughly. You don't need a lot of soil from each hole; the lab doesn't need more than a couple of teaspoons' worth to get an accurate analysis. Place each sample into a separate Ziploc bag, mark the bag with the exact location and name of the plot it was taken from, and seal it completely.

Special Note:

Many hunters think they can throw down several bags of lime on a plot with a low pH reading before planting to immediately raise the pH levels. Unfortunately, they soon discover to raise a soil's pH level, it takes a considerable amount of time for lime to be absorbed by the soil. If the soil requires a lot of lime—one to four tons per acre—it is crucial to apply the lime at *least* six weeks or more before planting your seeds and putting in fertilizer.

If you are only liming very small plots of a half acre or less, lime can be added close to the time of planting. However, it is important to apply enough lime even on small plots.

▲ Here are the tools needed to take soil samples. The bag is clearly marked with the name of the field from which the sample was taken.

▼ In March, my cousin, Leo, and son, Cody, prepare 300 pounds of lime to increase the pH in a 1/2-acre plot.

On large plots, depending on how low the pH reading actually is, it can take from 2,000 to 3,000 or more pounds of lime *per acre* to raise a soil's low pH level. It takes a few months for the soil to benefit from an application of lime. As mentioned above, to help the soil absorb lime more quickly, the soil should always be tilled thoroughly after the lime is applied. There are sites on the web that have online calculators to help determine exactly how much lime must be applied to a plot by entering the levels of the low pH reading.

Fertilizer 101

The sure-fire way to assure that a food plot will not grow to its maximum potential is to ignore that a plant requires fertilizer to grow healthy. All living organisms, including plants, require some form of nutrition to develop well. Most often, when a food plot manager has complications growing crops, it's usually due to a lack of planning to include fertilizer as a component in their food plot program.

Most times, fertilizer is applied and turned under the soil long before seeds are planted in the plot. A second application, often referred to as a top-dressing, should be applied at planting to increase a plant's production.

If food plots are afflicted by nutrition deficits, plot managers will quickly run into trouble. When plants lack nutrition, the result is a noticeable decline in their overall growth pattern. Once this happens, it is difficult for the plant to recover and regenerate. When a plant lacks the needed amount of nutrition, it quickly sets off a domino effect that begins with vulnerability to stress. This is particularly true when it comes to the plant tolerating extreme weather conditions. Lack of quality nutrition weakens the crop's natural immunity, making it much more vulnerable to stunted growth, a poor yield, disease, and insect infestation.

Therefore, it is essential for deer managers to pay close attention to their food plot's nutritional fertilizer needs to assure a long-term successful food plot program. Since plants naturally remove nutrients from the soil on a daily basis, the loss of these nutrients must be replaced if the plant is to grow healthy and have a good yield.

The way to accomplish healthy food plots is to provide each planting with the specific type of rec-ommended mineral fertilizer it requires and in the proper quantity. Once again, there are key elements needed to help plantings grow at their maximum levels. Managers should provide them with nitrogen, phosphorus, and potassium, often referred to as N-P-K. (The first number of the three elements always represents the percentage of nitrogen, the second stating the amount of phosphorus, and the third the percentage of potassium.)

Only a lab analysis can accurately determine exactly what a particular food plot will need in N-P-K. Reliable labs have typical amounts of N-P-K for a variety of crops. It is also wise to let the lab know what and when you are planting in each food plot when you send them your soil samples.

Some plants require much more fertilizer than others because certain crops remove more nutrients from the soil than other plants. One that comes to mind is alfalfa. While alfalfa is a top-notch crop for deer managers to grow, it needs constant attention and care to flourish. If alfalfa was a woman, people would say that she required high maintenance. The fact is alfalfa is a crop that does require *very* high maintenance indeed. So much so, I stopped planting it on my farm and replaced it with bird's-foot trefoil. Bird's-foot is a crop that requires much less care than alfalfa does while still providing deer and other wildlife with the high-yielding, nutritious forage benefits of alfalfa.

One notable disadvantage to alfalfa is that it draws enormous amounts of potassium from the soil, as much as 450 or more pounds a year. Since alfalfa has such a dramatic need for nutrients, it isn't the best choice for those managers who plant small plots or have limited time and money to spend on their plantings. Furthermore, on a small plot, alfalfa can draw an estimated 100 pounds of phosphorus and 400 pounds of nitrogen for a one-acre planting. You can see what I meant about alfalfa being a high-maintenance crop. When alfalfa is not regularly fertilized with the correct amounts of nitrogen and phosphorus, it will decline and eventually die off, leaving a weed bed in its place.

It becomes easy to see how important it is to provide the proper mixes of fertilizer for a variety of plants. Each fertilizer provides a mix of nitrogen, phosphorus, and potassium. For instance, many forage plants benefit from using a fertilizer called Triple-19, more commonly referred to as T-19. Triple-19 contains 19 percent nitrogen, 19 percent phosphorus, and 19 percent potassium. Another example would be 10-10-10; it contains 10 percent nitrogen, 10 percent phosphorus, and 10 percent potassium. Therefore, when a deer plot manager needs a particular blend of fertilizer, these names and blends make it easier for a manager to figure out exactly what each fertilizer contains.

It is important to note here, prices rise and fall in accordance with the price of fuel. Depending upon the size of your plots, fertilizer can be a significant out-of-pocket expense in the maintenance of forage crops to benefit deer and other wildlife. Frequently, cost is given as the prime reason why food plot man-

agers don't fertilize their plantings with the correct amounts—or, in some cases, at all. Food plot managers can save money on fertilizer applications if they *compare* the total cost of applying different fertilizer blends before purchasing them.

Rarely do crops need the three primary nutrients on a one-to-one-to-one basis. That means you may only need to apply one or two of the nutrients needed instead of three. Purchasing fertilizers individually, particularly in bulk amounts, can often save lots of money for food plot managers. That's why it is highly recommended that you take a soil test analysis first to determine the crop's exact fertilizer needs for nutrients and the rates at which those nutrients should be applied. There is absolutely no doubt that a soil test is *the best way* to determine the *exact* nutrient needs of a

▼ One-acre plots often require 300 to 400 pounds of fertilizer. Here, I am using 100 pounds of T-19 for a quarter-acre plot.

▲ When transporting several bags of fertilizer to our fields, we use an ATV to make the hauling easier.

soil. Soil tests will provide accurate information about the nutrient levels of the soil and the amounts of lime and fertilizers necessary to achieve a particular yield goal.

Nitrogen (N)

Nitrogen is part of the three essential soil minerals called N-P-K. Nitrogen aids plants in photosynthesis and their ability to produce amino acids. When a plant's leaves begin to turn yellow, this color indicates a lack of nitrogen in the soil. Other signs of a nitrogen deficiency in the soil usually show up in a plant when it grows slowly or becomes stunted.

Nitrogen occurs through the slow process of plant and animal life decomposition in the soil. That is why season food plot managers always include plant species like a variety of clovers, legumes, and other plants that fix nitrogen on their root nodules, thereby replenishing nitrogen naturally into the soil. In addition to these plants depositing nitrogen into the soil, land managers should also plan to add nitrogen to the soil. Some food plots will require at least one application of nitrogen during the growing season, and other plants may need additional applications. In any event, the savvy land manager pays particular attention to applying nitrogen to his food plots. A top dressing of nitrogen is particularly advantageous to grasses to enhance growth.

Phosphorus (P)

Phosphorus is also an important nutrient. Plant life is very dependent on having the proper levels of phosphorus to achieve a healthy root structure that aids plants in drawing water and other nutrients from the soil to promote rapid stem growth, buds, seed pods, etc. Since deer eat plant parts, they regularly contribute to the loss of phosphorus in the soil during the entire time the plant is growing. If a plant's growth becomes stunted, or its leaves turn a maroon color, these signs should set off a "red flag" to land managers, as they indicate a surefire phosphorus deficiency

in their food plots. Wise land managers will regularly include phosphorus applications to their plantings to ensure healthier plant growth. Knowing how much phosphorus to use and when to apply it is solely determined by a soil test analysis. Phosphorus is a crucial nutrient for deer (particularly mature deer), which accumulate phosphorus within their bones. For male deer, phosphorus is essential for antler development.

▼ Cody is fertilizing a small strip plot of turnips with a top dressing of 100 pounds of ammonium sulfate and a tiny amount of boron.

Potassium (K)

Potassium, along with other elements, helps a plant in many ways. It's critical in photosynthesis; it helps the plant retain moisture and provides production of protein. Potassium helps a plant build resistance to disease. The protein is essential to a buck's antler growth and development, which is a primary concern for most if not all deer and food plot managers. Potassium also helps regulate a deer's body fluids and their nerve and muscle function. A top dressing of potassium is usually applied to legumes to help give the plants a boost.

How Much to Apply

It is important to know that fertilizer application is always calculated on a per-acre basis. There are 43,560 square feet in an acre. To determine how much fertilizer, lime, and even seed should be applied to a particular plot, the area must first be measured. When it comes to putting lime and fertilizer in the soil or when planting seeds, remember that applying too much can be as harmful as applying too little.

How to Determine Calculation Rates

To determine the square footage of a plot properly, start by measuring its width and length. Let's say a plot is 225 feet long by 110 feet wide. Simply multiply the length and the width. In this sample, it would be 24,750 square feet. Take that figure and divide it by 43,560 and you will get a figure of 0.568181818 or 0.57 acres.

Use this formula when determining how much fertilizer and lime should be applied according to a soil analysis. Also use the same formula to conclude exactly how many pounds of seed should be planted or broadcast in a particular food plot according to the recommended pounds per acre on the bag.

When you achieve the best possible fertility on your plots, your plantings should reach their full growth potential from your liming and fertilizing efforts. Lime and fertilizer are two essential elements to successful food plot planting. They should never be overlooked.

4. Choosing the *Right* Equipment

*I*f you believe you can plant food plots that will grow healthy plants with high nutrition and tonnage for deer and other wildlife by simply tossing seeds over unprepared ground, you've been misinformed. Anyone undertaking a land and deer management program must recognize that a crucial element of food plot planting success is using the correct tools for the job at hand. For instance, using a large tractor with heavy-duty attachments to plant a small plot in the middle of a woodlot—or a quarter- to half-acre plot in a field—is overkill and not practical. It also wouldn't be realistic for you to use a hand rake and hand seeder to plant an acre field of clover.

The type and size of equipment needed to plant successful food plots should almost exclusively be coordinated to the total amount of acres to be planted. Therefore, the equipment needs of each manager will differ considerably and must be carefully selected to match the size of *your* food plot agenda and should follow general recommendations. Before you buy a single piece of equipment, realistically evaluate the limitations of your budget. Only buy what you can afford to purchase and you'll avoid breaking the piggy bank before you even get started.

Miniature Properties

Food plot planters who plant mini-sized food plots often get frustrated or give up because the equipment they use isn't well tailored to the size of their property and the food plots they want to grow. This leads many managers to go back to broadcasting seed by hand over improperly prepared ground, which is a plan destined for failure. The "throw and grow" plan *never* works as well as preparing the ground properly using well-matched planting implements for the job.

If you're planting small food plots, strip areas of about 12 x 50 feet in the woods, or a plot measuring about one-tenth of an acre in fields, understand there will be plenty of planting by hand and physical labor involved. In some instances, the hard work put into some plots can be downright back-breaking. It should be noted that the more work put into a hand-worked plot, the more you will get out of it—and that is a hardcore fact.

These types of plantings begin by thinking through everything you will need to make the plot grow to its maximum potential. A selection of necessary and sturdy tool choices include a:

- strong leaf rake
- sturdy garden rake with iron teeth
- heavy four-pronged pitchfork
- sharp, pointed spade shovel
- large pair of pruning shears
- small handheld pair of pruning shears
- chainsaw
- handheld or two-wheel seeder
- seed compacter (something as simple as a piece of fence with a cinderblock and rope to pull over the planted area to smooth it out)
- a handheld weed killer
- fertilizer spreader
- soil test kit

▲ Using a tractor to plant a woodlot food plot strip like this would be highly impractical for most food plot managers.

▲ When planting small plots, particularly in woodlots, hand tools may be the only practical choice.

I strongly recommend hand-planting your plots only if there is *absolutely* no other equipment option you can afford to purchase.

Small to Medium Properties

Small- to medium-sized properties can be realistically and effectively planted with an ATV as long as the ATV used has enough power to pull implements without straining the engine. If you don't already own an ATV, consider buying one with a lot of horsepower, such as a 650cc machine. Small 25 to 35 horsepower tractors will also do the job, but often don't work as efficiently as an ATV does in woodland or other tight places. The first important decision you must make is whether you need an ATV and ATV implements or a small tractor and tractor-sized implements. Therefore, it is particularly important to carefully plan what types of equipment are needed to grow quality crops and require the least amount of labor, and then determine what equipment is realistically affordable. Once again, this requires a frank evaluation with yourself about what you can afford to spend on the equipment without spending a large portion of the overall budget or, more importantly, getting a divorce.

ATVs

Today almost anyone who owns land also owns a 4x4 ATV. They are affordable, reliable, useful machines that are regularly used for multiple purposes including hunting, fishing, recreational riding, and as effective, practical pieces of equipment for food plot planting. Over the last several years, some ATV makers have manufactured a line of planting implements to compliment their ATVs. Pragmatically, buying an ATV and their planting attachments will more often than not be *the* most affordable choice for an overwhelming number of land managers.

▲ Cody removes his rifle from its case for an afternoon hunt from his favorite deer blind on our farm.

Depending on the manufacturer, the line of implements available range from meager to complete. For instance, I own Arctic Cat ATVs. Arctic Cat offers a complete line of well-suited farm planting implements, including cultivators, two and four point seeders, rack-mounted sprayers with 10-foot-long folding boom spray bars, four row planter/drill seeders, rakes, tandem discs, drag harrows, landscape rakes, rear blades, box scrapers, moldboard plows, single discs, brush movers, and finish mowers.

Other ATV manufacturers also offer a line of implements, but do not offer as many different types or machines as well-built as Arctic Cat's line. For the average food plot planter, the amount of ATV implements that are available within the marketplace will definitely fulfill any planting need for small- to medium-sized properties. I mention Arctic Cat because I have personal experience with the brand and can vouch for them; I have put the ATV and planting tools to the test and they have performed flawlessly for many years (as long as they are maintained properly, as any piece of equipment should be).

On properties where food plots range from one-tenth of an acre to about three acres, an ATV matched up with compatible farm ATV implements is the way to go. ATVs are much more appropriate to planting less accessible areas of land or when used to plant in hard-to-navigate woodland areas where the plot (more often than not) has to be shaped around trees and other natural woodland structures. This is particularly true in spots that require a lot of tight-turning.

For those with deeper pockets, a small tractor will also fit the bill when it comes to planting small- to medium-sized parcels. A 4x4 25 to 35 horsepower tractor is a practical choice. Once you decide on a tractor, the implements you purchase should be matched to the tractor as well. They will be more expensive than ATV implements and, like the tractor, they will require more storage room. Implements needed for tractors this size include:

- heavier multi-tined plows
- double-row, hydraulic disk harrow seeders
- heavy-duty PTO driven three-point seeder spreaders
- multi-nozzle herbicide boom-arm sprayers

▲ Every year we plant about 25 food plots ranging from 1/10 of an acre to an acre or more. About 50 percent of our plots are planted with an ATV and ATV implements. Photo courtesy: Arctic Cat.

- subsoilers
- cultipackers
- PTO driven box tiller and other farm implements

Tractors are also prone to turning over if not used properly. Therefore, if you are unfamiliar with operating a tractor, you should plan to use one first before making your decision. I know several land managers who after attempting to drive a tractor decided to abandon that choice and use an ATV instead to do their planting.

Large Properties

I define large properties as those with land over 500 acres and with total *planting acreage* that exceeds 50 acres. When it comes to planting and tilling large acreage of this size, the most logical choice of equipment is traditional farm machines and planting equipment.

Tractors

A large tractor and heavy-duty implements are the best choice when a manager's deer and food plot plan includes planting 50 or more acres of food plots. Turning under old, dormant fields into crop-producing pastures, or other types of farm work on large acreage, requires land managers to invest in 40 horsepower or larger tractors. This type of heavy-duty planting equipment makes the job quicker and easier to accomplish when planting big properties. They're big-farm friendly and will enable land managers to develop and grow the very best possible food plots. Big tractors basically need the heavy-duty three-point versions of all the same type of attachments including:

- disc harrows
- hay and brush cutters
- large multi-blade plows
- rotary cutters
- spraying rigs
- primary seeders
- compactors
- back-blades

▲ Cody is preparing to use a 45 hp tractor and corn planter to plant a 4-acres field of corn.

A quality front-end hydraulic bucket loader is also a necessary piece of equipment for large parcels of land that will be planted. They will be regularly used to move mounds of dirt or gravel quickly and easily or remove large, heavy rocks from fields. They will also be used to bring bucket loads of fertilizer, manure, or bags of seed from place to place and for hauling 5- to 12-foot trees to planting locations.

A hydraulic rear-mounted back-blade attached to a larger type of tractor will also make short work of grading farm roads and other trails. They are also handy when filling deep ditches created by run-off, holes, ruts, and much more.

Keep in mind that owning a large tractor and implements requires a land manager to be mechanically inclined, as needing to make routine maintenance and minor repairs to larger equipment is inevitable. In the end, however, big tractors and implements will make short work of planting large acreage.

The importance of purchasing the right planting equipment for the size of acreage and the number and size of the food plots to be planted is a crucial first step in developing a deer and land management program. Having the correct type of equipment comes before planting a single seed. Using effective equipment will not only make the overall undertaking of developing food plots quicker and easier, but will also make the process much more enjoyable and satisfying.

Maintenance

Finally, when it comes to ATVs, tractors, and their planting implements, to get many years of reliable service requires basic upkeep. One of the chief causes of farm equipment failure is lack of general maintenance. A good maintenance program starts with storing your equipment out of the weather, particularly during the winter months, when it is not in use. Before storing equipment for long periods of time, it is important to include the following procedures to ensure the equipment will be ready for use in spring:

- Add proper fuel line anti-freeze and stabilizers to the gas.

- Add diesel fuel supplements (for diesel equipment only).

- Check levels of other fluids and replenish additives as needed.

- Keep the battery on a low trickle charge with a 1.5A batter charger that allows safe charging of most batteries during long storage periods.

- Clean the battery's post and terminals and coat with a terminal protective spray or gel.

- Cover ATVs, tractors and planting implements with a tarp.

- Lubricate all grease point fittings.

▼ Make sure you have an ample supply of anti-freeze, fuel stabilizers, fluids, sprays, and chargers in your shed. This will pay big dividends when preparing your equipment for storage or spring plantings.

▲ Before storing our equipment over the winter, each tractor and ATV gets a complete maintenance inspection and oil and fluid replacement.

mendations regarding all levels, types of oil to use, etc., over any other suggestions. Keeping up a well-planned maintenance program for your equipment will ensure that the equipment will provide reliable service season after planting-season.

Safekeeping Tips for Equipment

No matter what type of planting equipment you purchase or already own—be it a tractor, an ATV, or other farming implements—the gear can be a substantial financial investment for most land managers. To keep your investment safe, consider taking some basic precautions.

▼ The wise maintenance manager always checks all the manufacturers' manuals before storing them for the winter.

During the planting season, be sure to develop a general maintenance and checklist program and chart. It should include daily, weekly, and monthly maintenance and verification of the following:

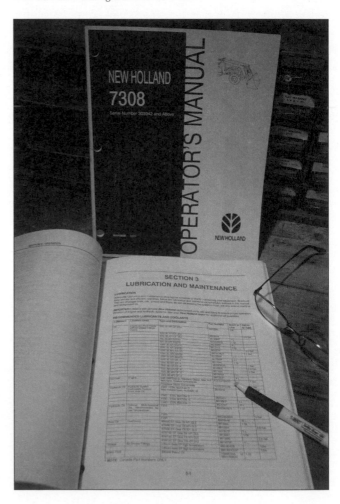

- Regular oil changes

- Check transmission and hydraulic levels

- Clean or change spark plugs

- Clean or replace all filters as necessary

- Replace worn hoses

- Check water levels frequently

- Check all fluid levels (brake, power-steering, battery, etc).

- Regularly inspect all belts and hoses

- Grease all fittings properly and completely with a multi-purpose lithium-based lube grease *each time the equipment is used.*

- Add fuel enhancers as a water remover and injector cleaner

- Sharpen all blades as needed or warranted (plow, disc blades, or other implements that may require sharpening

IMPORTANT NOTE: Always check the manufacturer's manual before doing any maintenance to your equipment. Follow their guidelines and recom-

▲ We store our ATVs in our heated shed through the winter.

▲ It's a good idea to remove the batteries on equipment that will not be used during the winter and place them on trickle chargers to keep them fully charged and ready to go in spring.

STORAGE, THEFT, FOUL WEATHER, AND INSURANCE

- When storing equipment over long periods, particularly over the winter months, it is best to keep it in a barn, shed, or garage that is heated if possible. All the equipment should be covered with a tarp secured with tie-downs.

- Use trickle chargers to keep all of the batteries fully charged during long periods of storage. This is especially important during the winter months.

- If you are an owner who doesn't live on your land full-time, it is crucial that your storage building has a high-quality, heavy-duty security lock to discourage would-be thieves from stealing your equipment. It's a sad state of affairs, but a reality of our times.

- Never leave your equipment in the field even for short periods of time without removing the key.

- If equipment must be left outside, particularly overnight in unprotected areas, remove the ignition key *and* the spark plug.

- Never make the mistake of not purchasing insurance for your valuable equipment. Insurance for ATVs, tractors, and implements is surprisingly affordable and easy to purchase. Ask your insurance agent if you can add a rider to your existing homeowner's insurance policy.

▲ Although we live on our farm, we still remove the ignition keys from our ATVs and tractor when leaving them out overnight.

5. Food Plot Placement

This chapter provides information about where to plant wildlife food plots in relation to the plants receiving the most advantageous direct sunlight and soil fertility. This is an element of planting that shouldn't be overlooked by novice food plot managers. In reality, selecting the right planting location is an important aspect of growing quality, high-yielding crops. To maximize a plant's growth success, it is important to provide the plant with the proper daily length of direct sunlight it requires. It is also important and advantageous to match a particular plant to the correct soil type it needs whenever it is possible or practical. For instance, place plants that thrive in moist soils in damp sites and plants that do best in well-drained soils in soils that stay mostly dry.

Fields

The *best* planting locations for growing healthy crops is unquestionably in existing agricultural fields, reclaimed openings, or overgrown pastures that have been out of cultivation and are in need of some work to make them amenable to wildlife food plot plantings. What all three of these locations have in common is they will all provide maximum daily sunlight and good soil conditions for the crops planted in them.

Other Locations

Other potential food plot planting sites include along the banks or edges of logging roads; along right-of-ways; old hiking, horse, or ATV trails; firebreaks; and cleared sections of woods. The latter group will *only* produce healthy food plots if the plantings receive enough *daily* sunlight, have the correct pH levels, and are fertilized accordingly. Historically, these locations don't provide more than a few hours of sunlight, which may be problematic. Sometimes it is necessary to either plant crops that are shade-tolerant or remove over-story to allow more sunlight to reach the plantings. Keep in mind many plants can be placed in nearly *any* plot, on practically any site, as long as the soil is *properly* prepared for the planting *beforehand*.

Woodland Clearings

Not all pieces of property include openings for planting food plots. Some properties may have open land to plant, but food plot managers may also want to create a plot in a hidden area in the woods. In either case, it is necessary to create an opening for such plots. By carefully choosing the best quality soils to create the plot, you will substantially reduce the amount of lime and fertilizer needed for these types of sites. Inevitably, plots made in wooded clearings require lots of lime and fertilizer. This is best accomplished by taking some pH samples and sending them out to be analyzed *before* finally clearing an area for a woodland planting.

Clover and Other Legumes

When planting any of the variety of clovers—bird's-foot trefoil, Lablab, cowpeas, lupines, and other legumes—it is important to remember that this entire group grows best when it receives at least six to eight

▲ A woodlot plot of subterranean clover. Studies have shown subterranean clover can reach over 90 percent of its potential growth when receiving 50 percent shade and it will even do well in plots with 75 percent shade!

hours of full sunlight. Managers also need to ensure the proper pH levels are met *and* the correct fertilizer is applied for their plantings. When this group receives the required amount of daily sunlight, you can be assured your plots will grow much better. Some legumes are sold as being shade-tolerant and only require a few hours of sunlight each day; if the pH is correct and the suggested type of fertilizer is used, they, too, will produce dandy food plots.

Grains

This group is classified as small and large grains. They include grain sorghum, oats, winter wheat, triticale, rye (*Secale cerale*), and corn. These plants need a lot of direct sunlight per day to grow. Before selecting a site, keep that in mind if you wish to have the best production and nutrition from grain crops.

Brassicas

Plants that fall into the brassica family consist of forage rape, several types of turnips, forage kale, canola rapeseed, radish, rutabaga, cabbage, cauliflower, and swede. Most food plotters plant the more common types of brassica plants such as turnips, kale, rape, and radishes.

▲ This shaded subterranean clover plot required 650 pounds of lime to raise its pH from 5.3 to 6.2. I fertilized the plot two weeks after this picture was taken with 300 pounds of T-19.

▼ This plot of mixed clovers was planted in a field that received a minimum of eight hours of direct sunlight.

◄ This brassica plot of forage rape was planted in a field that received a maximum of 10 to 12 hours of sunlight each day.

Another critical consideration with brassicas is that they do best in colder climates, particularly after a few hard frosts.

Brassicas are by far the easiest plants to grow. It is important, however, to pay specific attention to site location areas where brassicas will be planted. Brassica plants require *a lot* of sunlight to grow well. In fact, they need much more sunlight than the clovers and other legumes do. Therefore, when planting brassicas, it is crucial to select planting sites that will receive direct sunlight from sunrise to sunset.

Inside Corners

Another good place to plant food plots is near inside corners (see more about inside corners in the *Shooter's Bible Guide to Whitetailed Strategies* available on our website at www.deerdoctor.com). An inside corner, which is often referred to as an "interface," is where existing terrain features meet thicker cover and provide more security for deer as they enter the food plot. Not surprisingly, inside corners make deer feel much more comfortable and safer than food plots placed in fields or other more open areas. A food plot that takes full advantage of interface areas where the plot actually meets or borders thicker cover is a prime plot to see and bag more deer during daylight hours, particularly a mature buck.

As I have mentioned in previous writings, to encourage deer to use plots in large fields during daylight, I often break up a large field with a few rows of pines. It gives the deer the illusion that even a field as large as 5 acres is much smaller than it actually is. The rows of pines block off the view of the rest of the field, creating a few plots that appear to the deer to be more concealed, allowing them to feel that it is safe to enter the plots even during midday.

You can create land features that are used to maximize inside corners using your chainsaw or by employing specific habitat management land feature practices. On some properties, land features are a gift of Mother Nature and are naturally available. A thick row of tall pines, an island in the middle of the plot, a long section of manmade blow downs, or any other type of natural or manmade obstruction to block off a large view from a food plot will create an illusion of safety for a wise old buck. This will lure him from the edge of the woodlot into your food plot.

Irregularly shaped food plots also help to create a false illusion of safety for skiddish bucks.

Many of my irregularly shaped food plots are intentionally small and narrow down considerably from the wider points of the plot. Interface-type plots are easy to create in secluded woodlot areas where the cover is naturally thick all around the plot. Deer instinctively feel they can access the plot from all points of the

▲ Behind the row of pines is a 1-plus-acre field. Because the woods border it on three sides, it makes it an ideal inside corner. I planted the row of pines to partially obstruct the view of a 5-acre field above and make the 1-plus-acre field seem more secluded (for deer).

▲ This plot of Subterranean clover was intentionally planned as a woodlot planting because it is tolerant of shade.

compass without revealing themselves. Mature bucks will often use this type of plot at even midday to check out potential does that may be near or in estrus.

Conclusion

The ideal way to become a consistently successful wildlife manager and food plot planter is to *plan* each step in the process carefully beforehand—I know I have mentioned this before, but it can't be emphasized enough. If you lack the proper preparation, your food plots are destined at best for mediocrity and at worse for total failure. Those who believe they can simply spread some seed on the soil and expect to grow successful crops that will enhance the antler size of the bucks on their lands are in for a rude and expensive awakening.

Many of the other plants used for wildlife food plots have specific requirements and therefore benefit from a food plot manager selecting the proper planting sites. The savvy deer manager understands the nuances of the importance of site selection related to each plant and keeps that uppermost in his mind before arbitrarily planting a crop in a location where it will not achieve its maximum growth potential. Your food plots will not benefit from randomly selecting planting sites without taking into consideration the plants' soil and sunlight needs beforehand.

6. Plots & Planting Techniques

This is a short but vital chapter. The advice here will help you to grow more successful food plots and should not be ignored. One of the most overlooked aspects of planting food plots is to precisely measure the size of each plot. Knowing what a particular plot's measurements are will help you quickly establish the accurate amounts of lime, fertilizer, herbicide, and how much seed you will need. To get the exact measurements of a food plot doesn't require managers to be rocket scientists. Determining a plot's accurate dimensions can be done quickly and easily using a handheld calculator, range finder, GPS unit, or even a pad, pencil, and 200-foot surveyor's measuring tape.

▲ Cody uses a Swarovski range finder to measure the total square footage of one of our food plots.

Measure Each Plot Accurately

One of the chief causes of a food plot failing or not growing to expectations is that many times they suffer from too little or too much application of lime, herbicide, fertilizer, and *most often* too much seed. This happens simply because the food plotter either didn't think measuring the plot was important or didn't realize it was a necessary step to successful plot management.

The reality is that over-seeding a food plot is most often worse than under-seeding it. As the old adage goes, "Everything in moderation." This is particularly valid when it comes to preparing and planting a food plot. If too much herbicide is applied to a food plot, for example, the excess herbicide can either result in the plot's inability to grow a crop properly or, worse yet, render the soil of the plot dormant for long periods of time.

Placing either too much or too little lime in a plot inadvertently throws the pH levels off one way or the other. Putting too much fertilizer down can end up burning the plants. Not applying enough fertilizer can result in not providing the plants with the sufficient amount of minerals needed for maximum growth. If you neglect to accurately determine the overall dimensions of each food plot, not only will the plantings suffer, but you will also waste quite a bit of valuable time, work, and money. It will also result in frustration when the plots don't perform as expected. I strongly suggest that you take the time to measure each plot accurately and don't skip this very important step if you hope to grow better food plots.

An important figure to remember about food plot planting is that the overall dimensions of an acre of land measures out to be 43,560 square feet. Since a majority of plots are more or less square or rectangular in shape, simply measure the length of the plot by the width of the plot to get the plot's precise overall size. To determine what percentage the plot size is as it relates to an acre, take the plot's overall dimensions and divide it by 43,560 (the total number of feet in one acre). This will provide you with the fraction figure or percentage of an acre that is related to each plot.

For example: Let's say your plot is 75 feet by 120 feet. Multiply 75 by 120 and you'll get a figure of 9,000 square feet. Divide 9,000 by 43,560, and you get 0.20 or two-tenths (2/10) of an acre.

To eliminate having to recalculate food plots every season, store the dimension information either on a computer or in a handwritten log book for future reference. It will help eliminate unnecessary work the following spring, leaving you only to calculate the size of new plots that are created. To eliminate confusion, each food plot should be given a name or number. The dimensions should then be applied to that particular plot in your computer or handwritten log to prevent the final measurements from being confused with another plot. Obviously, if the size of a plot is extended or reduced, the plot needs to be measured again and the new dimensions re-entered into a log.

Knowing the exact dimensions of all your plots will save you lime, herbicide, fertilizer, seed, money, time, and, most important, the frustration and grief of a plot not growing as well as you hoped it would.

▲ Some food plots fail because of drought, over-browsing, flooding, or other natural elements. They shouldn't fail because they weren't measured before they were planted.

I want to emphasize again how important it is to know the exact size of each food plot so you will know *exactly* how much seed to plant or how much lime or fertilizer is needed.

This formula can be used to determine the size of irregularly shaped plots as well. It takes a little more math work in measuring and calculating asymmetrical plots, but it is still an *essential* step in the overall land manager's food plot program. It is worth the extra effort it takes to get the accurate dimensions of uneven food plots. Measure all sides of lopsided plots individually, then apply the same calculations to reach a close approximation of the overall size of the plot.

▼ If you don't have a range finder or a surveyor's measuring wheel, use a 200-foot tape measure. They are readily available and inexpensive.

7. Weed Management

Weeds are to a wildlife food plot what water was to the "Wicked Witch of the West"—*deadly*. Weeds will ultimately "snuff out" or at least severely limit a food plot plant's growth and the nourishment it provides wildlife. When a food plot fails, an overwhelming majority of the time they are lost to the presence of obnoxious weed growth within the plot. Weeds effectively compete with plot plantings for nutrients, light, and, most critically, water. Controlling weeds from overtaking a food plot can be a very a difficult problem to overcome.

The reality of weeds is that they are found everywhere. For the food plot manager, the element that helps weeds to grow in their plots is by the disturbance of the soil when cultivating a food plot. The more the soil is disturbed and the deeper the ground is turned over, the more the weeds will grow in the food plot.

In a test conducted on our farm, we selected a few half-acre plots that were individually planted with for-age radishes, turnip, or forage rapeseed. We did not use herbicides to prepare the plots and instead we allowed the weeds to grow naturally in each of the three plots. We wanted to compare how well our herbicide treatments were actually working to either eradicate weeds or severely limit their growth in our food plot program. The experiment did not have a surprising result, to say the least, but with the price of herbicide we felt it was worthwhile to conduct on a small scale.

What we learned was mostly what we expected to find out. Using the correct herbicides did, in fact, eliminate, or at least substantially reduce, the overall volume of weeds in our food plots. The plants in the food plots we used without herbicides grew taller, were greener, and more robust than the plants in the experimental plots were. What the test revealed was not a surprising result.

The real discovery came as we watched deer feed in our food plots throughout the summer and into late fall and winter. As usual, they ate the offerings of the

▼ This field is choked with dandelion, a broadleaf perennial. In spring, sprouts emerge from the soil. The yellow flowers turn into white puffballs containing seeds that spread by wind into other food plots. The taproot survives deep in the soil, making it hard to kill. I use Big N' Tuf herbicide to eliminate the taproots of dandelions.

▲ Disking a plot too deeply will always disturb the weed bank and encourage weed growth.

food plots where the weeds had been controlled with herbicides as eagerly as they normally do.

In the three plots where the weeds grew unchecked and competed with the plantings, deer fed in them less frequently throughout spring and summer. In fall, after the weeds died, the plantings were almost totally ignored by the deer and other wildlife. Even though the turnips and radishes were visibly abundant, the deer only browsed them briefly as they casually walked through them to get to more palatable food plots.

It took some time but finally the light came on and we realized the weeds had sucked the very *life juices* from the turnips, rape, and radishes. They significantly reduced the nutritional value. It eventually, albeit unexpectedly, became as plain as the noses on our faces that the deer not only found the plants to be much less nutritious they also found them to be much less flavorful. The weeds had changed the palpability

of each of the three plantings so much that the deer treated them as non-food items. Needless to say, our test clearly demonstrated the importance of controlling weeds in our food plots.

Eradicating or even reducing weed problems in food plots is a never-ending battle and it is rarely an easy problem to control. Basically, you can get an upper hand on weed management by mowing or using the correct herbicides. The use of chemicals is by far *the most effective way to control weeds in food plots*. Be forewarned, however, that it is essential to completely understand what a particular herbicide is capable of controlling and what type of weeds it is meant to kill. No matter what type of weed, grass, or broadleaf plant you want to eliminate, there is a chemical made to control or kill it. Whenever herbicides are used to kill or control weeds, it is a must to first *read the entire label slowly and carefully* before applying the herbicide

▲ Big N' Tuf is an affordable and effective herbicide that kills both grass and broadleaf weeds. It can be found in most farm supply stores.

▲ This plot was first sprayed to kill the weeds. Seven days later, we top-seeded turnips in a totally weed-free plot.

to the ground. I know that sounds like common sense, but I can assure you many times the warning is disregarded or overlooked.

Another important factor in effective weed control is best achieved by using the right equipment to manage or eliminate weeds. The quickest way to apply herbicides is by hiring a sprayer truck from a local farm supply company or co-op service. It is more costly, but in the end saves a lot of time and effort on your part. You can also effectively apply herbicides using a wick-bar arm applicator, a backpack sprayer, or a sprayer mounted on the back of an ATV or tractor. The longer the arms of the sprayer, the quicker the job will get done. *Before using any type of sprayer, however, it is imperative to first calibrate the sprayer.* This is an absolutely crucial procedure to managing weeds effectively, therefore do not ignore this step.

The management or elimination of weeds using herbicides is a complicated matter. It requires a serious understanding of how to use chemical herbicides safely and effectively. It also requires a detailed knowledge of the weeds on your land. The more you know about the weeds that are indigenous to your area, the better

you will be able to control your weed problem. There are many free guides available on the web. Knowing what herbicides kill what weeds will save you time and money. It will also help to ensure the successful growth of the plantings in your food plots.

Managing weeds in food plots is a combination of different types of methods, including, mowing, hand-weeding, light tilling, choosing the best plot sites, preparing the site for planting correctly, and using chemical herbicides safely, wisely, and exactly as instructed by the label. The most successful elimination of weeds is accomplished by combining a few of these methods rather than using just one of them.

I strongly recommend reading all you can on weed control and the identification of weeds. I found the following books to be information sources on this subject: *Invasive Plants* by Sylvan Ramsey Kaufman and Wallace Kaufman; *Weeds of the Northeast* (Comstock books) by Richard H. Uva; *Common Weeds of the United States* by the U.S. Department of Agriculture; and, for the more "green-minded" food plot planter, *Weeds: Control without Poisons* by Charles Walters—all available on Amazon. The web is

◀ This is "Mr. Big." He's standing in front of a failed rape crop overtaken by weeds before moving off to a more appealing planting.

It is more expensive but has been treated to reduce weed seeds in it.

• Prevent weeds from establishing themselves.

• Don't use contaminated seeds; they contain weeds. Instead, use only certified seeds, which state the contents are weed-free.

• If you use your mower to cut weeds or other obnoxious plants, wash it down from top to bottom before using it to mow clovers or other plantings in your food plots.

• Try to treat weeds prior to them going to seed.

• Pull weeds when practical and/or necessary.

• Other than herbicides, employ other weed-controlling methods such as mechanical weed control via mowing, mulching, or burning.

Not All Weeds Are Wicked or Evil

It should be noted, however, that not all weeds have to be eradicated from your land. Many weeds are an important element within a deer's overall diet. Deer feed four to six times per day (every four to six hours), actively seeking out a wide variety of food sources. They mostly eat browse (leaves, twigs, shoots, vines, etc.). They include all types of soft and hard mast (fruits and acorns), flowering plants, grain crops, legumes, clovers, vegetables, and some grasses in their diet. Grass compromises a very small amount of a deer's overall diet, less than 10 percent. They also actively seek out a large variety of weeds including sumac and poison oak. My point is, while weeds are evil in a food plot, they do play a vital role in a deer's diet, making them an important food source when they grow *outside* of your food plot planting.

also a terrific source for more detailed information on weeds and their control. It is also an excellent place to get further information on the safe and effective use of all types of chemical herbicides.

More Weed Control Tips

• Avoid using untreated manure as fertilizer in food plots. Untreated manure contains the seeds of many weeds. If you want to buy bulk manure as fertilizer, purchase commercially treated manure.

8. Growing Trees—An Important Part of Any QDM Program

GO CRAZY—PLANT NUTS

The most primitive native mast crops and their impact on game animals were noticed even by our earliest nomadic hunting ancestors. In fact, wild nuts have been a food staple for both hunter and prey since hunters first hurled their spears. Today, nut-producing trees are a vital food source and an important part of the habitat for white-tailed deer. Nut trees allow hunters the opportunity to see and harvest more game. The experienced manager is motivated to enhance deer and other wildlife populations and increase harvest numbers by planting, growing, and managing a variety of nut trees for both hunted and non-hunted game species alike.

To diversify and enhance a food plot and deer management program, it is *essential* to improve the numbers and varieties of nut-bearing trees on a piece of

▼ When acorns fall, whitetails typically abandon other natural food sources and even the most tempting food plots. They won't return to them until the acorns are gone. Photo courtesy: Ted Rose.

land. This includes trees already on the land and new plantings. If there is any single wildlife food source that will quickly attract deer to a property during the fall, it is the availability of a quality mast crop that provides a variety of highly nutritious nut-bearing acorn-type fruit.

Deer will temporarily abandon nearly all other available food sources natural and planted when acorns begin to ripen and fall to the ground. In fact, one study found that in years of an abundant acorn crop, as much as 80 percent or more of the food deer consumed were acorns. If a piece of land includes even a few varieties of high-quality nut-bearing trees, the mast they drop *absolutely guarantees* it will draw deer from far and wide and keep them there until they eat every last available acorn they can find—no matter what other types of wildlife food plots or natural vegetation is available to them.

There is an old adage that says, "One doesn't plant nut trees, particularly slow-growing oaks, chiefly for themselves. Rather, they are planted for generations to follow." While that is true of some of the slow-growing nut-bearing trees, such as white and other oaks, it absolutely doesn't apply to all mast-producing trees. This is principally true when planting orchard-type nut trees. While the typical white and other oak trees take years expending their nutrition to grow above the surrounding canopy, orchard-type nut trees used for wildlife provide faster nut production—sometimes production is as quick as three to five years. A complete nut-bearing management program therefore includes several varieties of slow- and fast-producing mast trees.

FAST-GROWING NUT TREES

Surprisingly, there are many fast-growing mast-producing trees in both the orchard and typical wildlife varieties than you may realize. Some will produce nuts within a few years, while others will take slightly longer to produce a viable mast crop. If your management plan requires quick-producing mast trees, here are some choices for consideration (Gobbler Sawtooth Oak, Live Oak, Pin Oak, Sawtooth Oak, and the best choice of all—chestnut trees).

At one time, the American chestnut (*Castanea dentate*) was *the* most important and abundant tree in America. Unfortunately, the American chestnut

◄ Notice how many Dunstan Chestnuts™ are growing on these trees. Dunstan Chestnuts are known for producing high-quality, blight-resistant trees with dense clusters of chestnuts. They are available at chesnuthillnursery.com.

became a rare tree due to it nearly being completely wiped out by the Chestnut Blight (*Endothia parasitica*) that began ravaging the American chestnut trees in the early 1900s. Today, scientists are crossbreeding blight-resistant strains in several species of chestnut trees, such as Japanese, European, and hybrid varieties. Most chestnut trees other than the Japanese and European varieties are cold-hardy and will grow as far north as Canada. Depending on the variety, they can reach heights of 40 feet and more.

Rather than planting traditional, slow-growing oak trees—especially if you want to see the mast crop in your lifetime—you should plant the faster-growing oak varieties. Some varieties like the Dunstan Chestnut™ tree begin to bear in only two to four years. You don't have to wait twenty years for them to start bearing acorns like with many of the traditional oaks. They are proven to bear ten to twenty pounds of nuts per tree within ten years of planting—before most oaks even start to have acorns. Chestnuts are sought out by game because the sweet-tasting nuts are very high in carbohydrates and protein, and they have no bitter-tasting tannin like many red acorns are known to have. Chestnuts bear their nuts from September to early November. They can be grown throughout the eastern United States, in zones 4 through 9, from Michigan and Illinois, west to eastern Texas, and south to central Florida. An excellent choice to consider is the more widely adapted tree than the blight-resistant Dunstan Chestnut™ (available from www.chestnuthillnursery.com).

According to my contact, Robert Wallace, of Chestnut Hill Nursery, "blight-resistant chestnut trees can be planted today thanks to Dr. Dunstan. In the 1950s, the noted plant breeder Dr. R. T. Dunstan found a surviving American chestnut surrounded by dead trees in Ohio. He took cuttings from that resistant tree and crossed them with the Chinese chestnut. The blight was from China so the Chinese were naturally resistant. He then crossed the seedlings from the first cross back to both parent trees. This second generation of trees is known as Dunstan Chestnuts™. Now, fifty years later, not a single Dunstan Chestnut™ tree has died of the blight. Hundreds of thousands of these trees have been planted all over the country by commercial orchardists who helped create a commercial chestnut industry in the United States. The major problem orchardists have is that deer eat a large percentage of their harvest. Did you register that last sentence?

Chestnut Hill Nursery is the exclusive producer of Dunstan Chestnuts™. I plant Dunstan Chestnuts™ on our farm. According to R.D. Wallace of Chestnut Hill Nursery, Dunstan Chestnuts™ are the most widely planted chestnuts in America, and they have proven beyond a doubt to be blight-resistant and to bear the best-quality nuts for the past thirty years.

If you don't have any chestnut trees in your management plan, take my advice and plant some as soon as possible. One-year-old trees are available for shipping by UPS in spring and larger sizes are available as well. You can call 1-855-386-7826 or visit www.chestnuthilltreefarm.com for more information. Chestnut Hill Nursery also grows other types of quality nut trees, fruit trees, oaks, and other wildlife trees using root-enhancing pots and advanced production techniques.

Robert Wallace also told me, "Chestnut Hill Nursery's Dunstan Chestnut™ variety is known for producing heavy yearly crops of very large and sweet-tasting nuts. The nuts average 15 to 35 nuts/lb, as compared to Chinese chestnuts (35 to 100/lb) and American chestnuts (75 to 150/lb). They are much better tasting than imported European nuts, as they are less bland or bitter to wildlife and people.

"The nuts break open easily, unlike imports that have clinging and ingrown pellicles (seed coats). The flat, shiny, mahogany-colored nuts ripen in autumn and deer can forage them well into November." Dunstan Chestnuts™ are one of the very best trees for providing food for wildlife other than deer including turkey, squirrel, bear, and many other hunted and nongame species. Dunstan Chestnut™ trees produce nuts on a yearly basis unlike the oak trees and other nut-bearing trees that produce nuts on a cycle ranging between heavy and light.

Another point about chestnuts is that they are a primary food source for many types of hunted and non-hunted animals. They are a primary food source for deer, bear, turkey, squirrel, hogs, and other wildlife. They can produce literally a ton or more of mast per acre. Dunstan Chestnuts™ are a highly favored food source for deer and other game in the fall because the sweet-tasting nuts are high in protein (40 percent) and carbohydrates (10 percent) and do not have bitter-tasting tannins like acorns. It doesn't take deer long to figure out they are better-tasting than other acorns because of that fact.

I'm told that chestnut-fed pork is the sweetest pork there is. In Spain, domestic hogs are raised on chestnuts because of the excellent-flavored meat it produces. Estremadura pork is regarded as an international delicacy. Venison from chestnut-fed deer tastes like corn-fed venison. The meat of deer that browse on natural oaks (acorns) can end up having more of a "gamey taste" due to the tannin in the bitter-tasting acorns.

Chinese chestnut trees produce nuts within five years. ▶
Deer eagerly seek them out as soon as they ripen.

Chinese Chestnut Oaks (*Castanea mollissima*)

Another blight-resistant chestnut tree is the Chinese chestnut. They are tolerant of most soils, including acidic soil. Some grafted species can produce nuts in a few acidic soils. Since the grafted varieties of chestnut trees are all sterile, two different cultivars must be planted to cross-pollinate them.

The Chinese chestnut (*Castanea mollissima*) is a medium-sized tree that can reach heights of about 40 feet. Although the flowers have an unpleasant odor and the nuts have prickly husks, these large nuts are highly attractive to deer. Chinese chestnut trees will produce nuts within five to six years and a viable wildlife crop in about six or seven years. They are available as either 18- to 36-inch seedlings or as three 3- or 7-foot trees shipped in pots.

Japanese Chestnut (*Castanea crenata*)

Japanese Chestnuts produce even larger nuts than the European chestnut. The tree reaches a maximum height of 35 to 50 feet. The nuts are very large and get about 2 inches in size and weigh about 1.5 ounces. The nuts are generally not as "sweet" as the American, Chinese, or Dunstan varieties of chestnuts. Additionally, Japanese chestnuts are usually not as cold-hardy as the other chestnut species. Although they have a resistance to chestnut blight, there can be wide genetic differences in their resistance. Some Japanese chestnut trees begin bearing nuts at a young age.

Importance of Nuts to Deer and Other Wildlife

All wildlife, particularly white-tailed deer, instinctively prefer the high-energy food sources which quickly help them to gain weight. Nuts and acorns (mast) influence the winter survival rate, physical condition,

reproductive success, and the overall size of the population rates as well, especially for female deer and other female wildlife.

As browsers, deer consume a huge portion of the available mast and appear to prefer acorns over browse. As mentioned earlier, one study documented that during years of an abundant acorn crop, mast will make up approximately 85 percent of deer's total food volume. Conversely, in poor years of production of mast, the volume of acorns in a deer's stomach was less than 8 percent. When mast is not abundant or available, deer quickly seek out agricultural, natural food sources. During times of poor mast is when deer will also visit food plots continuously. When mast production is light, these other food sources can comprise up to 50 percent of a deer's diet.

These factors are what make planting all types of mast-producing trees, including the traditional acorn-bearing trees as well as the non-traditional nut trees such as chestnuts, and other nut trees so important to wildlife managers. As I have stated, to complete a food plot and deer management program, you must include the planting of a wide selection of mast trees.

Where to Plant Nut Trees to Attract Wildlife

Where nut trees are planted is an essential element to attracting deer to their location. As with any food plot, the closer the plant is to secure heavy cover, or close to wooded areas, the more comfortable deer and other wildlife will feel in visiting the area. When trees are planted in very open areas, deer shy away from visiting them in order to avoid exposing themselves to predators; instead, they visit the area mostly at night. A better option when planting trees in open areas is to plan to create travel lanes, draws, or fence rows that lead from wooded areas. Nut trees can be planted along the draws or spaced out along a fence row. The important element is that all roads to the trees must be tied to the woodlot.

How to Select Nut Trees for Deer and Other Wildlife

Generally speaking, this could be a full chapter itself. Instead, here are some of the more important elements to keep in mind when buying nut-bearing trees for wildlife. Like all plantings, it is wise for managers to investigate the types of nut and acorn trees their land can support and the wildlife prefer. The more

homework you do about what kinds of nut trees are best suited to your land, the more production the tree will be able to provide.

- How easy deer and other wildlife can crack open a nut is a chief point in selecting nut trees. The easier the nut breaks open, the more preferred it is by deer and other animals. Chestnuts are a top choice in this category.

- The larger the crown and the diameter of the trunk of the tree (sometimes referred to as the bole), the better the chances are for the tree to produce a more plentiful mast crop.

- Species that produce mast between each crop are obviously better than other tree choices because they provide a more dependable source of mast.

- For all wildlife managers, plants that produce high-quality tonnage is an all-important element, therefore before selecting a certain nut tree species, first investigate how many nuts certain species of trees produce.

Some mast trees for the north, including shingle oaks, swamp white, and pin oaks, prefer wetland sites. In the south, Shumard, willow, and water oaks are the best choices for wetlands.

Shumard Oak is among the fastest growing Red Oaks.

OTHER MAST-BEARING TREES

Gobbler Sawtooth Oak (*Quercus acutissima*)

Gobbler Sawtooth Oak is the same tree as the Sawtooth Oak. The only difference between them is that the Gobbler Sawtooth Oak produces smaller acorns than the Sawtooth Oak does. The Gobbler Sawtooth Oak is one of the fastest growing oak trees. It can reach heights of 40 to 70 feet and can have an equal width (the length of its furthest branches). They are cold-hardy trees that do well in northern climates as far as Canada.

While the typical Sawtooth Oak produces acorns in about four to six years, Gobbler Sawtooth Oaks produce their nuts sooner. Gobbler Sawtooth Oak nuts are highly favored by wild turkey and deer. Under the right conditions, it is a persistent and prolific nut producer. In alternate years, the nut production will be heavier than the preceding year. Gobbler Sawtooth provides an excellent winter food source for deer and other wildlife.

DUNSTAN CHESTNUT™ COMPARISON CHART WITH OAKS

	DUNSTAN CHESTNUT™	WHITE OAK	SAWTOOTH OAK
Zones	4-9	4-8	5-8
Native	Hybrid with native	Yes	From China
Soil Type	Wide adaptability No wet areas	Rich upland soils	Best on sand to clay loams
Height	60-80'	80-100'	50-60'
Spread	30-40'	30-40'	30-40'
Growth Rate	10-12' Year 3	3-4' Year 3	4-6' Year 3
Years to Bearing	2-4	20-50	4-6
lbs/tree Year 10	10-25	0	10-30
lbs/tree Maturity	20-100	100+	20-125
Annual Bearing	Every year	Every 4-10 years	Every 2-3 years
Nut size	25-40/lb	60-100/lb	80-150/lb
Tannin	None	Low-moderate	High
Protein %	10	4	5
Carbohydrate %	40	10	10
Fat %	2	10	20

Chestnuts and Other Nut Trees as Agricultural Crops

It is reported that the United States imports $20 million of chestnuts yearly because there are fewer than 2,500 acres of chestnut orchards in the entire United States. It would take approximately 10,000 acres of productive chestnut orchards to supply what the United States currently imports. American-grown nuts can reach the market sooner, be fresher, and bring a higher price than imports, which are often low in quality, making growing chestnuts an excellent small-farm business opportunity as well as a wildlife food source. Growers who produce high-quality chestnuts in America should have a nearly unlimited market available to them for many years. Chestnuts are a very profitable crop as they bear nuts within four to five years, produce 1,000 to 2,000 pounds per acre each year, and live for about fifteen to twenty years. The wholesale prices for large, high-quality chestnuts are currently about $2 to $4 per pound and higher than that at retail. There are many other nut trees that can provide equal monetary gain as farm orchard crops and also make excellent choices as commercial nut crops. They include almonds, hazelnuts, hickory, pecans, walnuts, pine nuts, macadamia, and pistachio nuts.

Hazelnut (Corylus sp.)

A rather unique selection is a hazelnut. I have no personal experience with how well deer may like hazelnuts (a.k.a filberts). I have heard from commercial planters of hazelnut that deer and other wildlife do eat them, however. I'm always willing to experiment and therefore I'll give something new a try to see how deer and other wildlife respond to it. It is known that the catkins produced by the male flowers provide a great winter food source for many types of wild

▲ Commercial growers claim deer eat hazelnuts. I plan to experiment to see just how much deer like them by planting a hazelnut tree on our farm.

animals, including deer. (A *catkin* or ament is a slim, cylindrical flower cluster.)

While it is often referred to as "the perfect shrub for lands with limited space," it can reach heights of 8 to 12 feet and has a spread of about 7 feet or more when fully matured. However, hazelnut can also reach heights of 30 or more feet, making it more tree than a shrub.

The American hazelnut is a compact, low-maintenance tree that produces branches teaming with nuts every year—which should be highly attractive to deer and other wildlife. Hazelnut is a cold-hardy shrub that requires about 1,200 "chill-hours" for best production, which makes it an ideal choice for managers in northern zones. Because hazelnut is not self-pollinating, it needs at least two different cultivars or more if it is planted as a commercial crop. It is drought-tolerant and produces vibrant fall foliage.

The American hazelnut adapts easily to all soil types and thrives in full sunlight. The small nuts are easy to

crack and have sweet kernels that are rich in antioxidants and nutrients. The American hazelnut, whether it is a shrub or tree, will produce a bountiful crop of nuts from September through October, creating plenty of mast well into November. If the deer and other wildlife don't eat them, which I think is highly unlikely, it will leave more for you.

Almond (*Prunus amygdalus*)

Like the American halzenut, planting an almond tree is an experimental exercise in wildlife forage planting. The almond is related to apples, pears, and peaches. They will grow best in hot, dry climates in locations such as California's Great Central Valley. Almonds are relatively fast-growing and can reach heights of about 30 feet and produce nuts within five years. They, too, need two or more cultivars. (A *cultivar* is a plant or group of plants selected for desirable characteristics that can be maintained by propagation.)

Live Oak (*Quercus virginiana*)

Live Oak is a tree that will do well for managers whose deer and food plot programs are in southern areas. Live Oak ranges from the coastal plains to southern Florida and west into Texas. It is often found in a variety of habitats including grasslands, forested areas, and savanna-type terrain. More often than not, Live Oak can be found mixed with other hardwoods, pines, and junipers and is often decorated with Spanish moss.

Spanish moss hanging from a Live Oak tree. ▶
Live Oak trees grow well in southern areas.

This type of tree can grow to 50 feet in height. It develops a short, solid trunk that supports many of its huge, nearly straight, wide-spreading branches that form the trees, noted dense crown. Live Oak needs plenty of room to develop and does best when it is planted in large open areas. It isn't susceptible to many diseases or insects unless it is stressed by fire or other damage.

Live Oak produces an abundant amount of small- to medium-sized sweet acorns. Its mast is highly prized by deer, turkey, and other bird and mammal wildlife. It can produce acorns as early as age five, making it one of the fastest-growing oak-producing trees. For managers in southern zones, this Live Oak is a splendid choice to provide quality mast for deer and other wildlife.

Northern Red Oak (*Quercus ruba*)

Red Oak is found in many forested areas with other hardwoods and conifers, particularly pines. Red Oak grows best on deep, fertile, well-drained but moist soils. Red Oaks are the *cold-hardy, fast-growing* tree of the Oak family and they can reach heights of more than 150 feet. It is used in the restoration of wildlife habitat and degraded sites, particularly those areas with acidic soil conditions. Like other Oaks, it has a high timer value.

Northern Red Oak is one of the largest Oaks and is capable of producing large amounts of acorns. While red oak nuts are not as highly prized by whitetail deer as white oak acorns are, deer do seek them out as a secondary choice. Their egg-shaped acorn has a shallow cap and bitter seed. Red Oak often produces a reliable, abundant crop of acorns, making it a good choice to be included in a woodlot management agenda as well as a deer management program.

Pin Oak (*Quercus palustris*)

Pin oak is found from southwestern New England, west through extreme southwestern Ontario, to northern Illinois, southwest to northeastern Oklahoma, and east to Virginia. It is a moderately fast-growing tree than can reach heights of about 90 feet and live to about 150 years. It needs a spot in full sunlight to produce its best and it is partial to moist soils.

The brown acorns mature in the second year and are about a half-inch long, nearly round, and about

▲ Mature Red Oak trees produce reliable, abundant mast crops, making them a good choice for any deer management program.

one-third enclosed in a very shallow cap. The mast is small but highly favored by wildlife. Ducks particularly enjoy pin oaks but deer enjoy eating them too.

SLOW-GROWING NUT TREES

Other varieties of nut trees take decades to produce their nuts or acorns, but are highly valuable as wildlife forages and as commercial crops. These include White Oak, hickories, walnut, pecan, evergreen pinyons, pine nuts, and Swamp Oaks.

White Oak (*Quercus alba*) is highly prized as a premium mast by deer and other wildlife despite it taking decades to produce its acorns. It is yet another of those types of plantings that is a necessity in a forestry program or as a nut-bearing tree if, like my land, your property is absent of white oak trees. White Oak is a highly prized tree with conservationists, foresters, and land and wildlife managers because of its acorn production and its high timber value.

It has been reported that more than 23,000 acorns were produced during a good seed year by an indi-

▲ White Oak takes decades to produce its first mast crop. After that, nut production will be sporadic. However, the acorns are highly prized by deer and turkey.

vidual White Oak tree growing in Virginia that was sixty-nine years old. Average acorn production for White Oaks in good years for individual forest-grown trees, however, is a lot less than that—probably no more than 7,500 to 10,000 acorns.

Most deer hunters know that white acorns are the mast crop choice of whitetail deer. Many other animals also enjoy the sweet flavor of White Oak acorns, too. All acorns are the preferred deer food in autumn, but White Oak acorns are at the pinnacle of deer's preferred foods. Deer can taste the difference of the flavor of acorns (from very bitter to highly sweet) along with the level of tannic acid in the nut. White Oak acorns have the least tannic acid.

Without question, White Oak is the number one food choice of deer and turkey. It will provide food throughout the fall and winter. As such, it should never be left out of a land and wildlife program unless it will not grow in your area.

Hickory (*Carya sp.*)

Hickories are reported to have about twenty or more species. Two are found in Southeast Asia and the remaining species are located in eastern North America. They live long, reach heights of more than 50 feet, and are rated from being slow-growing to moderately quick. Exactly what "moderately quick" means is not clear, as most hickories take many years to produce nuts. This is one of the trees that's best planted

in a management program for others to benefit from because they live for centuries.

With that said, however, many grafted varieties may grow slightly faster and yield more reliable crops. They are extremely cold-hardy and as such make excellent choices for northern areas. They produce small, sweet nuts that are housed in very sturdy shells.

Other Acorn Tree Choices

Other than the nut trees mentioned previously that can be grown both for wildlife and commercial value, there are about twenty-five or more different types of oaks and beach trees that bear acorns throughout the eastern United States. The oaks represent the most important hardwood trees in the eastern forests. Before planting a particular oak, check with a local agricultural agency to be sure that the types of oak trees you want to plant will grow well in the zone where you intend to plant them.

1. **American Beach (*Fagus grandifolia*)** grows to heights of 60 to 80 feet and has a diameter of about 2 to 3 feet. The nuts are edible, but are not highly prized for human consumption. The acorns are triangular in shape, about ¾ of an inch long, and borne in twos and threes in prickly husks. The acorns begin to fall after the first hard frost, usually occurring in October and November. The acorns are an excellent food source for all types of birds and animals, including whitetail deer.

2. **Black Oak (*Quercus velutina*)** is a very common oak in the eastern forests. It can attain heights of 50 to 80 feet and generally has a trunk diameter of about 4 feet when it matures. The acorn is rounded and about ½ to ¾ of an inch long. It is encased up to half its entire length in a bowl-shaped cup.

3. **Blackjack Oak (*Quercus marilandica*)** is small compared to other oaks. Its thick, black bark is deeply divided into rough, nearly square plates. Blackjack Oak is a tree common of the Old South. It appears throughout the southeastern states from southeastern New York into Oklahoma and Texas. Its acorns are fringe-free and are no longer than 1 inch in length. It has a deep cup that covers the nut to about half its length. Wildlife from rodents

to all types of birds and mammals eat the acorns, including whitetail deer.

4. **Burr Oak (*Quercus macrocarpa*)** has several other common names including Mossy Cup Oak, Blue Oak, and Burly Oak. When mature, it can reach heights of 70 to 80 feet. It a slow-growing oak, but is one of the most massive with a trunk diameter of up to 10 feet. It is native to North America in the eastern and mid-western United States and south-central Canada. It grows best in well-drained sandy loam with full sun, although it can tolerate partial shade. The Burr Oak acorns are very large and can grow to be 2 inches long and 1.5 inches broad, which makes the acorns an important wildlife food source. Black bears love the acorns. Other wildlife, such as deer, turkey, squirrels, and rabbits, eat the acorns, as well.

5. **Chestnut Oak (*Quercus macrocarpa*)** is an oak tree found in mountainous upper elevations. It is one of the most abundant trees of the mountainous ridges of the Appalachian Mountains, extending from Maine to Georgia. It is particularly well suited to rocky upland forest and ridges. It is a small tree due to the nutrient deficiency of the environment in which it grows. It only reaches a modest height of about 55 to 80 feet. The Chestnut Oak is the shorter cousin of the venerable White Oak. The acorns of the Chestnut Oak are prodigious, growing to a length of more than an inch with a girth nearly as large. They are among the largest acorns of all American oaks. Though good crops of chestnut oak acorns are relatively rare, they mast every four or five years in lieu of the normal oak mast cycle of two to three years. They are an important food source for many animals, including deer, bear, and turkeys.

6. **Chinkapin Oak (*Quercus muehlenbergii*)** will on fertile ground grow to about 65 to 80 feet high. The trunk diameter can reach 2 to 3 feet. Chinkapin Oak is native to eastern and central North America, ranging from Vermont west to Wisconsin and south to South Carolina, western Florida, New Mexico, and northeastern Mexico. The acorns are dark colored, oval, and about ¾ of an inch long. They are encased about halfway into the cup. The acorns are very sweet and, like White Oak acorns, they contain less tannic acid than most other acorns. They are highly attractive

Burr Oak is a slow- ▶
growing oak. Its acorns
grow to 2 inches or more.
Black bear love to eat the
large burr oak's mast.

▲ Laurel oak acorns are eaten by all types of mammals and are favored by upland birds like this grouse.

to bear, deer, turkey, and many other forms of wildlife.

7. **Laurel Oak (*Quercus laurifolia*)** is a tree that is fast-growing, tall, and full. Laurel Oak grows scattered with other hardwoods in well-drained soils near the edges of streams and rivers. It grows throughout the coastal plain from southeastern Virginia to central Florida and west to southern Texas. Laurel Oak is abundant in Florida and in other parts of the south. Laurel Oak produces large crops of small ½-inch-long acorns with saucer-shaped cups. It produces its acorns regularly, making it an ideal tree for wildlife managers. It is an important wildlife food resource for whitetail deer, turkeys, ducks, squirrels, upland and other birds, and other wildlife.

8. **Live Oak (*Quercus virginiana*)** is a tree of the south and is the state tree of Georgia. Live Oak is a large tree of the lower Coastal Plain from southeastern Virginia to southern Florida and to southern Texas. Live Oak is a fast-growing tree. Sweet, edible acorns are usually produced in great abundance and are of high value to whitetail deer, turkey, wood ducks, squirrels, and many other birds and mammals. The acorns are three-quarters to 1 inch long, broadest at the base to almost uniformly wide and rounded at the tip.

They are light brown within the cap that covers about ¼ inch of the dark nut. The largest part of the acorn is dark brown to black and shiny. They occur solitary or in clusters of three to five. The Live Oak makes an excellent nut tree to plant for managers in southern areas.

9. **Northern Red Oak (*Quercus ruba*)** has nuts that are bitter, but still eagerly eaten by deer, turkey, grouse, bear, boar, and other non-hunted wildlife, particularly in the absence of White Oaks. The nuts require about two years to mature. Northern Red Oak grows almost everywhere east of the Mississippi except the extreme southern portions of the country and the state of Florida.

10. **Nuttall Oak (*Quercus nuttallii*)** is a species that is one of the most restricted in its range. It only grows in the mid-southern states bordering or close to the Mississippi River. It prefers moist bottomland soils. It can grow 60 to 90 feet tall and have a stout trunk 4 feet or more in diameter. The acorn is oval, about 1 inch long, and has a thick deep cup.

11. **Overcup Oak (*Quercus lyrata*)** is an oak within the White Oak group. It is native to lowland wetlands in the southeastern United States from Delaware to southern Illinois and down to northern Florida and southeast Texas. The tree can reach heights of 60 to 90 feet, but will usually be smaller. The acorns usually contain a single seed and are enclosed in a tough, leathery shell. Its acorns take between six and twenty-four months (depending on the species) to mature. The acorns are ½ to 1 inch long, spherically shaped, and almost entirely encased within it tough cup.

12. **Pin Oak (*Quercus palustris*)** can reach heights of 120 feet and its trunk can reach 3 feet or more in diameter. The acorn is very round and about ½ inch in diameter, light chocolate in color, and is stripped. The acorn production is a bit erratic, but deer and other wildlife eat them hardily.

13. **Post Oak (*Quercus stellata*)** is sometimes called Iron Oak. It is a medium-sized tree abundant throughout the Southeastern and South Central United States. It is a slow-growing oak that is considered drought resistant. The range of Post Oak extends from southeastern Massachusetts, Rhode Island, southern Connecticut and extreme south-

eastern New York (including Long Island); west to southeastern Pennsylvania and West Virginia, central Ohio, southern Indiana, central Illinois, southeastern Iowa and Missouri; south to eastern Kansas, western Oklahoma, northwestern and central Texas; and east to central Florida. The acorns mature in one growing season and drop soon after ripening during September through November. The acorns are sessile or short-stalked, borne solitary, in pairs, or clustered. They are about ½ to ¾ of an inch long, oval-shaped, broad at the base, and set in a cup one-third to one-half its length. The scales of the cup are reddish brown.

In common with many other oaks, Post Oak begins to bear acorns when it is about twenty-five years old. Good acorn crops are produced at two- to three-year intervals, although at several locations in Missouri over a six-year period, Post Oak consistently averaged only 200 seeds per tree per year while White, Blackjack, Black, and Scarlet Oaks of the same size on the same site bore from 500 to 2,400 acorns per tree. Isolated trees in open fields in east Texas consistently produced well. Elsewhere in Texas, trees less than 15 cm (6 in) in diameters at breast height (d.b.h.) had no acorns.

14. **Scarlet Oak (*Quercus coccinea*)** can reach heights of 70 to 80 feet. Its branches are small compared to its height and trunk diameter. A Scarlet Oak's acorns are usually about ¾ to 1 inch long. They are oval in shape and encased one-half to one-third of their length in a deep, basin-like cup. The end that sticks out is usually marked with circular lines. Hunted and non-hunted wildlife of all types eat their acorns.

15. **Shumard Oak (*Quercus shummardii*)** is native to the more southern states of the eastern United States, even reaching into the northernmost areas of Florida. The acorn is ¾ to 1¼ inches long, oval, and has a thick, rough cup that is flat and saucer-like. Most of the acorn fruit sticks out of the cup. It can grow to about 100 feet high or more and has a trunk diameter of 4 to 5 feet.

16. **Southern Red Oak (*Quercus falcata*)** occurs from southern New York to central Florida and west to southern Missouri and eastern Texas. It is a medium-sized tree reaching 50 to 70 feet tall, with a trunk 2 to 3 feet wide. The acorn are short, bright orange-brown, and enclosed for one-third to one-half of its length in a flat cup. The acorn matures at the end of its second season.

17. **Swamp Chestnut Oak (*Quercus michauxii*)** closely resembles the chestnut oak Quer*cus prinus*. However, the swamp chestnut oak is a larger tree. It typically grows to around 60 to 80 feet high.

The acorns of the Swamp Chestnut ▶ are among the largest at 1½ inches long. They are a favorite acorn for squirrels and other wildlife.

The swamp chestnut's fruit is an acorn 1 to 1 ½ inches long, ovoid, and covered about one-third of its length in a thick cup with rough scales. White-tailed deer, turkey, squirrels, and hogs eat the acorns.

18. **Swamp White Oak (*Quercus bicolor*)** has a mature height of 50 to 60 feet and is a rapid-growing tree that can reach 300 to 350 years old. It likes swampy situations, prefers acidic soil, is drought-tolerant, and survives in a variety of habitats. The mast usually grows in pairs on long stems. They are oval, about 1 inch long with about one-third of their length encased in the cup. The acorns are sweet and are eaten by deer, squirrels, wild ducks, several nongame birds, and animals.

19. **White Oak (*Quercus alba*)** grows throughout most of the Eastern United States. It is found from southwestern Maine and extreme southern Quebec, west to southern Ontario, central Michigan, to southeastern Minnesota; south to western Iowa, eastern Kansas, Oklahoma, and Texas; east to northern Florida and Georgia. The tree is generally absent in the high Appalachians, in the Delta region of the lower Mississippi, and in the coastal areas of Texas and Louisiana.

Several studies have shown that only a small portion of the total mature acorn crop (sometimes less than 20 percent) is sound and fully developed. The remaining acorns are damaged or destroyed by animals and insects. Healthy White Oak acorns have a germination capacity between 50 and 99 percent.

White oak can produce *seeds* prolifically, but good *acorn* crops are irregular and occur only every four to ten years. Sometimes several years may pass without a crop. Acorn yields range from nothing to heavy. This great variation in acorn production exists not only among isolated stands of oaks but also among individual trees within stands and from year to year.

When hunters fail to see deer in the fields or along the edges, they often attribute the infrequent sightings to a variety of excuses, including too many does being harvested, a hard winter, deer going totally nocturnal, too many coyotes, etc. Usually, the answer for what causes a sudden fall hunting season where deer seem to be much less abundant lies beneath the hunter's feet.

When the white acorn crop is abundant, the deer will forsake all other food sources and focus on the acorns entirely until they have eaten every last available one. The gorging within the woods greatly reduces the deer's need to travel longer distances between their bedding and feeding areas. If they can stay within secure areas, eating all the acorns they care to, there's little reason for deer to move. Instinctively, deer consume all acorns, but particularly white acorns because they provide sweeter, tasty nuts that are chock-full of fats, starches, and high levels of protein. In years of very heavy white acorn crops, I have seen deer in the Catskill Mountains in Delaware County, New York, abandon one of their other primary food sources—apples. Instead of regularly feeding in the apple orchards, they opted to remain within the deep woods and ridge-tops feeding on white acorns. Because deer find white acorns easy to digest, they eat lots of them per day. As I mentioned earlier, if White Oak can be planted in your hunting areas, they should be an integral part of your tree management program.

20. **Willow Oak (*Quercus phellos*)** regularly reaches heights of 90 to 100 feet, with a trunk diameter of about 3 to 4 feet. The round acorns are small, only growing about a half inch long with a thin, flat, scaly cup. Animals that eat their acorns include whitetail deer, turkey, wood and mallard ducks, and other non-hunted birds and mammals.

FRUIT TREES

For anyone planning a food plot and deer management program, it should be standard-operating procedure to include a planting of several different types of fruit trees. The most popular fruit tree planted is the common apple tree. There are many other equally good choices of fruit trees to choose as well. Some other choices other than apple trees include Common Pear, Jujube, peach, plum, Common or Japanese Persimmons.

A complete selection of a variety of fruit trees could include a few of each of the trees mentioned. It is important to remember when purchasing fruit trees that many varieties need to be pollinated by either a male or female tree of the same type and that the accompanying pollinating tree be planted within 30 to 50 yards away. Some varieties of fruit trees are "self-pollinating."

The fruit dropped by these trees quickly draws deer and other wildlife to their fallen bounty, much like a magnet draws iron. Deer temporarily abandon most other food items when ripe apples and other fruit begin to fall. In many cases, deer will eat the apples, pears, jujubes, or persimmons within hours after they begin to hit the ground. The fruit will remain a priority food source until it is *completely* exhausted by wildlife.

Fruit trees require particular care when being planted. Follow the planting directions carefully. For most trees, the hole must be at least twice as wide as the root ball and slightly deeper once a tree is planted. In the bottom of the hole, lay an inch or two of 10-10-10 fertilizer. If the tree is a year or more old, use Osmocote 18-6-12 fertilizer at planting; it provides excellent nutrition, but since it is a slow-release fertilizer, it won't burn the newly planted tree. (See Chapter 9 for more information on how to plant trees properly for best growing success.) For more information about where to order fruit and other trees from mail-order nurseries, see the listing at the end of this chapter.

SHRUBS

Planting a variety of shrubs will also enhance any quality deer management (QDM) program, such as the Allegheny Chinquapin (a medium shrub that produces an abundance of edible, small, sweet nuts relished by a wide variety of game and other wildlife) and the American Hazelnut shrub (whose nuts are a favorite of game birds and other small game). Like hardwood trees, the mast crop produced by shrubs will attract and hold deer, turkey, and other wildlife on your land until the mast is totally eaten.

▼ We have dozens of wild apple trees on our land. Deer will concentrate in apple orchards or under wild trees and continually visit them until they eat every last apple.

▼ Planting non-traditional fruit and nut trees like jujube (below) and persimmon will give you the edge over neighbors who most likely only have common apple and/or pear trees.

▲ It takes five to eight years for persimmon trees to bear their sweet orange fruit. Persimmon fruit will last well into the winter months.

▲ Deer love pears. Within hours of the fruit hitting the ground, deer will come in to eat them.

Other non-traditional shrubs that benefit from a QDM program include American Beautyberry, which produces purple berries and grows to about 6 feet tall. Its berries are enjoyed by a wide variety of game and non-hunted species. The Red Mulberry grows to a height of 60 feet and is also attractive to a wide variety of game and non-hunted species. The Common Pawpaw has a rich, sweet fruit with a nutty banana flavor; it, too, is savored by many species of wildlife. Chickasaw Plum grows like a thicket-forming small tree that provides excellent cover for quail, grouse, turkey, and other game birds. Deer and turkey seek out its sweet red fruit in late summer and eat it until it is gone. Buttonbush is a large, woody shrub that grows to be between 3 and 10 feet tall. Its seed is readily eaten by waterfowl. Lespedeza Bicolor is a large leguminous shrub that reaches heights of 8 to 10 feet. It can be planted to provide excellent cover for deer, game birds, and small game.

The longer a game and land manager waits to plant hardwoods, softwoods, and shrubs on their land, the longer the wildlife (and you) have to wait to reap the benefits of planting trees and shrubs.

The easiest and most productive way to do that is to contact county extension offices, or a professional forest manager and or logger, to evaluate the trees on your land. Timber-stand-improvement (TSI) is an essential management tool for land managers to include in their wildlife and food plot program. Enlisting the services of a professional, *trustworthy* forester is the first step to having healthy woodlands on your property.

An experienced forester will help you decide if the time is right for you to engage in a *selective* lumber-

▲ Professional logger and TSI expert Mark Decker of Quality Hardwoods, Inc., calculates the total board feet of a harvestable ash tree on our land. Mark's decades of experience assure us of a successful TSI management program.

ing program of mature trees on your land, including those trees that are not beneficial to deer and other wildlife. Removing a controlled portion of mature trees will improve the overall long-term financial value of the remaining lumber and allow sunlight to reach the forest floor to encourage understory growth as well. A percentage of the revenue received from a logging campaign could be reinvested into buying and planting more beneficial trees including fruit, mast, and other plants. At no additional cost, if asked nicely, some foresters will identify with a mark the "worthless" trees that don't have any future commercial value or nutritional value to the deer and other wildlife. Cutting down "useless" trees will allow more sunlight to reach the forest floor.

NUT AND OTHER TYPES OF TREE SOURCES

Chestnut Hill Tree Farm
  – www.chestnuthillnursery.com
Morse Nursery – www.morsenursery.com
Hallman Farms – www.hallmanfarms.com
Smith Nursery Company
  – www.smithnursery.com
Stark Bro's Nursery – www.starkbros.com
Cummins Nursery – cumminsnursery.com
Dave Wilson Nursery – www.davewilson.com

CONIFERS

A variety of conifer seedlings are made available to the public by many state Department of Environmental Conservation agencies at a low cost to the public in quantities of either 25 to 100 units per package. In some cases, they are available at no cost. State agencies do this to encourage tree planting that will improve wildlife habitat, control soil erosion, provide windbreaks, enhance the environment, and beautify the landscape. Many other local agencies include County Extension Offices and the Natural Resources Conservation Service office (NRCS). Sometimes even lumber companies provide a wide selection of softwood tree species as seedlings for free or at very reasonable costs.

Conifers are often referred to as softwoods. It is important to remember that different conifer species, like all trees, grow to maturity at significantly different rates of speed. For instance, white pine and Norway spruce trees are the *fastest* growing of the softwood trees, and balsam fir is ranked the *slowest* growing of the conifers. When planning a softwood tree either to provide wildlife protection from severe winter weather, wind breaks to protect planted fields, or as future stands of pine where wildlife can seek security from predators and hunters, your best choice will be to select the fastest growing species of conifer trees.

◄ The six-year-old trees in foreground are a variety of different fast-growing conifers. The other pines in far background were used to break up this large field into smaller-looking fields to deer.

▲ This half-acre of randomly planted conifers is six years old. In a few years, the trees will be more than twenty feet tall. Deer will use them to bed among and as a refuge from inclement weather..

Conifer trees are the least expensive to purchase when they are 6- to 8-inch seedlings. They are easily planted using a tool known as a dibble. Once you get used to using a dibble tool, you will be able to plant at least thirty to forty seedlings an hour. Before placing the seedling in the ground hole, trim its roots to a manageable length between 6 and 10 inches and then plant the seedling. While conifers will tolerate acidic soil, they do best in a pH of 6.0 and better. If the pH is lower than 6.0 at planting, they should be *correctly* fertilized at planting to promote quick and healthy growth. I strongly recommend paying a little extra to purchase the taller, older variety which will be from 10 to 18 inches in length. The older trees have a more substantial root system, which will give the tree a jumpstart after it is planted.

Many managers plant conifers in neat rows, but I don't. Once I select an area, I plant the trees randomly throughout the space. When the random planting reaches about 5 to 7 feet tall, it becomes very attractive to wildlife, much more so than row-planting. If deer and other wildlife can see the surrounding area through the pines, they will not use it consistently to seek cover. This is particularly true of mature bucks. If wily old bucks can see predators approach, they instinctively know they can be seen by predators as well and will avoid using the stand of pines as a place of security. A random planting grows tightly and irregularly enough to effectively hide wildlife from predators. It also helps conceal a hunter's approach, to hunting stands in the area. The planting will also look much more natural to wildlife and to the human eye instead of it looking like a landscape-type tree planting.

CONIFERS CREATE ILLUSIONS OF SAFETY

Another reason to plant conifers is the option they offer as breaks or "walls" to reduce the size of larger fields into smaller, more secretive sized fields. Deer, chiefly older bucks, feel much more comfortable entering a small, secluded field than they do a larger field. This is particularly true in daylight or under heavy hunting pressure. Deer perceive a small field to be safer and easier from which to escape.

A thick grove of pines, even one as small as a half to one acre will draw deer to the conifer patch to bed, escape hunting pressure and predators, and seek

▲ Before and after images; Kate planting more than 100 conifers to provide deer with a future stand of security. After: Five years later, the trees have grown significantly taller.

shelter in the pines when the weather turns cold and snowy. To ensure your conifer patch will be a magnet for your deer, plant them haphazardly and a little closer together than recommended. Don't let anyone talk you out of this by saying the trees won't grow well if planted too closely together. You're not planting trees for beauty—you're planting them to provide cover that is as thick as possible while still allowing for good growth potential.

However, when reducing a larger field of 5 acres into several smaller fields, I use a variety of conifers, but mostly white and Norway spruce. I also plant Red & Scotch pines and Douglas fir, which grow quickly as well. When I plant to break up large fields, I place the first row of trees in straight lines (unlike a random security pine planting) and then plant a second and sometimes a third row behind them in an alternating pattern to seal off unwanted views past the planting. This plan ensures that when the trees mature, they

I only plant conifers in ▶ straight double rows when I want to make a larger field look smaller to deer. This picture was taken seven years ago. Today, the pines have grown to more than 20 feet tall and have completely closed off the view of the other fields.

will shut down any potential views from other nearby fields.

To help conifers grow quickly, I fertilize them twice a year with a specialized evergreen mix like Hollytone or something similar. You can also use a general fertilizer mix of 16-4-8 or 19-19-19. Both can be used on trees and shrubs. Fertilize in spring and then again in fall. In just a few short years, your evergreens (especially the white pines) will grow to 6 feet or more.

One more point about pines: Unlike the eastern pines that deer browse mostly as low choice items, some pines in the west, particularly, the southwest, are more attractive to wildlife from September through early November—exactly the time that benefits southwestern hunters the most. This is a prime reason for hunters living in these areas who own or lease property and have instituted food plot and wildlife management plans to consider soft pine plantings to attract wildlife to their lands.

If you live in the southwest portions of the country you can plant soft pines as cover, or to break up large open areas. Soft pines, however, can also be planted as quality food sources for deer and other wildlife. Over a dozen species of soft pines provide nut crops in North America. They belong to one of the two taxonomic subdivisions called the stone pines and the pinyon pines.

When used as wildlife food sources, both the stone and pinyon pine nuts are nearly as important to deer and other wildlife as oak tree nuts. Wildlife of all kinds, both hunted and non-hunted species, readily eat pinyon and stone pine nuts. The foliage and twigs of the pinyon pine are browsed by mule-deer and mountain sheep. Stone pine nuts, however, are more highly sought after and the preferred food source for a wide variety of southwestern wildlife including turkeys, mule-deer, bears, pinyon jays, woodrats, squirrels, and other wildlife. They are a common food for deer, particularly during harsh winters with deep snows.

Pinyon-juniper woodlands provide habitat for a varied wildlife population, particularly mule deer, white-tailed deer, elk, desert cottontail, mountain cottontail, and wild turkey. It is easy to see that planting soft pines species that produce nuts can serve in more ways than just providing cover or breaking up fields.

Pine nuts were a favorite food staple thousands of years ago for the Native American Indians who resided in the southwestern parts of the country. Unfortunately, today pine nuts are most often found in food stores. They are sold as pignolias, pinyon nuts, and Asian pine nuts. Being of Italian descent, I have had a lot of experience eating pignolia nuts. They are used to adorn Italian cookies and in many other Italian recipes including sauces, soups, stuffing, candies, and in meat dishes. Pignolia are very sweet and delicious nuts.

Pinyon nuts apply to all pinyon pine species (Mexican Pinyon Pine, Colorado Pinyon Pine, and Singleleaf and Pinyon Pine). The nuts are all harvested by humans in North America. Pinyon nuts are also excellent sources of phosphorus and iron, and contain vitamin A, niacin, riboflavin, and thiamine. They are full of protein and are easily digested and, amazingly, they contain all 20 amino acids, many of which are found in large concentrations. They pack an unbelievable amount of food energy—as much as 3,000 calories per pound.

Stone Pine Nuts include species such as the Korean Nut, Siberian Stone Pine, Swiss Stone Pine, Whitebark Pine, Italian Stone Pine, Colorado Stone Pine, and Dwarf Stone Pine. Of the two taxonomic subdivisions (stone pines and pinyon pines), the stone pines are the faster growing group, particularly the Italian Stone Pine, which is the fastest growing of both groups. The Pinyon pines are all slower growers than the stone pines.

The Stone and Pinyon pines can make a serious contribution to enhance any deer and wildlife program that includes the more traditional food plot plantings instituted in any of the southwestern states.

TREE PLANTING TOOLS

Only a small financial tool investment is needed to make the job of planting trees go quicker and easier. It only requires some hand tools, including a dibble, which is a shovel-type tool that is designed with a beveled arrow point, allowing for fast and easy tree planting of all types of seedlings from 5 to 18 inches. For larger tree plantings, you'll need a few different types of well-built, spade-like shovels with different tip designs; a quality post-hole digger; and a sturdy pinch bar to help remove rocks while digging the hole. As long as the ground isn't frozen, you can plant trees with these tools and without any special preparation to the ground.

▼ A pinch bar makes quick work of making several fertilizing holes around a tree. Break the fertilizer sticks in half, place a half-stick in each hole, and cover it with soil. Fertilize in the spring and the fall for best results.

9. Easy Steps for Planting Trees

Whether you are planting fruit trees, hardwoods, evergreens, shrubs, or bushes, digging the hole correctly will help increase the tree or other type of plantings' survival rate dramatically. Planting trees and other plants the right way will also save you time, money, and frustration.

Begin by digging a hole twice as wide as, and slightly shallower than, the root ball. Roughen the sides and bottom of the hole with a narrow-bladed shovel so that roots can penetrate the soil deeper and more easily. The more you work the soil in the hole, the easier it will be for the roots of what you plant to expand into the surrounding soil.

If the tree is planted in a pot, remove it by rolling the container *gently* in your hands while applying pressure to the sides of the container. Once it becomes loose, lay the tree on its side with the container end near the planting hole. Tap the bottom and sides of the pot until the root ball is totally loosened. If you notice that the roots wind tightly in a circle at the bottom of the root ball, with a sharp knife blade gently cut through the roots on two sides of the root ball. If a tree comes in a burlap wrapping, it is better to completely remove the burlap bag. If you notice an exceptionally long root or two, trim them shorter and guide the shortened roots downward and outward so they will quickly establish themselves into the soil. This is necessary because root tips die when exposed to light and air, so this step should be done quickly.

The proper spacing for nut or acorn trees is about 30 feet apart. Remember that mast-producing trees like full sun. Fruit trees can be spaced a little closer, approximately 25 feet from each other. Shrubs should be planted about 6 or 7 feet from one another and planted in areas that provide full sun.

Before planting, put a slow-release type fertilizer at the bottom of the hole and then cover the fertilizer with about 2 inches of soil before planting the tree on top of the fertilizer. After the first year, fertilize the tree in early spring with Osmocote Classic 18-6-12.

Now put the root ball in the hole to check if the hole is at least twice as big as the root ball. If not, remove it and dig it larger. Then leave the top of the root ball, which is where the roots end and the trunk begins, at least ¾ to 1 inch above the surrounding soil. When planting trees with bare roots, make a mound of soil in the middle of the hole and spread plant roots out evenly over the mound. Do not set trees too deep. As you add soil to fill in around the tree, lightly pack the soil to squeeze all air pockets from it. Then, if possible, add water to help settle the soil. When planting trees in my fields or woods, I thoroughly wash out my fertilizer tank with clean water or I bring several gallon jugs filled with clean water with me for this purpose.

Form a temporary, but firm dip in the soil around the base of the tree to help hold rainwater and to help water penetrate to the roots of the tree. Water the tree thoroughly after planting it. I usually soak the trees

◄ When a tree is properly rolled free and out of its container, the root ball remains intact. This will make it easier to plant and is better for a healthy growth cycle.

▲ This hole is wider and slightly deeper than the root ball. The dirt in the sides of the hole was loosened to allow the roots to penetrate the soil easier.

well just prior to planting them. Most times, a dry root ball cannot absorb water as quickly as a moist one.

For best results, put some type of mulch around the tree when you are finished. Place as much mulch as needed to make a circle of mulch that will be at least 3 feet in diameter and about 4 inches deep for weed and moisture control. Check newly planted trees regularly to keep them as weed-free as possible.

I always use quality-type tree protectors called Plantra® Jump Start® Grow Tubes when I plant any type of trees, shrubs, or vines. Plantra® Jump Start® Grow Tubes are plastic tubes translucent to sunlight and are uniquely designed to provide both greenhouse benefits and physical protection for small, hardwood seedlings. Tube wall construction, tube diameter, and sunlight-optimizing properties of each design are a function of its intended purpose. Some Jump Start™ Grow Tubes are built for wild land, urban, and nursery

▼ Cody and his cousin Max plant a Dunstan Chestnut™ tree on our farm. It will only take two to five years before this tree produces chestnuts.

tree establishment while others are intended to quickly grow agricultural plants such as grapevines, orchard trees, and blueberry bushes. Jump Start® Grow Tubes begin doing their job the day you plant and are UV-resistant so they will last for years in the field or until your seedlings get established.

Tube heights for wildlife life plantings range from 2 feet to 6 feet with the height often matched to the multiple threats facing vulnerable seedlings. Shorter tube lengths (2 feet to 4 feet) protect against damage from smaller animals including mice, voles, and rabbits and also from chemical weed sprays and some equipment damage like string trimmers and mowers. Taller tube lengths (5 feet and 6 feet) shield against threats previ-

▲ This pine was destroyed by a buck. It would cost too much and be too time-consuming to use protective tree tubes on the hundreds of conifers we plant. However, we always protect the trunks of our newly planted fruit and nut trees with Jump Start™ Grow Tubes.

▲ We don't protect all conifer trees due to the expense. However, we always protect the tree trunks of our newly planted fruit and nut trees with Plantra Jump Start™ Grow Tubes. Photo courtesy: Plantra®.

ously mentioned but also protect against deer browse and bucks rubbing the trees with their antlers.

Unlike the Plantra® Jump Start® Grow Tubes, traditional tree tubes (sometimes called tree shelter tubes) are designed to provide physical protection for small seedlings. Physical protection is indeed important, but it shouldn't stop there. Jump Start® Grow Tubes combine the physical protection of tree tubes and tree shelters with sunlight-optimizing greenhouse benefits. Combining sophisticated light-diffusing construction with spectrally selective pigments, Jump Start™ is translucent to specific light wavelengths that plants need and delivers sunlight the way plants can best use it. This is an important combination that promotes healthy growth and maximizes the microclimate inside a rugged, protective tube. This is exactly what is needed to help young seedlings survive and rapidly grow toward maturity.

Threats to seedlings are many, and unprotected seedlings face a low probability of success. One of the biggest threats to seedling survival is chewing and gnawing by animals that too often eat and kill young seedlings. The vast majority of wild seedlings—and many planted by tree growers—suffer the fate of being eaten by deer or having their stems stripped of bark and girdled by a host of rodents including rabbits, mice, and voles. Another serious threat to seedling survival is desiccating wind. The Grow Tubes help retain leaf moisture, reduce water stress, and eliminate other negative impacts that hold unprotected seedlings back. Lastly, Jump Start™ Grow Tubes are designed to be used with Plantra's revolutionary Trunk Builder™ staking system. Staking trees is crucial to their survival and healthy growth. Trunk Builder™ is the first stake ever purposely built to support a grow tube or tree tube while helping the growing tree develop a stronger stem faster. Trunk Builder™ U-Stakes flex when the wind blows, but are engineered to stand tall with built-in super strong "memory" to return to a straight position even on the windiest sites. Trunk Builder™ stakes deliver benefits with a grow tube for wildlife plantings.

One of the chief causes of tree plantings not surviving is damage done by deer. Bucks particularly cause severe damage and sometimes even kill young tree plantings, especially during the rut when they will rub trees repeatedly. Always protect the trunk of a newly planted tree, particularly if it is a seedling.

10. Warm-Season Food Plots

Clover and most other legumes are the most popular plantings among food plotters. Clovers are by far the quickest seeds to establish, and some of the easiest seeds to start and grow (as long as they are inoculated properly). They are also land-manager friendly because many of them are perennials. What makes clovers even more attractive to food plot managers is that there is no question that deer eat clovers hardily because they are very palatable and they provide deer with high nutrition.

The most commonly planted warm-season group of clovers and other legumes include Alyceclover, American Joinvetch, burgundy bean, cowpeas, Kobe, lablab, soybeans, sweetclover, and some of the white and red clovers. Some of the clovers have several varieties such as ladino clover. Ladino clover has six different varieties including warm- and cold-season varieties.

Not all clovers can be grown everywhere in North America. Some do better in warmer climates and others in cooler climates. Most warm-season clovers can be planted alone, but do better when they are planted in a mix with other types of plantings.

For my money, however, some land managers plant too many stand-alone clover food plots. One of the problems with planting a lot of clovers is that many of the warm-season varieties can readily be found almost anywhere deer roam. Deer will almost always be able to locate some type of wild or planted warm-season clover on your neighbors' land, as well as most other properties. That fact reduces the attraction value of your warm-season clover plantings. This is why I strongly recommend not planting just warm season clovers and and other legumes, especially on small properties. Instead, limit the percentage of warm-season clovers and plan more space to plant other types of plants, such as cool and/or winter-hardy clovers.

With that said, however, planting a few warm-season clovers as stand-alone plots is still an important and practical plan in every food plot program. When they mix with other plants, they become even more attractive to deer, particularly when a neighbor has planted an overabundance of stand-alone warm-season clover plots. For better results to attract and entice deer to use your land more regularly, plan to plant a variety of different types of food plots mixed with warm-season clovers that deer can't find readily on surrounding properties.

This statement also applies to *all* plants grown in food plots, whether they include warm- or cold-season clovers, other legumes, grains, grasses, brassicas, forbs, herbs, or vegetables. By planting what can't be easily found by deer close to your property, you will attract more deer to your land on a regular basis. *You can take that to the deer hunting bank.*

Most land managers include several types of clovers and other legumes as part of their deer and other wildlife management program. Therefore, it is important to know what clovers and other legumes grow best as warm-season selections in your area and which of them provide the most nutrition. It is also important to know which plantings require a lot of acreage to grow best and which ones don't. Each specific variety mentioned below includes some of my favorite warm-season clovers and other legumes.

Although I plant some of them as stand-alone plots, most of them are planted in cover mixes with other warm-season plantings. Try planting warm-season clovers, other legumes, and other plantings like sunflowers, squash, or other plants that will be killed off after the first heavy frost and see what works best for your warm-season food plot plantings.

▲ This stand-alone plot on our farm is a warm-season clover. Stand-alone warm-season legumes take up about 20 percent of my overall food plot plantings.

Types of Clover

Crimson clover is a very popular clover for deer. It is an excellent choice as a warm-season planting. (I have grown it on our farm in western New York successfully as a cool-tolerant planting.) However, it is killed as the temperatures drop below freezing. Therefore, while it will withstand some colder temperatures, it is not a winter-hardy clover planting in northern areas. Although it is highly sought after by deer, I plant crimson clover also to attract honeybees. By attracting and holding bees on our farm, we help the pollination of our clovers, other legumes, fruit, and nut trees. Deer and turkey are very attracted to crimson clover. Like all legumes, it must be inoculated with Rhizobium bacteria (strain R) to grow best. I buy it pre-inoculated. It prefers well-drained soils and a pH level between 5.8 and 6.5.

Osceola clover is a variety of ladino clover. Deer enthusiastically seek it out. It can be planted in spring and will do well until early fall. It will die as soon as it is exposed to temperatures below freezing.

Durana white clover is a persistent, drought-tolerant, highly productive, and long-lasting clover that can be used as a warm-season clover or a cool-season planting. I had a stand of Durana that lived four years with regular mowing. Durana produces more runners than many other clovers, which allow it to spread quickly and aggressively. Durana clover withstands *heavy*

▲ Crimson clover is one of my favorite plantings. It lasts well into October unless it is exposed to temperatures below freezing for a few straight nights in a row.

▲ Warm-season clovers work very well with many other types of plantings. This clover is mixed with Rye (*Secale cereal*).

grazing pressure, making it an ideal clover to plant if your land has a high deer density problem. It also produces an abundance of flowers, which help to reseed it more dependably than other clovers. Durana will even grow in plots with a pH as low as 5.5, but like other clovers, it prefers a pH of 6.0 and higher. Durana is a good cool-season perennial legume. (See the complete Durana White Clover profile in Chapter 12).

Warm-season clover plots do well when they are fertilized and maintained properly by mowing them a couple of times over the summer when necessary. The warm-season perennial clovers will generally last a few years or longer if properly taken care of. When the life cycle of a clover plot begins to decline, it is a clear indication it is coming to the end of its productive life span and the plot will either have to be reseeded or replaced with another crop. Periodic selective mowing

practices once or twice a season help to rejuvenate a clover patch, which can then shade out weed growth. It should be noted, however, that mowing can also encourage weed growth. Mowing is best for keeping broadleaf competition low and using herbicides is more appropriate to eliminate grass competition. Never do either one earlier than six to eight weeks after establishing a clover plot. A clover plot will quickly lose its nutrients, water, and sunlight to weeds if the weeds are not held in check.

Warm-season clovers are best planted in the spring. While this is a standard practice, it isn't the only time to plant warm-season clovers and other warm season crops. When planting clovers and other legumes during spring, always try to put them in the ground just prior to when a steady rain is predicted.

Other Warm-Season Legumes and Plantings

Lablab is another tasty legume for deer. However, its downfall is that it can be quickly obliterated by overgrazing. Where deer numbers are high, Lablab requires large acreage to be planted for it to survive heavy grazing by deer. Lablab is best planted as a mix with other companion plants, including forage sorghum or corn. The sorghum and corn grow tall enough to defer over grazing problems and allow the Lablab to take hold as it climbs up their stalks. I don't recommend Lablab for land managers who have less than 10 acres of agricultural land to plant. It rarely survives in plots less than 5 to 10 acres in size. Most managers are working with less acreage than that for their food plot plantings.

Forage Soybeans are another excellent planting for deer. They contain high protein levels that can range from 20 to 35 percent. Like Lablab, soybeans need a lot of acreage to grow successfully. They are very susceptible to overgrazing. On our farm, deer have totally wiped out 5-acre plots before they got started. If you have enough land to plant them, however, forage soybeans should be included as a warm-season food plot in your management program.

Cowpeas and burgundy beans can also be included in the plants that require large acreage to grow without being overgrazed before they can grow successfully. If a manager has a large amount of land to plant, these are

▲ Lupine is a warm-season annual legume. It is a switch-hitter, however, and also works well as a cool-season planting in the south. The white variety is the best choice for northern plantings as it is the most winter-hardy of the three varieties.

▲ Lablab is a warm-season annual legume with twining vines and large leaflets. It contains up to 27 percent protein, making it ideal as summer forage for deer. Photo courtesy: Tecomate.

definitely two additional plantings that should be included in a food plot program. Deer absolutely love them and they provide quality nutrition and protein as well.

Lupine is a switch-hitter type plant because it is an excellent warm-season plant and works well as a cool-season planting, too. Lupines are an underused and underrated planting. Deer seek them to eat their tops. Turkey love lupine and use them as both a food source and a valuable brooding area. Lupines grow to heights of 3 or more feet. They provide about 30 to 35 percent protein levels. They should be planted in early spring. They come in three varieties, including

The following companies offer a wide variety of warm-season clovers as well as many other types of seeds.

SEED COMPANY SOURCES

- BioLogic 601-494-8859 www.mossyoak.com
- Cooper Seeds 877-463-6697 www.cooper-seeds.com
- Hunter's Specialties 319-395-0321 www.hunterspec.com
- Plot Spike 800-264-5281 www.plotspike.com
- SeedLand 386-963-2080 www.seedland.com
- Tecomate Seed 800-547-4101 www.tecomate.com
- Welter Seed & Honey Co. 800-470-3325 www.welterseed.com
- Whitetail Institute 1-800-688-3030 www.whitetailinstitute.com

▲ Ray Scott of Whitetail Institute launched the wildlife food plot industry with a variety of clover seeds. Today, the company has a broad line of seeds from which to choose.

white, blue, and yellow. Sweet blue lupine is best for deer and turkey food plots. Lupines grow nicely as far north as southern Canada. They are easy to grow and they make a beautiful-looking food plot as well.

Be cautious when purchasing designer clover blends. Countless seed companies now offer an almost unlimited variety of clover-mixed blends. It is crucial to find out where the company is established. For instance, if you live in the north, you don't want to buy seed from a southern-based company that has done all its research testing and product development in much warmer climates. The same holds true if you live in the south—you might not want to buy seed from northern-based companies.

Most companies provide a nationwide map depicting climate zones where their seeds have grown best. Check these maps out carefully before ordering seeds that are not designed to grow heartily in your area.

11. Cold-Hardy Food Plots

According to the latest research, the primary reason why the majority of hunters begin a deer management and food plot program is because they want to see more deer on each outing and to be able to harvest adult bucks with bigger antlers. In fact, according to a separate survey, another important element in developing food plots and deer management programs is to consistently attract and "hold" mature bucks on lands.

The reality of actually "holding or keeping" a mature buck on a piece of property for an indefinite period of time, however, boils down to one basic statement: It cannot be done. The myth is that planting food plots will create a foolproof method to hold a mature buck on smaller properties, or even larger acreage. However, it seems sensible to believe one can make plantings and deer management appealing enough to attract does and bucks to the land more consistently and to entice them to remain on the lands for longer periods of time.

▼ Taking adult bucks like this is the ultimate dream and goal of most deer hunters. It's the primary reason why so many hunters begin deer management and food plot programs. Photo courtesy: Ted Rose.

The most practical method to repeatedly draw adult bucks to your land is to protect male yearlings and to create a well-balanced wildlife and food plot management program. Such a plan must incorporate food, water, and cover. It also requires harvesting does every year on the property in order to keep the female herd at a sensible level. Healthy female deer—particularly the adult breeders—are essential to drawing and keeping adult bucks on well-managed lands. If any one of these elements is left out, it will throw a monkey wrench into your entire program. I can't emphasize enough that while food plots and management programs are excellent tools, they are not magic bullets. For hunters whose management plan is to significantly improve the number of deer they see and shoot on their lands, planning a variety of cool-season plantings is an absolute must in order to draw deer to the food plots during the months of October through January.

While the term "cool-season" is accurate to describe this group of plants, I feel strongly that the terminology is somewhat confusing, and it really doesn't convey the point as accurately as it could. I prefer to use the interchangeable phrases "cold-weather" or "winter-hardy" to define these types of cool-season plants. "Cold-season" or "winter-hardy" best describes how these cool-season plants survive and flourish in very low temperatures. Therefore, when I refer to a particular plant as either "cold-season" and/or "winter-hardy" plantings throughout this chapter, the two descriptions mean the same as the term used more often to describe this group.

Selecting what types of plants to include in cold-season food plots can be confusing. The considerations and variables of different plant species are many. Most cold-season plants can be seeded in either late spring, summer, or fall and remain attractive to deer long after the killing frosts occur; they remain particularly attractive as nutritional forage well into the late fall and

▲ A carefully planned deer and food plot management program can keep adult does from leaving your land. During the rut, healthy, mature does attract older bucks with big antlers, like this bad boy has. Photo courtesy: Ted Rose.

winter months. They are the best choice for northern climates and the wisest choice for deer stalkers who want to see and bag deer heading to their plots during the entire hunting season.

There are many cold-season species of plants that are commonly known and used by deer managers, and there are many other types of cold-tolerant species that are somewhat lesser known. All true types of cold-season plants are practical plantings meant to produce forage from late October through the frigid temperatures of January. Interestingly, the winter-hardy brassica and a few other plants reach their peak nutritional value and sweetness *only* after they are exposed to a few hard frosts. These cold-season plantings will survive well into the colder winter months, the time of year when most hunters want to have deer using their food plots during the hunting season.

Therefore, this chapter puts emphasis on the various types of cold-season or winter-hardy plant choices. It should be noted that the cold-season groups of plants are *the* most beneficial choices for managers for three primary reasons: They extend the growing season well past the first killing frost, particularly in places where the deer season runs into December and January. Cold-season plantings are excellent choices for those managers who plan to *hunt* over some of their food plots, and they also provide nutritional forage during the most stressful months of winter.

Throughout most of New England and the entire Northeast, the firearm season begins about mid-November. If you don't plan to use winter-hardy types of plantings, odds are the deer will not be feeding in your clover plots and, more importantly, they may feed somewhere else. Cold-hardy plants are highly attractive and beneficial to deer in the late season because most other warm season plantings have already been killed by several frosts. The native forage plants have also become dormant. Meanwhile your cold-weather plantings are active, palatable, and attractive to deer and other wildlife.

The cold and or winter-hardy plants included in this chapter are ones that I have planted for several years and that have provided the best success on our farm. I consider them top-choice, winter-hardy plantings that will definitely help you achieve your deer management goals.

One of the species of plants I always recommend as winter-hardy includes many of the annual plants within the *brassica* family. As a group, the brassicas are undeniably among the most winter-hardy of plantings; in fact, they could be classified as extreme winter-hardy plantings. Brassicas are high in protein and deer find them very digestible. When fertilized properly, the crude protein content of brassicas can range from 15 to 30 percent in the leaves, and from 8 to 15 or more percent in the roots. The leaves provide over 90 percent digestibility. Well-maintained brassica plots are extremely productive plantings and they can produce anywhere from six to more tons of forage per acre. This

▲ This photo was taken November 30. Deer fed almost daily in this brassica plot of Swede. By late December the deer ate all the bulbs seen here. The plot made the blind in the upper right background a choice hunting spot on our farm.

▲ I killed this 13-point buck during muzzle-loading season (December 19 at 11 AM). He followed a yearling doe in heat into a turnip plot. The buck was 50 yards away from the blind in the background.

volume of production makes brassicas a top choice for plantings, particularly on small acreage food plots. This is why brassica plants are commonly known to be favorite, cold-hardy resilient plantings among those who plant food plots.

Unlike other forage crops that become fibrous when they mature, the fiber content of brassica leaves doesn't increase with age. This means that brassica leaves remain very digestible to deer throughout their growing season. Additionally, deer tend not to eat brassicas in their early stages of growth as the leaves tend to taste bitter. This is one reason brassicas are rarely overgrazed by deer throughout the summer. Once the plants reach maturity in the late fall, however, the starches in the leaves convert into sugar, making the leaves sweeter and more palatable. The amount of time required for brassica plants to reach maturity depends mostly on the species and variety of types planted.

Most of the cold-tolerant plantings should be seeded between sixty and ninety days prior to the first expected killing frost. Forage kale and a couple of other varieties of winter-hardy plants are "slow-growers" and therefore they need extra time to grow to maturity.

They can be planted a little earlier than suggested in order for them to provide the best growth, nutrition, and the maximum amount of forage tonnage.

Many of the plants in the winter-hardy category are easy to grow, and require less work to maintain than other warm season clovers and other legumes, which require a lot of mowing, fertilizing, and other care. One of the most attractive points about many cold-tolerant plants is that they can be grown in tiny plots or larger areas ranging from a-half acre and up.

A vital point to consider when planting food plots is to always try and find out what your neighbors are growing in their food plots. Most often, they will be planting warm-season clovers, some other legumes, and perhaps the most well-known of the winter-hardy brassica plants—turnips. It also pays off to try and find out what local hunting clubs are planting in their lands. Local farmers will probably grow plenty of corn, clovers, soybeans, a few common small grains, and some grasses like Timothy. Discovering what the neighbors, farmers, and hunting clubs are planting will give you the edge in attracting deer to your food plots by using other types of plants—particularly the cold-tolerant varieties.

When planting food plots to attract deer during hunting season, you will benefit most by a well-thought-out planting strategy. The plan should incorporate some warm-season plantings and as many different types of winter-hardy crops as is practical to plant on the acreage. This type of plan ensures deer will use your plots during hunting season. Most importantly, discover what the neighbors are planting and be sure your food plots have a lot of items they don't. If you're limited to just a handful of food plots, this tactic becomes even more crucial to consistently draw deer to your land. This single maneuver will drastically improve your chances of enticing and keeping deer and other wildlife to your land more regularly, instead of having them visit your neighbor's food plots.

This ploy will significantly discourage your resident bucks and does from leaving your property for any extended periods of time. Once female deer realize they can secure palatable food on your land, when other natural and planted foods are dormant or dead, the chances are they will stay on your property instead of venturing off to find food elsewhere. *And you can take that advice to the deer-hunting bank.*

After you witness for yourself how much deer enjoy eating brassicas, you'll be hooked on them and will include them in all future plantings. Deer will turn your lush green food plots of forage rape, kale, Swede, and other types of brassicas into cleanly stripped, leafless stalks, leaving them to look like a miniature forest of tree trunks made naked by a tornado.

The brassica family includes the more familiar plants such as forage rape, kale, turnip, and canola rapeseed. The lesser known but equally attractive group of brassicas includes radish, rutabaga, Swede, mustard, cabbage, and cauliflower. All the brassicas make *excellent* food plot plantings. Their only downside is they should not be planted on the same plot for more than two consecutive years; this will prevent insect and root disease problems. Therefore, when planting several plots of brassicas, the plan must include some forethought about new locations to plant them every two years. However, it is worth the trouble.

Also incorporated in the cold-tolerant and/or winter-hardy section are other types of plants that range from being cold- and/or winter-hardy to being *extremely* winter-hardy plantings. They include both annuals and

▲ Our son, Cody, inspects a plot of forage rape. Rape is fast-growing and high-yielding. It is available to deer from November to January when other forages are dormant or less productive.

perennials such as herbs, forbs, cultivated type vegetables, cereal and other small grains, grasses, clovers, and other legumes. They are also an important part of any cold-hardy plan intended to provide forage from October through January.

Whether the plantings recommended below include any of the species mentioned above, they are all *generally* planted the same way. After preparing a plot, the soil depth of each of the plants below can range from top-seeding to planting either ¼ of an inch to ¾ of an inch below the soil's surface.

▲ Groundhog radishes don't require a lot of time to grow long and thick. This radish is only two months old. Photo courtesy: www.wildlifeperfect.com.

THE BRASSICAS
FORAGE RADISH

Forage radishes have long been a well-kept secret as a wildlife food crop within the family of the most popular cold-weather brassicas (forage rape, kale, turnip, radish, canola, hybrid pasa, t-raptor rapeseed, mustard, cabbage, cauliflower, rutabaga, and Swede). Over the last couple of years, however, managers across the country have learned that although it may take deer a season or two to discover what forage radishes are, once they do, deer are attracted to this new food plot crop in a really big way. This makes forage radishes the newest food plot buzz.

Radishes are large broadleaf annual brassicas that are very tolerant of cold temperatures. They can withstand temperatures of about 25 degrees and it will take several frosts of below-20-degree nights to kill them off. I have had excellent success planting a brand called Groundhog Radish from the Welter Seed and Honey Company.

Radishes not only provide forage for deer, but their long, wide root system acts as a soil builder by "till-

◄ This is a mixed planting of radishes and corn. Radishes also do well when mixed with other brassicas, sorghum, and other grains. Photo courtesy: www.wildlifeperfect.com.

▲ It may take deer a season to figure out what radishes are. Radishes have a strong odor to help deer locate them. This often leads to deer nibbling at the radishes and discovering that they like them. Photo courtesy: www.wildlifeperfect.com

ing" into the soil and naturally loosening packed-down soils. Forage radishes produce a large amount of root and leaf mass, providing about 200 units of nitrogen per acre, and they capture and recycle soil nutrients in this biomass. Radishes decompose quickly, helping to loosen soils and allow better water and air infiltration into the soil.

Radishes have large, long, fleshy taproots that can be up to 18 inches in length. The actual radish plant has wide, succulent leaves that are soft and palatable. It can grow semi-erect and reach about one to two feet high above the ground.

Radish leaf tops provide high nutrition and excellent production. Because of their fast establishment, they quickly suppress weed competition, too. They germinate ultra fast and grow heartily. They also provide dry-matter production of 5,000 pounds per acre of top growth plus 2,000 pounds per acre of root dry matter.

The forage radish looks like a long, green and white carrot, and it can reach lengths of 18 to 24 inches. Deer will eat the leaves as they turn green and succulent, unlike other forage crops such as rape, kale, and other brassicas, which deer often ignore until heavy frosts make them more attractive.

Radishes can be planted as late as August in the north and September in the south. By doing this, managers will ensure the crop will be mature at a time

▲ The top of the radish bulb is only the tip of the iceberg. A majority of the fruit lies underground. Deer will eagerly pull and dig radishes up soon after the plant undergoes a few hard frosts. Photo courtesy: Wildlife Perfect.®

radishes and are highly beneficial as cover crops and soil conditioners.

Radishes are much easier to grow than finicky sugar beets and are well adapted throughout the Northeast, Southeast, and Midwest. Like all other members of the Brassica family, radishes should not be grown on the same ground for more than two successive years because of a possible buildup of disease in the soil. Normally, a two-year rest period is enough before planting radishes again.

Incidentally, radishes are also good in stir fry or raw, as they have a crispy, crunchy texture and mild, sweet flavor. They are great in salads and are very nutritious, especially high in calcium, phosphorus, and iron. But best of all, your deer will love them.

Currently, Trophy Radishes are the only forage radishes on the market available to deer managers at a reasonable price. They are available at Welter Seed and Honey Company (www.welterseed.com) or Coopers Seed www.cooperseed.com. I have had excellent success with the brand GroundHog Radish which is available at Welter Seed & Honey Company.

RECAP

- **Seeding Rates:** Broadcast at 10 to 12 lbs per acre, or drill in rows at 5 to 9 lbs per acre. Seed prior to an expected rainfall.

- **pH Level:** Will tolerate 5.5 but prefers a pH is 5.9 to 6.5.

- **Planting Time:** Plant in spring or fall but no later than early September.

- **Depth of Seed:** Plant between ¼" to ½" depth.

- **Fertilizer:** Use 300 pounds each of 19-19-19 at planting.

- **Companion Mixes:** Plant alone or mix with other brassicas or with small grains and some clovers.

- **Overgrazing:** Limit grazing for about 60 days.

- **Extends Grazing Season:** Deer eat radish tops in the summer but devour the radishes from November to January.

- **Caution:** Do not plant radishes in the same food plot more than 2 consecutive years.

- **Avoid:** Do not plant radishes with other mustard family brassicas.

when they most want to attract deer—the archery or firearms seasons from October through January. I plant my radishes in July when I know rain is forecast.

Radishes can be planted alone or as part of a food-plot mix with small grains and clovers as long as *fewer* radish seeds are used in order not to shade out other mixtures. When planted with clovers or other mixes, they should be planted with no more than 15 to 20 percent of that forage mix and seeded at 1 to 2 pounds per acre. Radishes can also be planted in pure stands at about 10 pounds per acre for forage production or 15 pounds per acre to suppress weeds.

Other radish varieties include the Daikon radish (*Raphanus sativus*), which is also known as the winter radish, Japanese, Oriental, Asian, and many other names. Some varieties are also called forage or tillage

Although rape can be ▶ planted as late as August, I like to plant it in late May or early June to allow it to grow to its maximum potential. This small plot was planted in early June.

FORAGE RAPE

Forage rape is an exceptionally cold-weather brassica. Its leafy greens will draw deer to food plots throughout most of the United States and Canada. During my thirty years of planting food plots, I have found forage rape to be easy to plant, fast-growing, and easy to maintain. Deer will browse the rape leaves during the summer, but they really don't eat the plant aggressively until forage rape undergoes a few *hard* frosts in late fall. Forage rape is one of many winter-hardy plantings that can extend a deer's grazing season well into November and most times through January. When buying forage rape, be careful not to confuse it with oil-seed rape or canola rapeseed. There is rarely a season in which I do not include forage rape plantings in one or more food plots.

To give rape the best start possible, it should be planted early. In the north, plant it anytime after

◀ This plot of forage rape was planted near a corn plot. The deer ate all the corn by late October. The forage rape, on the other hand, lasted until late December.

the Fourth of July. I try to plant it when I know the forecast calls for rain within the next day or two. Rape will be ready to browse by deer about thirty to ninety days after it has established itself. For best results, plant rape in a plot that has good soil drainage. While forage rape will tolerate lower pH levels of between 5.3 and 5.9 it prefers a soil that ranges between 6.0 to 6.5 pH.

Rape seed is tiny and, like all tiny seed plants, it can be successfully top-sown on well-prepared soil. I prefer top-sowing rape on lightly tilled soil, assuring that I achieve proper seed-to-soil contact. Using a compactor will help achieve seed to soil contact. A 3-point hitch harrow attached to the back of your ATV will also provide excellent seed-to-soil contact. A harrow will level furrows or ridges and finish off the ground evenly.

Before planting, wait until the weeds emerge and when they reach about 2 inches in height, use a combination of herbicides to kill unwanted grass, broadleaves, and other noxious weeds. Be careful to follow all herbicide instructions exactly and wait to plant the plot at least seven to ten days later.

Disk the soil *lightly,* being careful not to turn it under any deeper than an inch or so in order to break up the compacted surface. By lightly disking the soil, you will prevent stimulating new weed growth.

Forage rape can be broadcasted at rates between 5 to 10 pounds per acre. Be sure not to use more seed than is recommended. Planting more seed than is recommended is among the biggest causes of growing spindly food plots, and sometimes over-seeding can cause complete plot failure. This is true of all types of food plot plantings. When it comes to brassicas, for the best results fertilize rape directly after planting it with 300 to 400 pounds of T-19 (19-19-19) per acre and then add about 100 pounds/per acre of 34-0-0. The fertilizer will help the rape attain maximum crude protein levels between 15 to 30 percent. Deer find rape to be very digestible forage.

I have had excellent success by planting brassicas in food plots by themselves, although sometimes I plant my brassicas with other brassica plants or even chicory. I will often plant cold-tolerant clovers or other types of legumes near my rape plots to help take the browsing pressure from deer off my brassicas plots from May to September. If you do decide to mix other plants in your brassica plots, use other winter-hardy plantings like sugar beets, radishes, or chicory. I plant cold-tolerant clovers like Kura, Kopa, alsike, sweet clover, and bird's-foot trefoil near some of my brassica plots too.

Deer will enthusiastically seek out forage rape as well as all the other types of brassicas particularly from November through January, the time of year hunters want to attract deer on their hunting lands. You will be amazed how many deer will visit your forage rape plot during hunting season. On our farm, deer regularly visit our brassica plots during daylight hours in the hunting season.

RECAP

- **Seeding Rates:** Broadcast prior to an expected rainfall at 4 to 9 pounds per acre. Drill at 2 to 6 pounds per acre.

- **pH Level:** Will tolerate low pH levels of 5.3 to 5.9 but prefers soil that range between 6.0 and 6.5 pH.

- **Planting Time:** Plant in early July in the north and September in the south. I plant my rape in mid-June.

- **Maturity:** 30 to 90 days.

- **Depth of Seed:** Plant no deeper than ¼ inch below the surface. Can be successfully top-seeded.

- **Fertilizer:** Fertilize with 300 pounds per acre of 19-19-19 and 100 pounds of ammonium sulfate (34-0-0) at planting. Planted with legumes eliminate the 34-0-0.

- **Companion Mixes:** Does very well alone but can be mixed with other brassicas, small grains, and clovers.

- **Overgrazing:** When planting dwarf varieties, limit grazing for at least 60 to 90 days.

- **Extends Grazing Season:** Deer browse the leaves lightly in summer but hardily from November to January.

- **Caution:** Rape needs good soil drainage.

- **Avoid:** Do not plant in the same food plot for more than 2 consecutive years.

THE BRASSICAS

FORAGE KALE

Kale is among the top three fall forage *brassicas*, and is a winter-hardy "green" that provides high nutritional value to wildlife with crude protein levels ranging from about 15 to 28 percent. The only downside to kale is that it is a slower-growing plant than turnips and rape. If you plant kale, you have to allow at least four months for it to grow to maturity, or about 100 to 150 days.

To give forage kale a head-start it should be planted as early as May or June in the north and later in the south. Plant it when the forecast calls for rain within a day or two. Kale prefers good soil drainage. The best pH levels will be between 5.6 and 6.5 but if the pH gets too high the leaves will begin to molt. Plant the kale seeds about ¼ inch deep.

Forage kale should be broadcasted at rates between four to five pounds per acre and not more than is recommended. At planting fertilize kale with 300 to 400 pounds of T-19 per acre. For best results, remember that kale requires a little more fertilizer than most brassicas including 2 to 4 pounds per acre of boron,

50 to 140 pounds per acre of magnesium, and about ⅛ to ⅕ of a pound of copper and zinc but only when a soil test suggests they are necessary. I use a variety called Maris Kestrel kale, but there are many types of forage kale available.

When planted early enough, I have had good success planting kale, particularly when I plant it alone. Like other brassicas, however, kale can be mixed with other brassicas. If you do decide to mix other plants in with kale, use sugar beets, radishes, or chicory. It is important to use less kale per acre when mixing other plantings to prevent kale from shading out the plantings.

As soon as there have been a couple of deep freezes, deer will march into your kale stand with a serious intent to eat as much as they can. I plant about an acre or more each year and I'm never disappointed by how it attracts deer to my land, and the results, during the hunting season. Once you plant kale and witness the use by deer in winter, it will become a vital part of your yearly plantings, too.

◀ Forage kale is one of the slowest-growing brassica plants and requires about 110 to 150 days to grow to maturity.

▲ Deer love kale. Kale needs a full four months to grow. So plan accordingly in well-prepared soil. Photo courtesy: Millborn Seeds.

RECAP

- **Seeding Rates:** Broadcast 4 to 5 pounds per acre in a properly prepared firm, moist seedbed.

- **pH Level:** Desirable pH levels are between 5.5 and 6.5. If the pH gets too high, leaves will molt.

- **Planting Time:** Can be planted almost anywhere in the United States in June or July.

- **Maturity:** Requires 110 to 150 days to mature

- **Depth of Seed:** Plant no deeper than ¼ inch below the surface. It can be top-seeded successfully.

- **Fertilizer:** When planted alone fertilize with 300 to 400 pounds of 19-19-19 per acre at planting. Also requires 2 to 4 pounds of boron, 100 pounds of magnesium per acre and trace amounts of copper and zinc.

- **Companion Mixes:** Does very well planted alone but can be mixed with other brassicas, or chicory.

- **Crude Protein Levels:** 15 to 28 percent.

- **Overgrazing:** Limit grazing of dwarf varieties to 60 to 90 days.

- **Extends Grazing Season:** Plants will be eaten enthusiastically from November to January.

- **Caution:** Prefers well-drained loam soil but will do nicely in other well-drained soils.

- **Avoid:** Do not plant in the same food plot for more than 2 consecutive years.

CANOLA RAPESEED

Canola rapeseed is a fast-growing brassica that is a quality form of rapeseed. It has a high yield when planted as directed. Canola's leaves have a crude protein level that range from 20 to 30 percent. The TDN (total digestible nutrients) can range from 50 to 75 percent dry matter and the dry matter can be from 10 to 18 percent fiber. Interestingly, when canola seeds are crushed they contain up to 40 percent vegetable oil.

It is a fall plant that deer find especially attractive from October through January. I have found that deer will feed on both the stems and leaves as soon as it is ready to graze, which is 60 to 90 days after planting it.

For this reason, I plant at least one acre or more to prevent deer from overgrazing a small plot. In the North canola can be planted in August or in early spring, April or May. I have found, however, the earlier it is planted the better your success will be. Canola takes about two to three months to mature.

Canola is a leafy brassica earnestly sought after by deer through the summer and particularly from November to January like the other brassicas are. I include canola in my food plots most years.

As with all brassicas, canola is cold-tolerant, and this particular plant is also tolerant of drought and heat. It needs a plot that has good drainage with a pH level

▼ Canola rapeseed is a fast-growing brassica. It can be mixed with clovers, chicory, and or small grains or strip-planted next to other brassicas. When crushed, canola seeds contain 40 percent vegetable oil.

THE BRASSICAS

between 5.5 and 7.5. It will do best, however in a pH of 6.0 or above. Test your soil and, if need be, apply lime accordingly.

Although the directions say to plant the canola seed about ¼ inch deep, canola seeds are very tiny. As such, you'll have excellent success top-sowing canola. Plant it in a firm, finely tilled, moist seed bed. Then broadcast 8 pounds per acre. It can be broadcast with a quality hand-operated Harvest Broadcast Spreader. Compact the soil to make good soil-to-seed contact using a harrow to level furrows or ridges and finish off the ground. Again, by planting the seed just prior to a forecasted rainfall you will greatly enhance the seeds' germination.

To allow canola to have the best production you will need to provide 200 to 300 pounds of 19-19-19 per acre and 200 pounds per acre of ammonium sulfate or 200 pounds per acre of 46-0-0 (urea). When a plot of canola is fertilized properly, it will provide 20 to 30 percent protein, and about 2 tons of forage per acre. When canola seed is crushed it will contain about 35 percent vegetable oil and what remains will have about 30 percent protein and about 10 percent fat and fiber.

While I like to plant most of my plots as "pure plots," meaning only one seed, I have had success planting canola with other brassicas such as kale and rape. When it comes to canola, it is important to plant clovers or other legumes nearby to help divert the deer from over-browsing the canola before November.

This plan has saved several of my canola as well as my kale, rape, turnip, and sugar beet plots from being overeaten by deer. They prefer the sweet, tender clovers, alfalfa, and bird's-foot trefoil from May to September—especially when the plots have been maintained well with fertilizer and mowings.

You will be pleasantly surprised to see how heavily deer will eat canola from November through January.

It will help bring deer on your property during the time you want them there—deer season. Give canola a try—you won't regret it. Like most brassicas, it should not be planted in the same plot for more than two consecutive years to prevent disease problems.

RECAP

- **Seeding Rates:** Broadcast at 4 to 5 pounds per acre in a properly prepared, firm seedbed prior to rain.
- **pH Level:** Requires pH levels of 5.5 to 7.5 but prefers a pH of 6.0.
- **Planting Time:** Can be planted in April or in early August.
- **Maturity:** Quick-growing, matures at 60 to 90 days.
- **Digestibility (TDN)** About 75 percent contains high moisture content.
- **Depth of Seed:** Plant ¼-inch below the surface. Can be top-sowed successfully. Plant prior to a rainfall.
- **Fertilizer:** Planted alone fertilize with 200 pounds of 19-19-19, 200 lbs of 34-0-0 (ammonium sulfate), *and/or* 150 pounds of 46-0-0 (urea) per acre at planting.
- **Companion Mixes:** Does well planted alone. Can be mixed with other brassicas, clovers, wheat, and chicory.
- **Crude Protein Levels:** 20 to 30 percent.
- **Overgrazing:** Generally not an issue after 30 days.
- **Extends Grazing Season:** Plants will be grazed heavily from October to January.
- **Caution:** Prefers well-drained soils.
- **Avoid:** Do not plant in the same area for more than 2 consecutive years.

TURNIPS

All varieties of turnips are closely related to swedes. Like other brassicas, turnips are classified as cold-weather plantings. Deer will eat the turnip leaves from mid-September until January, adding to their value for early-fall bow hunters. The leaf tops have between 15 to 25 percent crude protein content. Even the plants' roots contain 10 to 15 percent protein. They love to eat the bulb as well and will begin to do so as soon as the plant undergoes a few hard frosts. An acre of turnips can provide a crop anywhere from one to five tons per acre of dry matter, which includes the turnip bulb as well.

Sometimes it may take a season for deer to actually discover what turnips are. But once they do, they quickly become addicted to them and will seek them out feverishly as soon as temperatures begin to fall.

Turnips are an excellent choice as a food plot planting for the colder regions of the United States and Canada. They are also drought tolerant. And they can be planted late even in northern latitudes. Turnips can be planted as late as July or early August. In the southern regions turnips can be planted in August or September. I find that planting them no later than mid-June to the July 4th weekend gives them a longer growing period and helps them to fully mature, which usually takes about 90 to 120 days.

Turnips can tolerate slightly acidic soil but prefer a pH level between 6.0 and 6.5. I have had most suc-

▲ This is a field of Tecomate Barkant Turnips. Barkant is a hardy forage variety of turnip that produces more leaf top growth and less underground bulb growth. Photo courtesy: Tecomate Seed.

cess when I plant them in medium loamy soil or heavy loamy soil. They will not do well, however, in wet ground or heavy clay soils.

Forage turnip seeds are *really* tiny. Because of the minuscule size of the seed, turnips are best seeded using a quality drop seeder with strong wheels, a Pro Broadcast Spreader with a rain cover (it helps to keep the seed from bouncing out over rough ground), or a quality hand-operated Harvest Broadcast Spreader. I also use my Arctic Cat Planter/Drill Seeder that attaches to my ATV via a 3-point hitch.

As soon as they are planted, fertilize them with about 400 pounds of 19-19-19 per acre (300 pounds will work, too, if your budget is tight). For best results about six weeks later, top-dress the plot with about 100 to 200 pounds of ammonium sulfate (34-0-0) per acre. This will help increase the production of the plant and bulb.

When the plant gets to be about 10 inches high, deer will start eating the leaves. It will take 90 to 120 days for turnips to fully mature. Unfortunately, if the deer graze on the turnip plants before then, they can hurt the production of both the tops and bulbs. That is why I like to plant either the turnip varieties that have more top growth or winter-hardy clovers near my winter-hardy plants (sugar beets, turnips, kale, rape, canola, etc.). The succulent clover helps to distract and deflect the deer from eating *"my precious"* brassicas. I want them to be in prime condition from October to January, when I'm hunting deer.

You will find that turnips make an extraordinary crop that will prove be an integral part of your winter-hardy planting program. Once the deer discover what they are they will eat them until they are gone. But remember that all *brassicas* should not be planted in the same plot more than two consecutive years. It would be even better to rotate them yearly.

There are a lot of different forage varieties to choose from. I like Purple Top for their large bulbs. I also like Barkant Forage for its very high concentrations of protein. I also plant varieties that have been selected to produce more top growth than bulb size. By doing this I provide deer with leafy turnip forage as the other varieties are producing larger bulbs. Once you discover how well turnips draw deer during the hunting season you will be as addicted to them as the deer are.

▲ Deer eat both the leaves and bulbs of turnip plants from mid-September until January, depending on critical low temperatures and snow cover. Photo courtesy: Tecomate Seed.

RECAP

- **Seeding Rates:** Broadcast tiny seeds at 3 to 4 pounds per acre like all top-sown plantings, best planted prior to an expected rainfall.

- **pH Level:** Requires pH levels of 6.0 to 6.5.

- **Planting Time:** In the north plant in July or early August. Can be planted as early a June. In the south, from August to September.

- **Maturity:** Between 90 to 120 days.

- **Depth of Seed:** Plant ¼ inch below the surface. Turnips can be top-sowed successfully prior to an expected rainfall.

- **Fertilizer:** At planting fertilize with 300 to 400 pounds of 19-19-19 per acre. Top dress with about 150 pounds of ammonium sulfate (34-0-0) about 45 to 60 days later.

- **Companion Mixes:** Does very well planted alone. Can also be mixed with other brassicas, clovers, and chicory.

- **Crude Protein Levels:** Tops provide from 15 to 25 percent protein levels. Roots have 10 to 15 percent protein levels.

- **Overgrazing:** Is generally not an issue after 30 days.

▲ Turnips are ready for grazing when they are about 10 to 12 inches tall or about 85 to 110 days after they are planted.

- **Extends Grazing Season:** From October through January. Plots will look like they were dug up with spade shovels.

- **Temperatures:** Tops will survive in extremely cold temperatures between 15 and 20 degrees. Bulbs will survive in temperatures 10 degrees colder than the leaves.

- **Caution:** Prefers fertile loamy soil but also does nicely in clay that is not too heavy. Does not do well in wet or inadequately drained soils.

- **Avoid:** Do not plant in the same food plot for more than 2 consecutive years.

THE BRASSICAS

SWEDE

One of my favorite brassica plantings is swede, which is a close relative of rutabaga and turnips. Deer find it highly digestible. The late maturing swede is noted for high yields and excellent disease resistance. I found swede seed at Welter Seed & Honey. It is called Major Plus Swede. It offers wildlife enthusiasts high leaf yield and excellent deer preference. Major Plus Swede is characterized by its white, fleshy bulb and bronze skin color. The leaves are very high in energy and low in fiber. Deer will hardily graze the leaves, stems, roots, and bulbs but at different times. A plot of Swede can end up looking like a mine-field after the deer begin eating the bulbs.

This plant extends the grazing season well into January, if the deer don't eat it all before that. I planted a rather small test plot the first year and our deer began eating the leaves in late September and then the stems, roots, and the bulbs after a couple of extended cold snaps.

Major Plus can also be used as a break crop in order to convert older pastures to different species and newer varieties. An annual crop gives a bigger window to eliminate the old, undesirable forage through the use of herbicides, tillage, and the competition of the brassica crop itself.

Swede can be planted at ¼ inch depth. However, I planted it on top of very closely mowed plot of hay. This is a method of planting I have been experimenting with for a few years. First I cut the hay or grass as close to the ground as possible. Then I use Big N' Tuff herbicide to kill the hay or other type grass. Although the directions of the herbicide say to wait seven to 10 days before planting, I wait no more than six to secen days to seed

▼ This is a small plot of a variety of Swede known as Major Plus Swede. This photo was taken in July. Swede can be successfully top sown over a prepared plot if it is seeded before a predicted rainfall.

▲ This is a Swede plot in July. Five days after the grass was killed with herbicide, the tiny seeds were top-sown. Note how well the plant grew using my unorthodox planting method.

definitely reduces a lot of work used when preparing a plot in the traditional recommended ways for seeding. Most importantly, it has helped to almost totally eliminate weed problems in plots I plant using this method of seeding. You may want to try planting a couple of plots like this as an experiment of your own. If it works as well for you as it does for me—well, then you can expand on it. Otherwise, swede can be top-seeded on a well-prepared plot.

RECAP

- **Seeding Rates:** Broadcast tiny seeds 1 to 2 pounds per acre prior to an expected rainfall.

- **pH Level:** Requires pH levels of 6.0 to 6.5.

- **Planting Time:** In the north plant in April or May.

- **Maturity:** About 180 days.

- **Depth of Seed:** Plant ¼ inch below the surface. Swede can be top-sowed successfully prior to an expected rainfall.

- **Fertilizer:** At planting fertilize with 300 to 400 pounds of 19-19-19. Six weeks later, finish off with 100 to 150 pounds of 34-0-0 (ammonium sulfate).

- **Companion Mixes:** Does very well planted alone. Can also be mixed with other brassicas, clovers, wheat, and chicory.

- **Crude Protein Levels:** Tops provide from 15 to 25 percent protein levels. Roots have 10 to 15 percent protein levels.

- **Overgrazing:** Is generally not an issue after 30 days.

- **Extends Grazing Season:** From October through January. Plots will look like they were dug up with spade shovels.

- **Temperatures:** Tops will survive in extremely cold temperatures between 15 and 20 degrees. Bulbs will survive in temperatures 10 degrees colder than the leaves.

- **Avoid:** Don't plant in places with a high rate of sulfur in the soil. Does not do well in wet or inadequately drained soils.

- **Avoid:** Do not plant in the same food plot for more than 2 consecutive years.

the plot and try to do it when there is a predicted rainfall. I do this once the grass shows signs of being dead, which usually takes four days. Then I use a hand-seeder to plant the seed directly on top of the closely mowed dead grass. Next I use a compactor to press the seed firmly into the ground. I make a few passes to ensure that the seed is making good contact with the soil. I have had excellent success using this method with all types of seed, particularly the tiny seeds of a lot of brassicas.

The system of planting seed has proven to me to be a terrific way for plants to get a quick jump start over weed growth. I plant using this planting technique. It

The Vegetable-Type Brassicas

Brassica is a genus of plants within the mustard family (Brassicaceae). Botanists have long argued about the classification and status of the Brassica species and its subspecies. Some brassica plants particularly the forage varieties of turnips, rape, and radishes and kale, and canola, are the more commonly selected brassicas to plant as wildlife food plots. The members of this genus are grouped as cruciferous vegetables including: cabbage, cauliflower, broccoli, Brussell sprouts, mustard spinach, rutabaga, squash, kohlrabi and mustard. I refer to this group of brassicas as the "other vegetable-type" brassicas. While they are grown more commonly by farmers for economic value to humans, deer love to eat them as well making them an ideal wildlife food plot. In order for the vegetable type brassicas to grow successfully, however, as wildlife food plots, they can't be allowed to be over browsed by deer before they reach maturity. Therefore each type of plant should only be planted in very large plots of five acres or more. Even taking this precaution may not be enough to keep deer from wiping out an entire five acre field of any of the vegetable type brassicas. Erecting a temporary electric fence may be the only solution to keeping deer out of vegetable type brassica wildlife plots.

Cabbage is a non-traditional brassica crop that deer find attractive from October to December. Cabbage is an easy-to-grow plant that is hardy, and deer find it delicious. It is ideal for small and large food plots. Cabbage thrives best in cool weather and should be planted in areas that get some shade during the dog-days of summer. By planting types with different maturity dates, you can ensure that forage will be available during hunting season.

MUSTARD is an aromatic, leafy brassica that is both delicious and nutritious to deer. It is easy to grow and an excellent source of vitamins and minerals. Mustard is cold-tolerant and produces green leaves with an aroma that deer smell easily. They can be planted in small or large food plots. Mustard is truly an unorthodox food plot plant. Although some traditional wildlife seed mixes may include some mustard, it is best to plant an entire plot with this crop. Mustard seed can be found under vegetable seed in most farm seed outlets.

Although mustard and cabbage are not as popular as the more familiar brassica seeds are, they should not be overlooked by managers as possible winter-hardy plantings. They are almost assuredly *not* grown by bordering neighbors or nearby farmers. Planting the lesser-known or popular brassicas is just what the doctor—*the Deer Doctor*—ordered to create the entire food plot illusion—*you can take that to the deer hunting bank*.

Cauliflower, summer squash, rutabaga, and pumpkin are also terrific cold-season vegetable and/or brassica plantings that will also provide top-quality nourishment. They can extend grazing opportunities from October to December. However, finding places that sell bulk seed for cauliflower, summer squash, rutabaga and pumpkins can be problematic and expen-

◄ Deer are quickly attracted to mustard plots as it is an aromatic plant. It is one of several vegetable species of brassicas.

THE BRASSICAS

sive. You can purchase affordable vegetable type seeds including pumpkin in bulk at www.mcgoughsinc.com or in smaller amounts at www.monsterbuckfoodplot.com.

All the brassicas mentioned are *ideal* winter-hardy plantings that managers can use to attract and keep deer using their lands regularly. They will all provide *superlative* winter-hardy hunting plots that will survive the harshest winter conditions.

BUTTERNUT SQUASH

Butternut squash is in the plant family known as Cucurbitaceae that consists of various squashes, melons, gourds, cucumber, pumpkins, luffas, and watermelons, all of which are attractive plants as food plots for wildlife. Deer are particularly fond of butternut squash and some of the other varieties of squash. By following a few simple rules, squash can make even the most novice food plot manager a success.

It doesn't take deer and other wildlife long to discover what squash are. Many food plot managers have reported excellent success planting butternut squash. One manager told me he "witnessed the same group of deer return to a squash plot over and over again during a single day." Once there are several *hard* frosts deer will enthusiastically and relentlessly visit a food plot of squash until they have eliminated the crop.

▲ Deer love butternut squash. They are easy to grow and provide quality nutrition for deer.

▲ Butternut squash is highly attractive to deer. However, the plot should be at least one acre or more or the deer will consume it long before hunting season.

Like sugar beets and other winter-hardy plantings, squash is erroneously thought of as a brassica. In fact, squash is a biennial vegetable. Squash is a cold-hardy planting that offers deer a succulent vegetable with a high rate of digestibility. Their sugar content can range as high as 20 percent. Their protein content is between 12 to 15 percent as well.

In northern areas squash can be planted in late June or early July because they have a short growing season of only about 60 days. I plant my squash in late July prior to an expected rainfall. As long as there isn't extended period without rainfall, a late-August planting will provide a mature squash crop by very early October.

If you are going to include summer squash in your food plot program make sure you lime the intended squash plots heavily *long* before planting them. It should be fertilized with 400 pounds per acres of

19-19-19. I plant it ¼ inch below the soil. As long as the seed makes good seed-to-soil contact and it is compacted properly, top-seeding squash will work.

It is not recommended to plant butternut squash in the same plot two years in a row in order to avoid disease. Once you see how much deer like squash you'll include them as one of your primary food plots for many years to come.

RECAP

- **Seeding Rates:** Broadcast alone at 2 to 4 pounds per acre.
- **Maturity:** Short growing season 60 days.
- **pH Level:** Prefers pH levels of 6.2 to 6.5.
- **Planting Time:** Plant in early spring when soil temperatures reach 70 degrees Fahrenheit.
- **Depth of Seed:** Plant ¾ to inch below the surface in a well-prepared plot that is compacted for best soil-to-seed contact prior to a rainfall.

- **Fertilizer:** In the absence of a soil test use basic NPK formulas for vegetables including 5-10-10, 10-10-10, or 16-16-8. Use 21-0-0 as a side dressing.
- **Companion Mixes:** Plant alone.
- **Crude Protein Levels:** Protein 5 percent.
- **Crude Fiber Content:** About .22 percent.
- **Digestibility:** Near 98 percent.
- **Overgrazing:** Generally not an issue after 30 days.
- **Extends Grazing Season:** From October through November.
- **Temperatures:** Withstands cold temperatures.
- **Caution:** Plant no more than two years in the same plot and then rotate summer squash to other plots.
- **Avoid:** Planting in soils of pure clay.

THE BRASSICAS

THE GRAINS

Grain corn is more aptly referred to as an annual warm-season planting than a cold- or winter-season planting. However, it is an important crop into late October and early November for deer. I included grain corn in the cold- and winter-hardy category for managers to grow it as a food plot to be left standing into the dead of winter.

Grain corn is also called feed corn and is an excellent early-fall crop that is ranked as an apex food preference of deer. In fact, corn is among the plantings that deer consider as *candy*. I want to be perfectly clear that I feel corn is a prime choice food plot planting, although I do so with several reservations.

There should be no doubt that if you have enough acres of agricultural land (fields), and plenty of money, time, farm equipment, and experience in growing corn, grain corn is a *must-have* plant for your deer management food plot program, particularly if it is left standing throughout the deer season. If, on the other

▼ This is the last field of corn ever planted on our farm. I don't plant forage corn anymore; it costs too much per bag and fertilizer and herbicide are cost-prohibitive too.

◄ A field of corn on our farm. For best results corn should be planted in large fields. Otherwise the corn seed will be dug up by deer, turkeys, crows, squirrels, skunks, and raccoons.

hand, you lack some or all of the above-mentioned necessities to grow corn successfully, you may want to reconsider planting corn as part of your management program.

I stopped planting corn for a wide variety of practical and financial reasons. My primary motivation, though, was that there are hundreds if not thousands of acres of corn grown by every farmer around our farm, making grain corn *the* most *prevalent* planting available in my area by far. Growing several acres of corn on our farm would be redundant as our deer have enough corn to eat without me having to offer it to them as well. It would also require a large portion of our fields to plant corn successfully, which would limit the number of acres I could dedicate to other crops, particularly those crops that are much more winter-hardy than corn.

Corn seed can also be expensive to plant. At this writing, a 50-pound bag of Round-Up Ready deer forage corn is $239! Add the cost of lime, the different fertilizers (T-19, nitrogen, and ammonium sulfate), and the herbicides for weed control (which is a critical factor to grow corn successfully), plus other fertilizers equally as expensive such as nitrogen, ammonium sulfate. In addition to that, add the cost of the chemicals needed to control weed growth (which is the most crucial factor in growing corn successfully), and it quickly becomes apparent how planting corn is one heck of an expensive undertaking as a food plot. There is no getting away from the fact that planting corn is expensive, time-consuming, and involves a lot of hard work and farm machinery to plant successfully.

If that isn't enough shock therapy about including corn as a food plot, here are some other realities about planting corn. I had a 2-acre field of feed corn quickly laid to waste by deer and other wildlife before it even got close to deer season. I have a friend who planted 20 acres of sweet corn that was totally devastated by deer and other wildlife by mid-August.

Corn is eaten by countless critters including bears, turkeys, squirrels, and a wide array of non-hunted animals including crows, blackbirds, skunks, possums, raccoons, pigeons, and even beavers. It generally takes at least a 5-acre plot to get past being totally eaten by animals other than deer. Even more so, corn is drought-sensitive.

By now you might be asking why I even bothered including corn in this chapter. Well, as I said at the start, when you have the land, equipment, time, money, and know-how, food plot managers should definitely make grain corn part of their food plot program. But unfortunately, grain corn is, without a doubt, not a crop for the beginner or average food plotter.

But don't be troubled: There is an alternative choice to grain corn that managers, particularly those who have small acreage, can plan to use that is *much less* expensive per bag, requires less fertilizer, herbicide chemicals, and it is easier to plant. It is also attractive to deer and provides them with quality nutrition. It is especially beneficial to those managers who have grain corn grown all around their land (see Grain Sorghum).

THE GRAINS

GRAIN SORGHUM (Milo)

Grain sorghum, a.k.a Milo, is an erect, short-growing annual unlike the taller silage and hay varieties. The grain selections are the only varieties that are nutritionally beneficial to deer. Grain sorghum can be grown almost anywhere within the United Sates as long as the growing season allows it to mature before the first frost occurs. Grain sorghum needs about 90 to 120 days to reach maturity. It makes an excellent substitute for corn.

Grain sorghum can be planted alone or as a mixture. It can be mixed with other plants including any of the beans, peas, even jointvetch. I plant my grain sorghum alone and use a mix of clovers along one side of the planting and a mix of other legumes on the other side. The deer will feed actively on the clovers and legumes, heavily overlooking the sorghum seed heads, which are attractive to deer. Deer will occasionally begin to feed on grain sorghum as early as August. However, deer make the most use of sorghum after the plant matures and feed on the seed heads from fall to late winter depending on the type of grain sorghum that is planted.

I plant grain sorghum in late May, but it can be sown as late as June. In the south it can be planted in April or May. It doesn't like acidic soils and prefers a pH between 5.9 and 7.4. Try to purchase the bird-resistant varieties that can be identified by their red seed heads. The red selections are more attractive to deer than the lighter colored varieties are. Taller varieties are better than the dwarf types of grain sorghum.

Grain sorghum, like corn, is a terrific summer and early food plot planting. If left standing, both crops will last into late fall and early winter providing forage for your deer. On our farm, grain sorghum attracts deer well into December when corn cobs are often frozen solid.

▼ Grain sorghum is a close relative to corn and provides most if not all of the same nutritional value. The seed is much less expensive and doesn't require as much fertilizer.

▼ I have had excellent success with replacing grain corn with grain sorghum (Milo). Purchase the bird-resistant varieties that have red-seed heads.

THE GRAINS

▲ When planting grain sorghum do not plant the Sudan, sweet sorghum, or cane varieties for deer. Grain varieties are the only type of sorghums beneficial for deer.

RECAP

- **Seeding Rates:** Broadcast alone at 8 to 10 pounds per acre or drill alone at 6 pounds per acre prior to an expected rainfall.
- **pH Level:** Likes pH levels of 5.9 to 7.4.
- **Planting Time:** In the north plant in May or June. In the south plant in April or May.
- **Maturity:** 90 to 120 days.
- **Depth of Seed:** ¾-inch to 1-inch deep. Can be top-sowed successfully in a well-prepared plot compacted well for best soil-to-seed contact just prior to a rainfall.
- **Fertilizer:** At planting 300 to 400 pounds of 19-19-19 and top with 100 pounds of actual nitrogen.
- **Companion Mixes:** Does well planted alone. Can also be mixed with beans, peas, or legumes like jointvetch.
- **Overgrazing:** Generally not an issue after 30 days.
- **Extends Grazing Season:** From October through December.
- **Temperatures:** Withstands late-winter temperatures.
- **Caution:** Do not plant sweet, Sudan, or cane sorghum as deer forage.
- **Avoid:** Short-growing varieties.

GRAIN RYE ANNUAL BUNCHGRASS

Rye (*Secale cereale*) is a top-shelf cold-season bunch-grass that is *the* very best winter-hardy deer attractant of the other five small grains, including oats, wheat, sorghum, triticale, and wheat. All of these grains come in spring and winter varieties. The winter varieties are best for food plotters. Rye is grain rye, not ryegrass. It is a cereal rye.

Rye is the most well-liked of the small grains among food plot managers. It is even more tolerant of cold temperatures than winter wheat. Rye reaches heights of 2 to 5 feet. Deer eat the seed heads and leaves. Rye is also nutritious providing 10 to 25 percent protein levels.

Rye is very easy to plant and grow. I have never experienced a crop failure when using rye. Plant rye as early as possible in the spring. I generally try to plant it in April if the weather is cooperative. Winter rye can be planted in mid-August in the north and October in the south. If you plant rye alone it can be broadcast at about 100 to 120 pounds per acre. In mixed plots, use about half that amount. Winter rye, like all the winter hardy small grains is inexpensive. A 50-pound bag of the winter hardy small grains averages about $15 to $20 per bag.

There are countless varieties of cereale rye to choose from. Some forage varieties include Winter King, Wintermore, and Wintergrazer 70.

Rye is an attractive food plot particularly in fall and winter. If you have never planted cereale rye give it a try. You'll be pleasantly surprised by how easy it is to plant, how well it grows, how trouble-free it is, how much the deer like it, and how long it will last into the cold weather. It is a must-plant food plot on our farm.

▲ A 1-acre field of grain rye (*Secale cereale*) on our land. Don't confuse grain rye with annual or perennial ryegrass.

THE GRAINS

▲ Grain rye is an excellent late-fall or early-spring cover crop that germinates quickly. I plant it in August when rainfall is predicted. By October, deer begin to feed in it regularly.

RECAP

- **Seeding Rates:** Broadcast alone at 100 to 120 pounds per acre. When drilled or planted in a mix, use half that amount. Seed prior to an expected rainfall.

- **pH Level:** Tolerates acidic soil but prefers pH levels when they are of 5.9 to 6.5.

- **Planting Time:** In spring plant rye as early as possible. Winter rye can be planted in mid-August.

- **Maturity:** 90 to 120 days.

- **Depth of Seed:** Plant ¼ inch deep. Can be top-sowed successfully prior to a rainfall.

- **Fertilizer:** At planting use 300 to 400 pounds of 19-19-19.

- **Companion Mixes:** Does very well planted alone. Can also be mixed with a variety of clovers, other legumes, peas, wheat, and chicory.

- **Overgrazing:** Generally not an issue.

- **Extends Grazing Season:** Deer eat rye October through January.

- **Temperatures:** Withstands late-winter temperatures.

- **Caution:** Don't confuse rye grain with perennial ryegrass.

- **Avoid:** Don't apply the nitrogen if rye is planted with clovers or legumes.

WHEAT

Winter wheat is the "mother" of fall cereal grain forage food crops. Deer eat wheat in spring, fall and especially winter. Winter wheat provides 10 to 25 percent protein levels. It is second to cereale rye as the most winter-hardy grain but more palatable than rye.

Wheat is generally planted in September in the north and October in the south. It can be planted in the spring as well. When planted alone, broadcast about 100 to 120 pounds per acre. If wheat is planted in a mix reduce the amount by half 50 to 60 pounds per acre. Wheat sprouts before freezing occurs, then becomes dormant until the soil warms up in the spring. The wheat grows and matures until ready to be harvested by early July.

Wheat likes a soil pH of 6.0 and higher and will produce best under these conditions. Fertilize it with about 300 to 400 pounds of 19-19-19 when it is planted.

Winter wheat is compatible with a variety of clovers, other legumes including Austrian winter peas, bird's-foot trefoil, and chicory. The clovers and legumes also help the wheat by "fixing" nitrogen in the soil—which the wheat uses. Deer find winter wheat irresistible.

As with other grains, when seeding wheat, first firm the plot using a cultipacker behind an ATV or a light drag. Broadcast the seed evenly across the food plot. Don't cover the seed more than about one inch deep. To ensure successful establishment of wheat or any grain make sure there is good seed-to-soil contact. As with all seeds the best time for planting is just prior to an expected rainfall.

There are many varieties of wheat from which to choose. Many wheat varieties have been designed as forage selections which are the most appropriate varieties for deer.

◀ Deer eat the tender, nutritious foliage from fall to spring. Winter wheat has a protein level of about 15 to 30 percent.

▲ I have had excellent success with this hybrid cross of wheat and rye known as Tricticale. Deer, turkeys, pheasants, and geese are all attracted to Triticale. It is an easy plant to grow and it isn't expensive either.

RECAP

- **Seeding Rates:** Broadcast alone at 100 to 120 pounds per acre.

- **pH Level:** Prefers 6.0 to 6.5.

- **Planting Time:** Plant in September in the north and October in the south.

- **Depth of Seed:** Plant one to 1.5 inches deep. Can be top-sowed successfully in a well-prepared plot that is well compacted for best soil-to-seed contact just prior to a rainfall.

- **Fertilizer:** At planting use 300 to 400 pounds of 19-19-19.

- **Companion Mixes:** Does well planted alone. Can also be mixed with legumes.

- **Crude Protein Levels:** From 12 to 25 percent.

- **Overgrazing:** Generally not an issue after 30 days.

- **Extends Grazing Season:** From October through December.

- **Temperatures:** Withstands late-winter temperatures.

- **Caution:** Before planting a particular variety of wheat, check with Agricultural Extension agents to see what varieties do best in your area.

- **Avoid:** Don't plant with run wheat.

TRICALE

Triticale is a hybrid cross of wheat and rye and it makes an ideal winter-hardy grain planting. I have had a lot of success with winter triticale on our farm. Triticale's protein levels range between 15 to 25 percent. It's terrific forage for deer, turkey, pheasants, and geese. Triticale is rated higher than wheat or rye by many wildlife managers. It can be planted earlier than wheat generally in August or September in the north and earlier in the south. If the ground is open I will plant spring triticale as early as April; otherwise I plant it in May.

Planted by itself, use 100 pounds per acre. It can do well by itself or even better when planted with other grains, clovers or other types of legumes. Companion grains include wheat, cereale rye, oats, or barley. I have successfully used crimson clover, Kura, and Kopa clover in my mixed triticale plots.

Triticale will provide its best height of production when pH levels are between 6.0 and 6.5. At planting, fertilize triticale with 400 pounds of 19-19-19. As with any planting get a soil test done at a certified lab prior to prescribing your own mix of fertilizer. In late winter, add about 150 pounds of nitrogen (46-0-0) to your planting.

There are a lot of triticale varieties from which to choose. Some varieties have been created particularly for fall and winter production. They are the wisest choice for those managers looking to increase the winter hardy offerings. I use Tritigold-22. Triticale is sold as both grain and forage varieties.

RECAP

- **Seeding Rates:** Broadcast alone at 100 pounds per acre. With legumes, half that amount. With clover and other grains, about 25 pounds per acre.

- **pH Level:** Likes pH levels of 6.0 to 6.5.

- **Planting Time:** In the north April or May. In fall August or September. In the south plant in September or October.

- **Depth of Seed:** Plant ¼ of an inch deep. Can be top-sowed successfully in a well-prepared plot that is well compacted for best soil-to-seed contact just prior to a rainfall.

- **Fertilizer:** At planting use 300 to 400 lbs of 19-19-19 and 100 lbs of 46-0-0 in late winter.

- **Companion Mixes:** Does well planted alone. Can also be mixed with other grains or legumes.

- **Crude Protein Levels:** From 15 to 30 percent.

- **Overgrazing:** Generally not an issue after 30 days.

- **Extends Grazing Season:** From October through December.

- **Temperatures:** Withstands late-winter temperatures.

- **Caution:** Use winter forage varieties for deer.

- **Avoid:** Don't use in acidic soils.

The two remaining small cereal grains that can be considered to plant as wildlife food plots include oats and barley.

OATS: One of the most popular and most often planted of the annual small cereal grains is oats. In fact, some say oats may very well be the best small grain food plot for deer. It can be grown for hay, pasture or silage and can produce up to four tons of quality forage per acre. Oats are highly preferred by deer and other wildlife and some managers report wildlife prefer oats over all other small cereal grains. Oats contain 10 to 20 or more percent protein, tolerate heavy browsing, and are very digestible. They are exceptionally winter-hardy and can survive in temperatures of zero to 10 degrees, making them an ideal choice as a wildlife food plot. Varieties include: Buck Forage, Buck Magnet, Certified Shelby 427, Registered Horsepower, IN09201, Woodburn, Certified Jim Oats, Morton, Frank Forage, Cover Crop and Harrison.

BARLEY: Is an inexpensive sweet cereal grain that grows quickly and can be planted in spring or winter. It is said that the deer attraction to barley can range from heavy to none and everything in between. Some managers in the Midwest report heavy use by deer while others report that deer were seldom, if ever, seen eating in their barley crops. I have never grown barley but I simply can't imagine that deer and most other wildlife would not find it an attractive food source. In fact, Montana Fish, Wildlife & Parks reports that barley is "utilized by big game." However, I recently spoke with a friend of Kate's and mine, Jack Curtin, who owns and

THE GRAINS

farms about 3,000 acres with his partner and brother Bob and members of both their families. They operate Curtin Dairy which is one of the largest dairy farms in New York State. Jack told me, *"The times I have planted barley on our farm I've noticed the deer didn't eat it at all. But I generally plant barley in spring when deer have so many other agricultural crops and natural forages to eat. They don't bother the barley."* So it seems the jury is out on the value of barley as an attractive wildlife food plot. With that said, however, I plan to plant barley on our land this year as a test. What the heck, if the deer don't eat it, I can use it to make homemade beer.

Barley has more protein than other cereal grains commonly used for livestock or for wildlife food plots. Starch is the chief element in barley kernels. Its dry matter has 7.5-18% protein and a total digestible nutrient (TDN) value of 80-84 percent. The NRC (84) lists crude fiber values of 5.7 to 7.1 percent for barley. Fiber levels in barley are normally greater than those of grain sorghum or corn and it contains more phosphorus than corn or milo. Those types of figures are all the more reason why I definitely plan to plant barley on our farm this coming year. Varieties include: Foxtail, Robust Spring Barley, and Valor Winter Barley.

THE GRAINS

OTHER PLANT TYPES

SUGAR BEETS (biennial vegetable)

Sugar beets are a cultivated tuber that is planted primary as an agricultural crop throughout the United States. Take my word for it: Sugar beets are to deer what ice cream is to children. Once deer discover what sugar beets are, they will consume them enthusiastically. We have had excellent success planting BuckLunch sugar beets on our farm. They have helped tremendously to draw deer into my food plots from October through January, making them an ultimate planting for hunting season.

Deer will paw them up even when the sugar beet plots are covered by several inches of snow. They will continue to dig them up until they have eaten the entire crop. Many times I have witnessed the same group of does or an individual buck returning to a sugar beet plot several times in one day. Once there have been several *hard* frosts, deer will enthusiastically and relentlessly visit sugar beet crops until they have unearthed and devoured every single sugar beet they can find.

In another book, I mentioned during the 2009 New York deer season on our farm, the regular firearm season proved to be frustrating. We had a hard time seeing good bucks the entire three weeks of the rifle season as the weather was milder than normal. It wasn't until two days before the muzzleloader season opened that the temperatures dipped quickly and radically, never getting higher than in the single digits.

▲ A sugar beet like this will make a terrific attractant for deer, particularly as the temperatures begin to drop. Note the yellowish color of the bulb. Photo courtesy: BuckLunch.

The dramatic drop in temperature quickly helped to "sweeten up" the sugar beets, making them the number one food source on our farm. Our plot of sugar beets looked like a minefield with deep holes everywhere. If you saw the holes you would swear the deer were digging the sugar beets up with shovels. On the third day after the temperatures crashed, I killed a wide 8-point buck at 11 AM during the *fourth week* of New York's firearm season. The buck marched into the sugar beet plot like he had nothing to worry about. Obviously the buck's craving for the sugar beets outweighed his need for caution.

Only two and a half days later, another hunter shot another terrific buck in the same sugar beet plot at 1:30 PM. He said he watched well over a dozen deer come in and out of the plot all morning. When he saw his dandy 9-point buck visit the sugar beet plot, he didn't hesitate for a moment before placing the crosshairs on the buck.

There's cold, hard proof that sugar beets are a top-notch choice for deer managers who want to assure themselves of seeing deer in their food plots from November to January. Sugar beets are a must-plant part of our late-season winter-hardy plantings and they should be for you too.

Some food plotters think that sugar beets are classified as a brassica. In fact, they are a biennial vegetable. What makes them a top rated winter hardy planting, however, is that sugar beets have a very high digestibility rate. Some managers swear that sugar beets provide the highest digestibility of any forage up to 98 percent. Their sugar content can range as high as 20 percent. Their protein content is between 12 to 15 percent as well.

Sugar beets can be planted in early spring. For northern areas they can be planted in late June or early July because they have a short growing season of only 90 to 100 days. I plant my beets no later than the Fourth of July. By the end of September and no later than the first week of October, they have matured.

The first time I planted sugar beets I was surprised to discover that deer also eat the tops of the plant as well. Speaking of that, don't mow the leaves of the sugar beets as they are growing. It will encourage additional leaf growth, which ends up decreasing the sugar content in the plants root system, which is the key to attracting deer.

▲ Jeff Elliot, (left), with his hefty 9-point buck and the author's buck killed a few days earlier. Both bucks were taken in the same sugar beet plot during a late-December New York muzzleloader hunt.

◄ This 10-point buck contently feeds on the tops of sugar beet plants. Deer will eat the tops and the bulbs, making sugar beets an ideal planting for any food plot manager. Photo courtesy: BuckLunch.

I have heard some deer managers say it took "a couple of years" before their deer discovered that they loved sugar beets. If that is the case when you plant them, you may have to dig up a few for the deer to help them discover the sugar beets (check the legality of your local game laws before doing this). Since the beet itself can stick above the ground by one third of its entire length, it shouldn't take the deer long to figure out what sugar beets are and how much they love eating the beet.

Sugar beets should be planted in a medium to heavy loam soil that receives an ample amount of moisture. Be careful about the site you select, however. While the beets will need adequate water in the summer, as immature plants they are vulnerable to drowning if they get too much water. Broadcast sugar beets at about 6 to 8 pounds per acre.

It is absolutely crucial to make sure that the plot you intend to plant sugar beets in is weed-free prior to planting the seeds in order to assure a successful crop. Once the plants begin to shoot up, their leaves will sufficiently block out the sun and thereby suppress weed growth and competition. I spray my intended sugar beet plots with Big N' Tuf about 10 days to two weeks before I plan to plant the sugar beets.

If you intend to plant sugar beets, lime the plots heavily *long* before planting your beets. First take a soil test to determine what the exact pH level is. If it is lower than 6.0 you'll need to lime it heavily in order to get the pH level to 6.5 to 7.5, which sugar beets prefer.

Plant sugar beets in April or May in the north. At planting, fertilize the beets with at least 400 pounds of T-19 (19-19-19) per acre and about 20 to 30 pounds of manganese sulfate (if your soil test comes back suggesting you need manganese sulfate). Turn both fertilizers under the soil slightly (about an inch or so to limit disturbing the weed bed). When the plants are almost fully grown (about 8 weeks later), broadcast about 100 pounds of urea (46-0-0) per acre.

If your plot is smaller than one acre, calculate your seed, fertilizer, and lime amounts by first measuring the plot accurately. Then take the total square feet of the plot you measured and divide it by 43,560 (the total square feet of an acre). It will give you the exact size of the plot in acres. As mentioned earlier, this formula will help you break down approximately how much fertilizer, seed, and lime is required for a particular plot.

I always plan to plant my sugar beets when there will be an expected rainfall. Although it is recommended

This plot of sugar beets is ▶ completely weed-free. Once the plants begin to grow, the leaves will totally shade out any future potential weed problems.

◀ Sugar beets are available uncoated (L) and coated (R) to protect the seeds from diseases. I buy them from www.bucklunch.com because they specialize only in sugar beets and provide customers quality planting tips and other support. Photo courtesy: www.bucklunch.com.

that the seed is planted about ¼ inch deep, I have had good success with top-sowing sugar beets. As long as you make sure the seed gets good seed-to-soil contact by using a compactor, top-seeding sugar beets will work.

There was one year when Roundup Ready sugar beets were available. At this writing they have not been Roundup Ready–approved. That is really unfortunate because as young plants sugar beets really don't compete very well with weeds. Hopefully, the scuttle-butt is that Roundup Ready seeds are in the works again and may be available soon. So before you purchase your sugar beets, make sure you check to find out if Roundup Ready seeds are available. If they are, it will make a considerable difference in controlling weeds and in the production of the crop. Roundup Ready seed will most definitely be more expensive but they will be absolutely worth the extra cost.

Sugar beets must be rotated every year. It is not recommended to plant them in the same plot two years in a row. In fact, it is highly suggested sugar beets should not be planted in the same plot for another three years.

◀ One year, sugar beets were available as Round-Up Ready (RR) seeds and the plot grew without any problems from the weeds. Hopefully, sugar beets will be available again, sometime soon, as RR seeds.

Once you discover how enthusiastically deer seek out food plots of sugar beets, plant them and see how they will not stop eating them until they have gulped down every last sugar beet. You will become as much of a die-hard sugar beet fan as I am.

RECAP

- **Seeding Rates:** Broadcast alone at 6 to 8 pounds per acre

- **Maturity:** Short growing season 90 to 100 days.

- **pH Level:** Prefers pH levels of 6.5 to 7.5.

- **Planting Time:** Plant in early spring.

- **Depth of Seed:** Can be sowed successfully at ¼-inch depth in a well-prepared plot that is compacted for best soil-to-seed contact prior to a rainfall.

- **Fertilizer:** At planting use 400 pounds of 19-19-19 and 25 pounds of manganese sulfate if necessary.

- **Companion Mixes:** Plant alone.

- **Crude Protein Levels:** From 12 to 15 percent.

- **Sugar Content:** About 20 percent.

- **Digestibility:** Near 98 percent.

- **Overgrazing:** Generally not an issue after 30 days.

- **Extends Grazing Season:** From October through December.

- **Temperatures:** Withstands extreme late-winter temperatures.

- **Caution:** Plant no more than one year in the same plot and then rotate sugar beets to other plots for three (3) consecutive years following.

- **Avoid:** Planting in soils of pure clay.

PUMPKIN (gourd)

I have only been growing small plots of pumpkins for the last few years. I have also included some pumpkins in plots with mixed plantings as well. The ones I have grown have definitely proven to be successful food plot attractants. However, I know several farmers who plant small and large fields of pumpkins to sell during Halloween every year. Some of them have told me that they over-plant the plots in order to have extra pumpkins to attract deer during the hunting season. They assure me that deer are very fond of eating pumpkins when they begin to overripen and are easy to break open with their hooves. I intend to plant at least a one-acre patch of pumpkins this coming spring on our farm.

From what I am told, most farmers plant their pumpkins differently from what is recommended in the seed catalog or on Internet sites. They claim planting pumpkins isn't as difficult as most instructions say.

If you want to grow pumpkins for deer and other wildlife, using small pumpkins is the best choice as deer can easily penetrate the outer layer in order to get to the fruit inside. One farmer friend, Alex Henderson, told me that "buying good seed is an important first step." In order to get a high germination percentage, and healthy and vibrant plants, start with fresh seed from a reputable company. Try to purchase seed that is the exact variety you want, not a generic seed like often found at big box stores or bargain seed at drugstores.

▲ A primary plot of purple-top turnips mixed with a small amount of pumpkin, sugar beets, rape, summer squash, and daikon radishes. I plan to plant an acre of stand-alone pumpkins next year.

▲ This is the same small mixed plot in December. Deer regularly feed in this plot from November to January. The blind in background. This mixed planting made it a popular post.

OTHER PLANT TYPES

The second step is to plant pumpkins where they will get full sun, at least 6 full hours of sun per day. The vines get quite long (usually 20–30 feet) and need room to grow. This doesn't mean you have to have a big plot. The site should have good drainage. If a plot allows water to stand, it is a poor selection site to plant pumpkins.

Pumpkins are very frost-sensitive. They should be planted when the average temperatures are at least 70°F and the last chance of frost has passed. Generally, the best time to plant pumpkins in the north is in May or no later than the first week of June, depending upon where you are in the United States. If you plant any later than late June, large pumpkin varieties won't be mature until after Halloween, and both large and small varieties can be damaged by fall frosts. Most pumpkin varieties take between 85–125 days to mature. Most of the heirloom and larger varieties are on the longer end of the spectrum.

Plant your seeds 1 to 2 inches deep. With any luck, the seeds should sprout in seven to ten days. Pumpkins can be fertilized with Osmocote. It is time-released, which makes it almost impossible to over-fertilize or burn a young plant. Pests that can attack pumpkins are Cucumber beetles, four line bugs, squash beetles and aphids. To eliminate bugs from your pumpkin plot you may have to resort to a pesticide.

If you need to spray your pumpkins try to do so in the early evening after the bees have headed back to their hives.

Generally pumpkin leaves will shade out weeds rather quickly. A lot of weeds can be problematic. Weeds directly compete with your pumpkin plant for water and for nutrients in the soil. Some weeds also can be a host for diseases or bug populations. You may have to spray the weeds after the pumpkin seedlings sprout and have five leaves on the plant. When applied around your plant it can keep additional weeds from germinating. Once the vine starts to grow in size, the large leaves quickly help to shade out small weeds that may germinate later. Pumpkins are in the plant family known as Cucurbitaceae that consists of various squashes, melons, gourds, cucumber, luffas, and watermelon.

RECAP

- **Seeding Rates:** Broadcast alone at 1 to 2 pounds per acre.
- **pH Level:** Likes pH levels of 6.0 to 7.5.
- **Planting Time:** Plant as soon as soil temperatures reach 70 degrees Fahrenheit soil-to-seed.
- **Depth of Seed:** Plant ¾ to 1 inch deep in a prepared plot that is well compacted for best soil-to-seed contact prior to a rainfall.
- **Fertilizer:** Use an NPK including 5-10-10, 10-10-20, or 16-16-8.
- **Companion Mixes:** Plant alone.
- **Crude Protein Levels:** 60 to 70 percent.
- **Digestibility:** High.
- **Overgrazing:** Generally not an issue after 30 days.
- **Extends Grazing Season:** From October through November.
- **Temperatures:** Withstands late-winter temperatures.

FORAGE CHICORY (perennial herb)

Chicory is an herbaceous cool season plant that is a highly nutritious broad-leaved perennial herb part of the sunflower family. It can be planted almost anywhere throughout the country. When it is properly maintained, chicory food plots can last for several years. Good management requires that you mow this plant before the flower stems get bigger than 6 inches. Chicory is quick to seed, and because it has a deep taproot, it is also drought-tolerant.

Forage chicory will withstand heavy grazing pressure, which makes it a good choice in areas with high deer densities. It is one of the finest forages for extracting nutrients from the soil and transferring them to deer

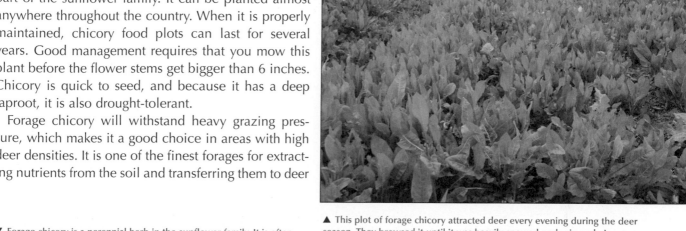

▲ This plot of forage chicory attracted deer every evening during the deer season. They browsed it until it was heavily snowed under in early January that particular year.

▼ Forage chicory is a perennial herb in the sunflower family. It is often mistaken for common plantain because they look so similar.

to help provide them with heavier body weights and larger antlers. Its protein levels range from about 10 to 30 percent.

Chicory should be planted in late July or early August prior to a rainfall. It can withstand acidic pH levels as low as 5.1 but does best when the pH is between 6.5 and 7.0. Chicory seeds should be planted about a ¼ inch below the soil's surface. Cultipacking the soil will assure the seeds get the best seed-to-soil contact. Since chicory seeds are very tiny, they are also easy to plant directly on top of a prepared food plot. I have had very good success top-seeding chicory particularly when I plant it just prior to a rainfall.

When planted by itself, the seeding rate is 4 to 5 pounds per acre. Many managers recommend planting chicory as a mix with clovers or other legumes. Chicory can also be planted with small grains and brassicas. I recommend planting a pure plot of chicory and a mix of chicory, a brassica of choice, and a couple of clovers. If you mix your chicory you will have to reduce the seeding rate of chicory to about half.

Directly after planting the plot, fertilize your pure or mixed chicory plot. It is always best to use a fertilizer that is recommended after a specific soil test is done. However, I have had good luck using 300 to 400 pounds of 19-19-19 fertilizer in my chicory plots.

OTHER PLANT TYPES

Chicory is a terrific plant to extend the grazing season well into December. Over the years, I have noted in my logs that deer are attracted to chicory all year long, but seek it out more often from late October into November through December. I've have grown chicory for many years and consider it one of my best food plot choices either planted alone or mixed with other crops. I also consider it a top choice as a winter-hardy planting.

Once you discover how easy it is to grow and how attractive it is to deer, chicory will quickly become one of your favorite and most successful winter plantings as well.

RECAP

- **Seeding Rates:** Broadcast at 4 to 5 pounds per acre just prior to an expected rainfall.

- **pH Level:** pH levels of 6.5 to 7.0.

- **Planting Time:** In the north plant in late July to early August. Can be planted as early a June. In the south from August to September.

- **Maturity:** 30 to 60 days.

- **Digestibility (TDN):** Extremely high, about 95 percent.

- **Depth of Seed:** Plant ¼ inch below the surface. Can be top-sowed successfully prior to a rainfall.

- **Fertilizer:** At planting 300 to 400 pounds per acre of 19-19-19.

- **Companion Mixes:** Does well planted alone. Can also be mixed with other brassicas, clovers, and small grains.

- **Crude Protein Levels:** From 10 to 30 percent.

- **Overgrazing:** Generally not an issue after 30 days.

- **Extends Grazing Season:** Deer eat chicory intently from October through January.

- **Temperatures:** Withstands winter temperatures.

- **Caution:** Requires high fertility and nitrogen (N) fertilization for best production.

- **Avoid:** Do not allow flower stems to exceed 10 inches in height.

▲ This field of cold-hardy chicory and a mix of clovers is being sprayed with fertilizer using a Chapin 60-gallon tank with boom arms (model #6327) during the summer to ensure a healthy and productive crop in fall and winter; a time when most hunters want deer in their food plots. Photo courtesy: Chapin, Intl.

SMALL BURNET (perennial forb)

Small burnet is a top evergreen perennial forb (a herbaceous flowering plant) that remains green well into winter. It is an excellent cold-hardy planting that is a highly favored planting for all wildlife including whitetail deer. It is an enduring plant that can live for long periods of time. It does well in open areas but will grow in areas that are somewhat shaded too.

Small burnet is adaptable to most parts of the country and some areas of Canada. It is a favorite among deer managers in northern zones as part of their wild-life food plots.

It does best when planted in well-drained soils and needs at least 10 inches of rainfall per year. It prefers pH levels between 6.0 and 7.5.

I have had my best success when broadcasting small burnet. It can be broadcast at 15 to 20 pounds per acre alone or three to five pounds per acre when planted in a mix. It is recommended to plant small burnet no more than ½-inch deep. I have planted it in May at a depth of ¼ inch deep successfully using a cultipacker or drag. As with a majority of my plantings, I seed it when I expect a rainfall.

Small burnet germinates quickly with its flowers blooming as early as May. Small burnet is notoriously slow to establish itself, making it susceptible to over-grazing by deer. To avoid this problem small burnet should be planted as a mix. It can be planted with grains like wheat, triticale, or with clovers like Durana or ladino or other legumes. I plant small burnet with chicory and fertilize it with 200 to 300 pounds of Triple-19 (19-19-19) at planting.

The one variety of small burnet seed I have used is called Delar. It is available from Welter Seed and Honey Company (www.welterseed.com). Delar seed grows from 12 to 18 inches tall and comes in 50-pound bags.

What also makes small burnet intriguing to plant as a food plot, at least to me, is that it is literally a food plot for deer and people. As a Ferengi of Star Trek would say, *hu*-mans can eat small burnet too. The leaves can be used in cold drinks and salads. They have a very pleasant flavor that tastes like a cucumber.

▼ Small burnet germinates very fast, but it is also susceptible to overgrazing. So, if you want to plant this, be sure to plant it in an area that is large enough to sustain grazing during the first few months. Photo courtesy: www.midwestfoodplots.com.

RECAP

- **Seeding Rates:** Broadcast at 15 to 20 pounds per acre prior to a rainfall.
- **pH Level:** Likes a pH level between 6.0 and 7.5.
- **Planting Time:** In the north plant in April or May.
- **Germination:** Very fast.
- **Depth of Seed:** Plant ¼ to ½ inch below the surface.
- **Fertilizer:** At planting 300 to 400 pounds of 19-19-19.
- **Companion Mixes:** Can be planted alone. Can also be mixed with grains, clovers, other legumes and chicory.
- **Overgrazing:** Very susceptible.
- **Extends Grazing Season:** From October into early December.
- **Temperatures:** Withstands cold temperatures.
- **Caution:** Requires mowing in late summer for best production.
- **Avoid:** Top seeding

THE GRASSES

TIMOTHY GRASS

Timothy grass is a perennial cold-hardy bunchgrass that is adapted to northern climates. It grows best in fertile, medium to heavy soils. It is among the most palatable grasses for horses, cattle, and deer. Timothy is also ideal as a nesting and brood-rearing cover. Timothy grass grows well on sandy loam soils that are fairly well drained. The stiff, erect stems of timothy create good fall roosts for pheasants and other non-hunted birds.

When Timothy is planted as a mix with ladino or red clover it produces an even more desirable crop for deer. When the clovers die back after five or six years, timothy will form a pure stand. Timothy reaches heights of 2 to 5 feet tall. It is among the quickest germinating and maturing bunchgrasses. When planted as a pure plot it can be seeded at a rate of 6 to 10 pounds. Planted with clovers, it should be planted at two to three pounds per acre.

Barfleo, in addition to high yield, offers excellent disease resistance and persistence. Barfleo is a versatile variety of timothy, being suitable for intensive grazing for deer and other wildlife as well as cattle and horses.

Timothy should be planted in a well-prepared seed bed, firming up the soil before planting. Plant the seed at a depth of ¼ to ½ inches. Be cautious not to plant timothy seed deeper than ½ inch below the soil's surface. Timothy does not take early grazing pressure, but once it is established it tolerates considerable grazing. Deer will graze on timothy until late spring and then as green-up takes hold they move off to forage elsewhere, making timothy's lack of tolerance of intense grazing a non-problem for deer managers. I like to plant timothy with some of the winter-hardy clovers such as bird's-foot trefoil, Kura, and Kopa. They deflect any early stages of heavy grazing and help to keep the plot attractive throughout the summer and into November.

For deer managers who want to include a grass within their management program, timothy is a logical choice. It is considered by many to be the highest quality cold-season of the bunchgrass family. We avoid planting rye grass, tall fescue, or orchard grass in lieu

▲ For those managers in the north a wise choice for a grass that deer will eat is timothy grass. Timothy is the most palatable grass for deer and it is a very cold-hardy bunchgrass.

of planting only timothy grass mixed with cold-tolerant clovers on our farm.

Timothy comes in a few varieties, including Barfleo, Dolina, Braliza, and Bart. Barfleo is marketed by Welter Seed and Honey Company (www.welterseed. com). The other varieties are available from the producer Barenbrug on their website at www.barusa.com.

RECAP

- **Seeding Rates:** Broadcast 4 to 6 pounds per acre of timothy as a mix with other clovers. Plant alone at 10 to 15 pounds per acre.
- **pH Level:** Prefers pH levels of 6.0 to 6.5.
- **Planting Time:** Plant in fall, late winter or spring.

- **Depth of Seed:** Plant ¼ to ½ inch deep in a well-prepared plot that is well compacted for best soil-to-seed contact just prior to a rainfall.
- **Establishment:** Timothy is easy to start.
- **Fertilizer:** At planting use 300 to 400 pounds of 19-19-19.
- **Companion Mixes:** Plant with winter-hardy and or cool-season hardy clovers, other legumes.
- **Crude Protein Levels:** From 10 to 12 percent and a good source of copper and zinc.
- **Palatability:** Very high.
- **Overgrazing:** Generally not an issue after spring green-up.
- **Extends Grazing Season:** From October to December.
- **Temperatures:** Has excellent winter hardiness.
- **Avoid:** Planting timothy as a stand-alone crop for deer.

While we only plant timothy grass, I don't mean to imply the other grasses should not be ruled out as viable wildlife plantings. Certainly many of the native grasses and some of the more common grasses used for agricultural and as wildlife plots make good choices within a food plot and management program as well.

NATIVE GRASSES

Native grasses are often planted with a wide variety of wildflowers or when mixed with a couple of different clovers and/or other legumes. There are many different types of native grass varieties. Some are gaining popularity for use in pastures, as bio-mass crops, or for wetland plantings and wildlife habitat restoration. Native grasses are regional in regards to climate, soils, etc. They are known to be very slow to establish. Native grasses are also used in pasture and crop production programs. Weed control is vital when they are first planted. Native grasses are ideal plantings for deer as top-notch fawning and nursery areas. They serve many other types of wildlife in the same way. There are countless varieties. Some of the more popular include: Switchgrass, Indiangrass, Little Bluestem, Big Bluestem, Cave-In Rock, Side Oats Gama, Canada Wild Rye, Buffalograss, and Canarygrass.

COMMON GRASSES

BROMEGRASS: Bromegrass is mostly used as livestock forage, but if it is mixed with different types of clovers it becomes more attractive to deer and other wildlife. It can be planted successfully on a wide variety of soils. Bromegrass is a very palatable, high yielding grass that has *exceptional* winter-hardiness. It is also more drought tolerant than many of the other cold season grasses. Some varieties include: Lakota, York, Lincoln, Fleet Meadow, Hakari Mountain and Free Flow.

ORCHARDGRASS: Orchardgrasses are medium to long lived, cold season bunchgrasses that do best on well drained soils. They produce quality pasture grass that is mostly used for horses and cattle. However, they can also be used as worthwhile food plots for deer, turkey and other wildlife. Orchardgrass is an excellent hay production crop, particularly when it is planted with a couple of different winter-hardy clovers such as Kura, Kopu II, Ladino (white) clover or red clovers. It tolerates heavy grazing and it has a high nutrient content. It is also tolerant to shade and is fairly drought resistant. Some older varieties have moderate winter-hardiness with the newer varieties being more winter-hardy. Varieties include: Potomac, Tekapo, Profit, Latar, Baridana, Baraula, and Persist.

ANNUAL RYEGRASS: Annual Ryegrass is a quick establishing crop. It is mainly a pasture crop that provides supplemental feeding for livestock and wildlife during fall and early spring months when other warm season grasses are dormant. It is a cold-season annual or perennial grass that grows best on well drained soils with good water holding capabilities. It can be an attractive forage to deer when planted in a mixed seeded food plot. Because it has good cold-tolerance, perennial ryegrass is often used in northern areas and should be planted with clovers or other legumes as companion mixtures. Varieties include: Gulf Annual, Rival Annual, Bruiser Annual, and RG Pasplus-50.

ITALIAN RYEGRASS: This annual variety of ryegrass is easy to establish. It can be top-sown if the seeds receive sufficient moisture soon after they are sown. Italian Ryegrass is often called the "improved annual ryegrass," because it is very affordable. It is used mostly to over-seed pastures. As with most grasses, it does better when planted with clovers or other legumes. It can also be used for winter cover. Annual ryegrass is hardy enough to re-seed itself in pastures as long as it is not overgrazed by livestock, deer or other wildlife. Varieties include: RG-ANN-50, Feast II Italian, and Green Spirit Italian. Perennial varieties include: Power Perennial, BG-34 Perennial, BG-24T Perennial, and Linn Perennial.

SUCRASEED GRASS: Sucraseed High Sugar Grass (HSG) mix is a new perennial ryegrass that has been developed specifically to contain high levels of Water Soluble Carbohydrates (sugar). These mixes have demonstrated significant increases in meat and milk production for livestock. This makes me believe Sucraseed HSG could also be highly beneficial when planted for deer and other wildlife. I plan to experiment with it. The only place I have found it available is through Welter Seed & Honey Co. Varieties include: Cash Cow, Beef Bank, Great Gains, Sweet Silage and Pasture Sweet'ner. By the sound of those names, you can understand why I'm going to give it a try as a wildlife food plot.

FESTULOLIUM: Festuloliums are a hybrid cross of perennial ryegrass and meadow fescue. They have the palatability of ryegrass and the toughness of fescue. Varieties include: Duo and Barfest.

TALL FESCUE: Tall fescue grass is grown for pasture, hay, silage and as a companion crop with other forage grasses, clovers and other legumes. It is easily established and hardy. It is one of the more drought resistant field grasses and will tolerate low fertility. Varieties include: Bronson, STF43, Barolex, Bariane, HDR Meadow, Fawn Tall, Kentucky 31, Baroptima Plus E34 and Creeping Red which is shade tolerant.

SUMMARY

All of the winter-hardy plants mentioned previously in this chapter will withstand cold temperatures and extend the grazing season from fall and well into winter throughout the country. However, within the plants listed above there are some that can actually be classified as being *extremely* winter-hardy plantings. The term, extremely winter-hardy, refers to any plant's ability to withstand (survive and thrive) in the most frigid temperatures and other winter conditions found generally in northern zones. Most importantly, extreme winter-hardy plants remain productive and provide quality forage from late October well into January, or until they are deeply snowed under. All of the plants listed previously fall into these two categories and therefore they are highly advantageous fall and winter plantings that will be unquestionably attractive food plots to deer during the late fall and winter months. I strongly recommend all as food plots to habitat and deer managers in northern zones who plan to hunt over some of their food plots.

A field being prepared to plant with a mix of winter-hardy seeds. Using a heavy-duty push-spreader like this Chapin model (No. 6321) makes short work of planting 125 pounds, of seed on uneven terrain. For more information on Chapin products visit their website at www.chapinoutfitters.com. Photo courtesy: Chapin, Intl. ▶

MEMO

Before I get into the winter-hardy clovers and other legumes I want to make sure you understand that I'm not advocating only planting cold-season clovers. Warm-season clovers and legumes have their place as an important element to successful food plot planting, as mentioned in Chapter 10.

A majority of managers cut their food plot teeth planting *mostly* warm-season clovers and legumes. While there are definitely many valid management reasons for planning warm-season plantings they are often overused by deer managers. With that said, however, I do include *a few* warm-season clover plots such as Alyceclover, lablab, and sweetclover. They provide quality nutrition in early spring when the pregnant does could use nutritious forage; these clovers are used heavily by fawns after they are weaned, and mostly because many warm-weather clovers can tolerate

heavy spring and summer grazing as well. However, as I have said before, I'm not a big fan of planting *too many* warm-season clovers. That's why I only set aside about 3 percent of my food plots to warm-season plantings.

My main purpose of planting warm-season clovers serves another *crucial* function other than providing spring and summer forage to wildlife on our farm. We want to attract honeybees so they can help us pollinate our fruit and nut trees and other plantings. Honeybees gather and eat a wide variety of sweet items including, but not limited to, nectar, pollen, sugar, juices from fruits, and syrups. Pollen is one of the purest and richest natural foods, containing all of the nutritional requirements of a honeybee: sugar, carbohydrates, protein, enzymes, vitamins and minerals. Each honeybee colony collects more than 60 pounds of pollen per year. Nectar is the sweet fluid found in flowers.

▲ Warm-season clovers, fruit trees, and other plantings attract and "hold" honeybees. In turn, the bees help to pollinate our plantings.

COLD/WINTER-HARDY
CLOVERS AND OTHER LEGUMES

Honeybees collect pollen and nectar from a variety of flowering plants, including milkweed, dandelions, *clovers and other legumes*, goldenrod, and a variety of fruit trees. So naturally we want to attract and actually *"hold"* wild honeybees on our land. It's no secret that for thousands of years, human beings have recognized the important value of honeybees in agriculture. Honeybees are *the* single most *effective* pollinators of plants in the world. They are an irreplaceable resource to agriculture productivity.

To that end, I rent at least one beehive a year from a local beekeeper, for $100 a season. Honeybees will significantly bolster the overall health and productivity of all your plantings. This simple strategy will quickly encourage *wild* honeybees to set up homes on your land and help you in your pursuit of a more productive food plot program. Consider renting a beehive for a couple of seasons as well. To encourage wild bees into your plots, plan to include the three warm-season clovers mentioned above, as well as other warm-season legumes in your management program.

COLD/WINTER-HARDY CLOVERS AND OTHER LEGUMES

Most references about clovers and other legumes list them as either warm-season or cool-season plants. While these designations are absolutely correct, I prefer to divide clovers and other legumes into three more self-explanatory groupings; warm-season, cold-season, and extremely winter-hardy. Each of the three categories more clearly describes clovers and other legumes based on how well they fare under different weather conditions.

The two groups covered in this chapter are the cold-season and the extremely winter-hardy season plantings. The cold-season plantings are diverse enough to double as both warm-season and cold-season plantings. However, it is important to keep in mind that even though they are cold-tolerant and can be categorized as cold-season plantings they can't endure temperatures below 10 degrees Fahrenheit for extended periods of time. (Freeze-out occurs from zero to 15 degrees Fahrenheit).

Both the cold-season and extremely winter-hardy groups can be mixed with other winter-hardy plantings, including small grains such as winter wheat, oats, rye, sorghum (Milo), and triticale. A few of the extremely winter-hardy clovers and legumes can be planted as stand-alone plots due to their ability to withstand extreme winter temperatures. This group is the type of clovers that managers who live in cold, northern areas who want clovers to be viable during their deer hunting seasons should definitely plan to include as food plots.

▲ Managers who plant clovers that can survive through winter will benefit by luring deer to their plots from May to December. This is a winter-hardy plot of mixed clovers and other legumes planted on our land.

▲ A buck killed in the late December muzzle-loading season. He and a doe pawed through snow at 11 am in plots planted with several cold and winter-hardy plantings including timothy, sugar beets, turnips, and kale. Note that the patch of corn stalks where he expired was completely void of actual corn ears by December.

ALFALFA

Alfalfa has long been a prime perennial legume of farmers and deer managers alike. It provides top-quality forage that is highly sought after by deer as a palatable and nutritious crop. It is rich in protein, vitamins, and minerals. Many varieties have been bred to withstand cold temperatures, resist heavy grazing, and are insect-resistant.

As a food plot planting for me, however, alfalfa has more negatives than positives. It is a very demanding and finicky crop. Even longtime experienced farmers say alfalfa is a "difficult" crop to plant and grow. To begin with, alfalfa is a very expensive seed to buy. It is susceptible to poor soil drainage, and it is very sensitive to competition when mixed with other plantings, including clovers and other legumes, even when the seeding rates are reduced. Choosing the correct variety of alfalfa can be daunting as there are countless types available.

Although grazing-tolerant varieties have recently been developed, alfalfa doesn't do well when it is planted in small ¼-acre plots. It does best when planted in one-or two-acre plots. I have planted alfalfa several times on our farm in plots ranging from ¼ to ½ acres. Each time the plots grew in nicely but were quickly eaten to the ground by deer.

Alfalfa prefers a pH level of 6.5 or more and is a heavy user of plant nutrients. Weeds can cause severe problems when planting alfalfa and preparing a weed-free seedbed is critical. Alfalfa also needs to be mowed a few times a year and the cuttings should be removed for new growth to do well. By now you should be getting the point that to grow alfalfa as a deer food plot requires a major commitment. When you grow alfalfa you're developing a long-term relationship with the plant. And, like any relationship, it demands a lot of attention and obligation. Rather than continue to list other shortfalls of alfalfa let's just say unless you have already planted it successfully you may want to exclude it from your plantings and replace it with another cold-hardy annual or perennial legume that is much easier to grow productively. My choice is bird's-foot trefoil, which can withstand severe winter temperatures.

◀ Alfalfa is one of the top choices as a food plant for deer. However, it requires a lot of attention. For the average food plot manager alfalfa is not the "magic bullet" plant.

SAINFOIN

Sainfoin clover is a disease-free perennial legume that is highly nutritious and very palatable for deer and other wild animals. It contains a high level of the major and micronutrients and as such provides excellent high-quality forage for deer, elk, and all grazing species.

Because sainfoin has an extended period of flowering it is very attractive to bees. This can lead to high yields of honey; also, it can provide a habitat for wild bees threatened with extinction. It must be considered a very environmentally friendly plant. Bees readily take nectar from its beautiful pink flowers.

Sainfoin does not require a lot of fertilizer because it has nitrogen-fixing capabilities. Sainfoin is not only very winter-hardy it is also very drought-resistant. However, it will not tolerate wet conditions and performs best on well-drained soils.

Sainfoin is very similar to alfalfa, which makes it a perfect choice to replace the finicky and expensive alfalfa seed. Sainfoin is taller than alfalfa but it is shorter-lived. It will bloom one to two weeks earlier than alfalfa. Sainfoin is resistant to the alfalfa weevil and is resistant to the root rot phase. It has lower fiber content than grass or other legumes with the exception of white clover.

Sainfoin has many tall, hollow stems, 60-80 cm or more. Sainfoin leaves are compound with five to fourteen pairs of oval-shaped leaflets and a single leaflet on top. It produces cone-like clustered pink flowers at the end of long stem stalks. A planting of sainfoin will last for many years.

▲ Sainfoin clover is a perennial that places high on the "like to eat" list of deer. They find it very palatable and nutritious, making sainfoin an ideal cold-season planting.

RECAP

- **Seeding Rates:** In a stand-alone plot 20 to 30 pounds per acre. When mixed, reduce to 10 to 25 pounds per acre.

- **Inoculate With:** Buy pre-inoculated.

- **pH Level:** Prefers pH levels of 6.0 to 7.0.

- **Planting Time:** Spring.

- **Depth of Seed:** Plant about ¼ inch deep.

- **Establishment:** Matures early.

- **Fertilizer:** Use 300 lbs of 19-19-19 per acre.

- **Companion Mixes:** Plant alone or with other cold-hardy clovers, grains, and grasses.

- **Crude Protein Levels:** High protein levels up to 25 to 30 percent.

- **Digestibility:** Very high.

- **Overgrazing:** After establishment not an issue.

- **Extends Grazing Season:** Well into December.

- **Temperatures:** Has very good winter-hardiness.

- **Caution:** When cut at full to mid bloom it recovers slowly.

SWEETCLOVER

Sweetclover is a biennial legume that is available in three species: Two are yellow and one is white. The root system can reach depths of 4 feet, making sweetclover one of the most drought-tolerant plantings.

Sweetclover is extremely drought-resistant, and heat-tolerant, and a very winter-hardy legume planting that grows quickly. It is most often used as a mix to accompany sorghum, corn, and other grains and clovers. Sweetclover has a digestible crude protein level of 30 percent.

Sweetclover produces best in May to August. It can be sensitive to heavy early grazing. However, grazing in late spring and fall is actually helpful to both the plant and the roots. After the second year, overgrazing is not an issue from then on. It produces more vegetative growth the first year than other legumes do.

Food plot varieties include Norgold, Denta, and Polara. Coumarin varieties affect the taste of sweetclover and deer prefer the lower content varieties.

RECAP

- **Seeding Rates:** Planted alone broadcast 10 to 15 pounds per acre. In mixes plant about half that rate.

- **Inoculate With:** Rhizobium bacteria (strain A).

- **pH Level:** Requires a high pH levels between 6.5 and 7.0.

- **Planting Time:** Plant in northern areas mid to late August.

- **Establishment:** Grows quickly once established.

- **Overgrazing:**

- **Fertilizer:** Use 300 lbs of a 0-20-30.

- **Companion Mixes:** Can plant along or with other cold-hardy clovers, grains, and grasses.

- **Crude Protein Levels:** From 25 to 30 percent.

- **Palatability:** Extremely high.

- **Overgrazing:** Susceptible to overgrazing during the first year. Exceptional tolerance once plant reaches its second year and continues to be tolerant from there on.

▲ Sweetclover is often listed as a warm-season clover, but it is actually winter-hardy. Sweetclover seed must be properly inoculated (strain A) and scarified for best growing results.

- **Extends Grazing Season:** From October to December.

- **Temperatures:** Has good winter hardiness.

- **Avoid:** Don't plant as a stand-alone crop for deer.

- **Caution:** Seeds can remain viable in the soil for dozens of years.

LUPINE

Lupines are switch-hitters. They are classified as both warm- and cool-season plantings. The three most common that are commercially available, include white, blue, and yellow flowered lupines. The most winter-hardy variety is white lupine, although I have had good winter-hardy success with blue as well. Inoculate lupines with the proper Rhizobium bacteria type H.

Lupines grow to heights of about 3 to 5 feet. The plant makes beautiful flowers that are 4 to 10 inches long. Lupine is said to provide 25 to 35 percent levels of protein. They can be planted in the north in April and May, earlier in the South. Lupine can be mixed with grains, clovers, and even chicory.

Avoid planting lupines that are high in alkaloids as deer and other wildlife will avoid grazing them because they have a bitter taste. I plant Blue Lupine which is low in alkaloid.

If your deer have never been exposed to lupine it may take them a season to discover what they are. Once they do, however, they will become addicted to eating blue lupine. Lupine is also a very attractive food source to wild turkey and other hunted and non-hunted species of birds.

▲ A food plot of lupine is both visually beautiful and an excellent food plot attractant for deer. The most winter-hardy variety is white lupine.

RECAP

- **Seeding Rates:** Planted alone broadcast 100 pounds per acre. Drilled or mixed with other plant about half that rate.
- **Inoculate With:** Rhizobium bacteria (strain H).
- **pH Level:** Requires a high pH levels between 6.0 and 6.5.
- **Planting Time:** In northern April or May.
- **Seeding Vigor:** Good.
- **Overgrazing:** Can be overgrazed.

- **Fertilizer:** Use 300 pounds of a 0-20-20 if planted alone.
- **Companion Mixes:** Can be mixed with clovers, all small grains, and chicory.
- **Crude Protein Levels:** From 25 to 35 percent.
- **Palatability:** High.
- **Overgrazing:** Susceptible to overgrazing during the first 60 days.
- **Extends Grazing Season:** From October to November.
- **Temperatures:** Has very good winter hardiness.
- **Avoid:** Lupines high in alkaloids.
- **Caution:** Deer use of lupine can range from heavy to slight during the first year.

ALSIKE CLOVER

Alsike clover is a palatable perennial that does well when planted in acidic soil (5.6 to 5.9). It also can grow in very wet areas. Many varieties of alsike clover can be mixed with grasses and grains, making good winter-hardy candidates.

The two alsike clover varieties, Aurora and Dawn, were developed in Canada and are winter-hardy varieties. They were specifically developed to withstand extreme winter conditions and are the only two varieties I would use as cold-season plantings. Alsike clover is very palatable to all deer. It can be planted in early spring or late summer for best results.

The recommended mixes include cereale rye, wheat, triticale, and oats, as long as you reduce the grain seeding rates per acre by at least half. Alsike can also be part of a grass mix with timothy or perennial ryegrass. It can also be mixed with bird's-foot trefoil.

Alsike responds well to 19-19-19 fertilizer and lime. Any needed fertilizer should be incorporated during seedbed preparation whenever possible. Soil pH should be brought up to at least 6.0 when a new stand is established. Weed competition needs to be controlled until the stand is established.

Alsike clover provides excellent nesting cover when planted in grass mixtures.

RECAP

- **Seeding Rates:** Planted alone broadcast at 8 to 12 pounds per acre in a prepared seedbed. On fertile ground use 300 pounds per acre of 8-24-24. On new ground 400 pounds per acre of 0-20-20.
- **Inoculation:** Use the proper strain (B) Inoculate.
- **pH Level:** pH levels of 5.8 to 6.5.
- **Planting Time:** April to May or late summer.

▲ When planting alsike clover, remember that it does best when planted with other grains, grasses, or legumes.

- **Depth of Seed:** Plant ¼ to ½ inch deep.
- **Fertilizer:** When planted in a mix use 300 pounds per acre of 19-19-19. In late summer fertilize again with 200 pounds per acre of 0-20-30.
- **Companion Mixes:** Can be planted alone, but does better when mixed with small grains rye, triticale, wheat, and oats or Timothy grass, bird's-foot trefoil.
- **Overgrazing:** Once established resistant to heavy grazing pressure.
- **Extends Grazing Season:** From September to November.
- **Caution:** Use winter-hardy varieties Aurora and Dawn
- **Avoid:** Don't plant alsike alone—plant as a mix with grains, grasses, and other legumes.

COLD/WINTER-HARDY CLOVERS AND OTHER LEGUMES

ARROWLEAF CLOVER

Arrowleaf clover is an annual that has large leaflets that are rounded at the base with visible V-shaped markings with a pointed tip. Arrowleaf can be used for soil improvement, as a wildlife food source, and a winter cover crop. It is an upright, cold-hardy clover that can reach heights of 3 to 5 feet.

It is a prime cold-weather planting for managers because it can withstand temperatures of 5 to 15 degrees Fahrenheit. The forage brands rank high in digestibility and are readily fed on by deer and turkey. It is high in protein, with a level of approximately 20 percent, and a very high digestibility content of about 75 percent, making it an excellent choice as a cold-tolerant planting.

Arrowleaf can be planted either in spring or fall and requires a smoothly prepared cultipacked seedbed. The seed should be planted at about ¼ to ½ inch deep. When planted as a stand-alone food plot, plant at about 15 pounds per acre. It prefers a pH level of 6.0 to 6.5. Either purchase Arrowleaf pre-inoculated or inoculate it with Rhizobium bacteria (strain O).

It is most often mixed with other small grains as long as the seeding rates of the grains are reduced, in order not to shade out the Arrowleaf. Arrowleaf can also be mixed with clovers and other legumes as well.

▲ Although arrowleaf clover has good winter hardiness, freeze-outs do occur at temperatures between 0 and 10 degrees. Photo courtesy: Cooper Seeds.

RECAP

- **Seeding Rates:** Planted alone broadcast 15 pounds per acre. In a mix 10 pounds per acre.
- **Inoculate With:** Rhizobium bacteria (strain O).
- **pH Level:** Prefers pH levels of 6.0 to 7.5.
- **Planting Time:** April/May or September/October.
- **Depth of Seed:** Cover seed about ¼ inch deep.
- **Establishment:** Establishes quickly.
- **Fertilizer:** Without a soil test fertilize with 300 lbs of 0-20-20 per acre.
- **Companion Mixes:** Oats wheat, rye grain. Lessen grain rates so as not to shade out the Arrowleaf. Also plant with red or crimson clover.
- **Crude Protein Levels:** Approximately 20 percent.
- **Digestibility:** Very high, about 75 percent.
- **Overgrazing:** After establishment not an issue.
- **Extends Grazing Season:** From September to December.
- **Temperatures:** Has good winter hardiness.
- **Caution:** Some managers report problems establishing the brand called Yuchi.
- **Avoid:** Planting alone, best used as a mix with small grains to extend its cold-season value.

BERSEEM CLOVER

Berseem clover is a fast-growing clover that is rated as a winter annual with a quick recovery from grazing by deer and other wildlife. Tests have shown that Berseem is very palatable to deer and domestic animals (cattle love it). Berseem forage contains from 18 to 28 percent crude protein, which is comparable with alfalfa.

The commercial use of Berseem clover (also known as Egyptian clover) is relatively new in the United States. It has been an important crop in the Mediterranean, Near East, and India for many years. Until recently, Berseem clover was only used in the southern states as a winter forage crop. However, with the development of new varieties, Berseem is finding its niche in the Midwest. Berseem has tremendous potential for providing high-quality forage and improving soil conditions and its capacity to fix nitrogen into the soil (Tests show that it can produce well over 100 units of nitrogen to the acre.)

Berseem will thrive in wet conditions but it will not tolerate drought or hard soil conditions well. Although Berseem grows in a variety of soils, medium loam soils that are slightly alkaline will produce the best crop.

Berseem will grow best in a firm, well-prepared seedbed. Plant the seed with a ¼-inch of soil or culti-pack prepared seedbeds to press the seed into the soil surface and to conserve moisture. Establishment has been successful by broadcasting the seed into a plot that has been scarified.

Berseem clover is characterized by its oblong leaves, hollow stems, upright growth habit, and yellowish-white flowers. Berseem looks much like alfalfa and they usually grow 20 to 30 inches tall (dependent on soil fertility and moisture). It has been reported that Berseem will grow as tall as the oats and other grains when it was planted with them.

Establishment of Berseem is very similar to the practices of other cold-season clovers and legumes. Berseem can't take as much freezing as other winter-hardy clovers can however. Once Berseem plants bloom, the growth cycle is over, so it is important for it to either be grazed on by deer or mowed before it flowers.

Because Berseem is a cold-tolerant clover it can be planted with turnips, rape, any of the brassicas successfully. It can also be planted with small grains like oats, triticale, or rye grain. If Berseem is planted with a grain crop it is recommended that the Berseem be broadcast 30 days later to slow down the development of the Berseem. Sow Berseem on top when the grain crop is 2-4 inches tall. Then cover the Berseem by using a rotary hoe, if possible. Berseem responds to liberal applications of phosphate and potash.

Grazing can begin when the stand reaches 10 inches in height, and when basal shoots begin to grow.

◄ Berseem works very well in companion crops with Italian Ryegrass or any of the brassicas, such as rape, tylon, or turnips.

Depending on the planting date, climate, and temperatures this may take anywhere from thirty to sixty days. Subsequent cuttings can be taken every twenty-five to thirty days, down to three inches, until the first serious freeze. Graze or clip to encourage new shoot production.

Common brands include Bigbee, Trialex, Topcut, and Mulicut. Bigbee is the fastest establishing brand.

RECAP

- **Seeding Rates:** Planted alone broadcast 10 to 20 pounds per acre. In a mix 8 to 12 pounds per acre.

- **Inoculate With:** Purchase pre-inoculated at www.welterseed.com or from other sources, otherwise inoculate with bacteria (strain O).

- **pH Level:** Prefers pH levels of 6.0 to 6.5.

- **Planting Time:** April/May or September/October.

- **Depth of Seed:** Cover seed about ¼ inch deep.

- **Establishment:** Establishes quickly (particularly with Bigbee brand).

- **Fertilizer:** Responds well to liberal amounts of phosphate and potash.

- **Companion Mixes:** All small grains, white clover, and brassicas.

- **Crude Protein Levels:** Above average.

- **Digestibility:** Very high.

- **Overgrazing:** After establishment not an issue.

- **Extends Grazing Season:** From September to late November.

- **Temperatures:** Has fair cold-temperature hardiness.

- **Caution:** Do not frost seed Berseem clover.

OTHER COLD/WINTER-HARDY CLOVERS AND LEGUMES

- A variety of different brands of red clovers
- Durana White Clover
- Hairy Vetch
- Ivory II White Clover

CRIMSON CLOVER

Crimson Clover is a very popular annual clover among wildlife managers, particularly in the south. It is rated as a cool-season clover but with the reservation that it will not "do well in extreme winter temperatures." With that said, however, I have been pleasantly surprised with the crimson clover ability to withstand cold temperatures on our New York farm and that is why I'm including it here. I have had crimson clover plots last into mid-November, despite crimson being rated as a cool-season annual best planted in the more temperate winter climates of the south. I'm not recommending it here as a winter-hardy planting, but as a test planting. Crimson clover has proven to be a worthwhile cold-season northern planting for me and perhaps it will prove to be for you as well, as long as you realize it won't tolerate extended winter temperatures or last past mid-November. I have witnessed deer foraging on our crimson clover plots during the first week or two of November, particularly when we had light snow during that time.

Crimson clover is also an excellent crop to attract honeybees. It prefers pH levels of 5.9 to 6.5. Crimson should be planted either in early April or May. Plant it in a well-prepared seed bed with good seed-to-soil contact. Make sure crimson is either purchased pre-inoculated or inoculate as directed with Rhizobium bacteria (strain R). According to many deer managers, not inoculating crimson clover properly is the chief cause of crimson failure. Crimson clover is inexpensive, easy to grow, and productive after planting. It is very palatable to deer and it has good protein levels.

RECAP

- **Seeding Rates:** Planted alone broadcast 25 to 35 lbs per acre. In a mix 10 to 15 lbs per acre.
- **Inoculate With:** Rhizobium bacteria (strain R) just prior to planting. Buy it pre-inoculated at (www.welterseed.com).
- **pH Level:** Prefers pH levels of 5.9 to 6.5.
- **Planting Time:** In the north plant in May and August in the south.
- **Depth of Seed:** Cover seed ¼ deep.
- **Establishment:** Quick-starting.

▲ Don't confuse crimson clover with red clover. Crimson leaves have more rounded tips and are deep red.

- **Fertilizer:** In a stand-alone plot 300 pounds 8-24-24 per acre. In a mixed stand use 350 pounds per acre of 19-19-19.
- **Companion Mixes:** Mix with small grains at reduced grain rate seedlings of about 50 lbs per acre.
- **Crude Protein Levels:** Very high.
- **Digestibility:** Very high.
- **Overgrazing:** After establishment not an issue.
- **Extends Grazing Season:** From October to early November
- **Temperatures:** Has limited winter tolerance.
- **Caution:** Will not tolerate poorly drained soils.
- **Avoid:** Inoculating crimson clover yourself. Instead buy it pre-inoculated.

COLD/WINTER-HARDY CLOVERS AND OTHER LEGUMES

LADINO CLOVER

Ladino clover is often called a cool-season perennial but would better be referred to as a cold-season planting. Ladino, particularly the giant leaf variety, is a clover that is a productive, high-quality white clover used for wildlife food plots, or pasture, hay, or silage for domestic animals. Other cold-tolerant white clovers include Durana White clover, a product created (bred) by Dr. Joe Bouton, and the common white Dutch clover. White clovers are the most commonly used clovers in the world. Ladino clover is a versatile planting that can be planted alone or, better yet, used as part of a mix. Ladino clover prefers pH levels of 6.0 to 6.5 and it responds well to potassium fertilizer.

I have found ladino clover to be a favorite of the deer on our farm and I suspect that it is also highly favored by deer in other locations across the country. Ladino has high protein content levels of 25 to 30 percent and it provides 50 to 75 percent digestibility. It is also disease-resistant and withstands winter conditions well.

Ladino seeds should be spread on a clean, firm seed-bed, covered lightly, and can be planted with a culti-packer seeder, a grassland drill, or by broadcasting. The seeds are available pre-inoculated or they should be inoculated with a commercial culture (strain B) that is specific for white clover.

It mixes well with perennial grasses such as ryegrass or, better yet, timothy grass. It can also be mixed successfully with any of the small grains including rye, oats, winter wheat, Milo, or triticale. An excellent northern mix includes 5 pounds per acre of ladino mixed with 7 pounds of red clover, and 5 pounds of timothy grass. Fertilize ladino clover using either 400 pounds of 19-19-19 per acre or 300 pounds of 8-24-24 per acre.

▲ Ladino can be identified by its leaves that are marked with a white "V." Ladino has an early freeze-out and will quickly kill off when temperatures fall below 10 degrees. We planted ladino in the lane next to the rye grass.

RECAP

- **Seeding Rates:** Planted alone broadcast 2 to 4 pounds per acre. In a mix, 1 to 3 pounds per acre.
- **Inoculate With:** Rhizobium bacteria (strain B) or buy it pre-inoculated (www.welterseed.com).
- **pH Level:** Prefers pH levels of 6.0 to 6.5.
- **Planting Time:** Seed at least 40 days before heavy frost.
- **Depth of Seed:** Cover seed lightly.
- **Establishment:** Slow-starting.
- **Fertilizer:** Use either 400 pounds of 19-19-19 or 300 lbs of 8-24-24 per acre.

- **Companion Mixes:** Plant with other cold-hardy clovers, grains, and grasses.
- **Crude Protein Levels:** From 25 to 30 percent.
- **Digestibility:** Very high.
- **Overgrazing:** After establishment not an issue.
- **Extends Grazing Season:** From May to November.
- **Temperatures:** Has fair winter hardiness (freeze-out occurs from 0 to 10 degrees).
- **Caution:** When planted with perennial grasses, mow at least twice per summer.
- **Avoid:** Don't mow below 2 to 3 inches for best results.

COLD/WINTER-HARDY CLOVERS AND OTHER LEGUMES

RED CLOVER

Red clover is a perennial clover that is described as a northern cold-hardy planting. Like all the cold-hardy clovers it won't withstand extended northern temperatures below 15 degrees Fahrenheit, especially for extended periods of time. It will, however, withstand some cold temperatures especially when red clover is planted with any of the small grains.

Red clover will reach heights of 2 to 3 feet or more. It is inexpensive and it grows best in northern portions of the country, although they are short-lived in the north, lasting only three or four years. It tolerates acidic soils with pH levels as low as 5.6, but does best when the ph levels are kept at 6.0 to 7.0. Red clover does not do well in wet soils.

There are many varieties of red clover and most are low-maintenance crops that produce a high-quality food plot for deer. Red clover establishes readily because the seeds are very energetic. It can be planted from June to August in the north and October in the south in a well-prepared seedbed with good soil-to-seed contact and plant prior to a predicted rainfall.

Red clover is a high-yielding planting that also has a long growing season from April to October. It provides palatable forage throughout its growing season. Deer will forage on it into late November.

As with many of the clovers, red clover will respond well to phosphorous and potassium. It is often mixed with other clovers including ladino, white, trefoil, and it does particularly well when planted with Arrowleaf clover. It also combines very well with the small grains (winter wheat, oats, rye, triticale, and sorghum [Milo]).

Red clover is available in many different varieties, including Kenstar, Bulldog, and several others. Check with your local county agent to see what variety grows best in your area. For managers who want the most cold-hardy red clover variety I suggest buying a variety called Persist Brand Red Clover, which is available at www.welterseed.com.

Persist has also done very well in deer plots as a red clover variety that is long-lasting and that the deer savor. Through developmental breeding, improvements have been made on these characteristics.

RECAP

- **Seeding Rates:** Planted alone broadcast 10 to 12 lbs per acre. In a mix 3 to 6 lbs per acre.

▲ Plant red clover with timothy grass or any small grains (wheat, rye, triticale, and oats).

- **Inoculate With:** Live bacteria culture (strain B). Better yet, buy it pre-inoculated.

- **pH Level:** Prefers pH levels of 6.5 to 7.0.

- **Planting Time:** April or August.

- **Depth of Seed:** Cover seed about ¼ inch deep.

- **Establishment:** Establishes very quickly.

- **Fertilizer:** Use 30 pounds of phosphate and 90 pounds of potash per year.

- **Companion Mixes:** Plant with small grains or ladino or Arrowleaf clovers.

- **Crude Protein Levels:** From 10 to 30 percent.

- **Digestibility:** High.

- **Overgrazing:** After establishment not an issue.

- **Extends Grazing Season:** From May to November.

- **Temperatures:** Will not withstand extended temperatures below 10 degrees.

- **Caution:** Be sure to buy improved cold-tolerant brands.

- **Avoid:** Planting alone, best used as a mix with small grains to extend its cold-season value.

SUBTERRANEAN CLOVER (Shade Tolerant)

Subterranean clover, a.k.a sub-clover, is a highly nutritious cold-hardy annual that will tolerate winter temperatures as low as 15 degrees—freeze-out takes place between 0 and 15 degrees. In the fall its productive seasons are from October to November. It is shade-tolerant and as such is popular with many managers who use sub-clover to plant food plots in wooded areas. It is also very tolerant to heavy grazing pressure by deer.

It can be seeded in spring or fall (September to October). Sub-clover germinates and emerges quickly and it is a terrific re-seeder. Sub-clover can be planted as a stand-alone plot or, better yet, in a mix with grains, white clovers and even vetches. It is recommended not to plant sub-clover more than a ½ inch deep. There are many varieties of subterranean clover to choose from, including Nangella, Oregon, Woogenellup, and Mt. Barker.

Subterranean clover is an ideal planting for managers who have more areas of woods and pines than they do open fields to plant. However, sub-clovers planted in very thick stands of pines or mature hardwoods are less likely to be successful.

Sub-clover develops differently than other clovers and legumes. After it pollinates the flowers develop a burr. The burrs weigh down the stems and by doing so they deposit seeds into the soil, allowing for continued grazing to occur without limiting seed production. Surprisingly, seed production is reduced if the sub-clover is not kept tightly grazed to heights of 2 to 4 inches. The stoloniferous growth habit of subterranean clover makes it an ideal plant for the close-type grazing of deer and other domestic animals.

RECAP

- **Seeding Rates:** Stand-alone plots broadcast 15 to 20 pounds per acre.
- **Inoculate:** With a specific inoculant for sub-clover (WR strain).
- **pH Level:** Prefers pH levels of 5.5 to 7.0.
- **Planting Time:** April or September.
- **Depth of Seed:** Cover seed about ¼ to ½ inch deep.
- **Establishment:** Establishes very quickly.
- **Fertilizer:** Use 300 lbs of 8-24-24 per acre at planting.
- **Companion Mixes:** White or crimson clover, small cereal grains, or vetch.
- **Crude Protein Levels:** Average.
- **Digestibility:** High.
- **Overgrazing:** After establishment not an issue.
- **Extends Grazing Season:** From June to November.
- **Temperatures:** Will not withstand extended temperatures below 10 degrees.
- **Caution:** Unreliable re-seeding, intolerance of poor drainage and drought.
- **Avoid:** Planting in very thick stands of woods and pines.

Sub-clover is shade-tolerant. ▶
It usually will not withstand
temperatures below 10 degrees.

EXTREME WINTER-HARDY CLOVERS AND LEGUMES

This clover and legume group can actually be classified as being *extremely* winter-hardy because they can survive in temperatures of zero to 10 degrees Fahrenheit, albeit not for extended periods of time. However, the term clearly refers to these clovers being able to withstand (survive and thrive) in the most frigid of temperatures and other winter conditions. Extremely winter-hardy clover plants remain productive and provide quality forage well into December and January or until they are deeply snowed under.

The group includes Austrian Winter Pea, Kura, Marathon, and Kopu clovers. They are my "survive and thrive" top clover choices and help to keep deer coming into my food plots from November until late December, when the deer season closes in my home state of New York.

▲ Kura is the most winter-hardy clover. It will tolerate the harshest of winters better than other winter-hardy clovers and legumes including alfalfa, Birdsfoot trefoil, red clovers, and winter peas. Stands of Kura often remain productive for several years when properly mowed and fertilized.

BIRD'S-FOOT TREFOIL

A better choice than alfalfa for the average food plotter is bird's-foot trefoil. It ranks among my favorite perennial legumes to replace finicky alfalfa. Deer find bird's-foot trefoil nearly as irresistible as they do alfalfa. In fact, trefoil is often called the "poor man's alfalfa."

What is even more attractive about bird's-foot trefoil is that it tolerates *severe* winter temperatures. There are specific varieties that were bred to be adapted to the northern states and Canada. The Empire brand trefoils are better tailored for wildlife food plots. Bird's-foot trefoil is better than alfalfa when it comes to cost and maintenance. It will provide an excellent alternative to alfalfa and therefore should be an integral part of any cold-season planting program. It will be a highly attractive planting addition as a mix with other winter-hardy plantings for deer, turkey, and other wildlife.

▼ Bird's-foot trefoil is a practical choice to replace alfalfa. It can withstand severe winters and cold temperatures, making it an ideal planting to attract deer from October to December.

RECAP

- **Seeding Rates:** In pure stands broadcast 10 pounds per acre. When mixed cut rates in half.
- **Inoculate with:** Rhizobium bacteria strain (k) prior to planting.
- **pH Level:** Likes pH levels of 6.2 to 6.5.
- **Planting Time:** In the north seed in late August or early September and October the south.
- **Depth of Seed:** Lightly cover seed ¼ of an inch deep. Can be top-sowed successfully in a well-prepared plot that is well compacted for best soil-to-seed contact just prior to a rainfall.
- **Fertilizer:** Use 300 to 400 pounds of 0-20-30 at planting.
- **Companion Mixes:** Best used as a mix with all small grains, some grasses and other clovers.
- **Protein Levels:** 10 to 15 percent.
- **Pliability:** High.
- **Overgrazing:** Generally not an issue once established.
- **Extends Grazing Season:** Well into winter.
- **Temperatures:** Withstands severe winter temperatures.
- **Caution:** Inoculants used for alfalfa and covers will not work with bird's-foot trefoil.
- **Avoid:** Be mindful of weed competition and correct as needed.

AUSTRIAN WINTER PEA

Austrian winter pea is an annual legume that ranks way up on a deer's preferred list of food sources. It is often referred to by experts in the field as the cool-season "ice-cream plant."

It is a good winter-hardy planting choice as long as managers understand that it can't tolerate prolonged frigid temperatures of below 0 degrees.

Austrian winter peas can be planted alone but do better when planted in a mix. They do nicely when combined with clovers, grains, and oats. This is a crop that can be very helpful for managers who intend to hunt over some of their winter-hardy food plots and as such winter peas should be an essential part of a cold-season planting program.

Other similar plantings including soybeans, lablab, cowpeas, and burgundy bean are classified as warm-season plantings and they are excellent choices for food plots. I would not include them as even cool-season crops, however. Even when they are planted as *strictly* warm-season plantings they can be troublesome for managers who do not have enough acreage to plant these legumes successfully. Cowpeas, burgundy bean, and soybean need large acreage plots from 5 to 10 acres each to escape being devastated by deer before they can mature.

RECAP

- **Seeding Rates:** Planted alone broadcast 40 to 50 pounds per acre. In mixes plant about half that rate.

- **Inoculate With:** Rhizobium bacteria (strain C).

- **pH Level:** Prefers pH levels of 6.0 to 7.5.

- **Planting Time:** Plant in late August.

- **Depth of Seed:** Cover seed ½ to ¾ of an inch deep.

- **Establishment:** Slow-starting, vulnerable to overgrazing.

- **Fertilizer:** Before planting mix 300 to 400 pounds of 0-20-20 into the soil. When planted with clovers or gains fertilize with 19-19-19.

- **Companion Mixes:** Plant with other cold-hardy clovers, grains, and grasses.

- **Crude Protein Levels:** From 25 to 30 percent.

- **Palatability:** Extremely high.

- **Overgrazing:** Susceptible to overgrazing.

- **Extends Grazing Season:** From October to December.

- **Temperatures:** Has excellent winter hardiness.

- **Avoid:** Don't plant as a stand-alone crop for deer.

- **Caution:** Will not survive extended frigid sub-zero temperatures.

▼ Austrian Winter Peas are winter-hardy; however, during severe winters when the peas are susceptible to extended periods of sub-zero weather, they will be killed off. Photo courtesy: www.plantcovercrops.com.

KURA CLOVER

Kura clover is a spreading perennial clover that is among the most extreme winter-hardy clovers. As such, it is able to withstand the most frigid of winter temperatures. Kura clover is a robust, perennial clover that is similar to but significantly different from red and white clovers.

It will survive the onslaught of winter well after clovers and other legumes are long dead. It is my number one choice as the most reliable winter-hardy clover planting. It is the perfect match for small grains like winter-wheat, oats, and cereale rye.

Once Kura is established it can tolerate intense heavy grazing even into late December. Both elements make Kura a prime planting for all deer managers, particularly those who want to extend the grazing season into November and December.

Kura spreads easily and it has an extensive root system which helps it to be more tolerant of drought than most other clovers, which makes it perfect to plant in more arid locations. If you want to attract honeybees,

Kura is the clover to plant as it is one of their most favorite of all the clovers.

Because it is so extremely winter-hardy and endures severe heavy grazing, Kura makes an ideal nurse crop. It does very well mixed with any of the grains, brassicas, and grasses.

The only downside to Kura clover is that I have noticed is that it establishes slowly. Once it gets going, however, Kura stands can last for many years. Kura can tolerate a pH range from 6.0 to 7.5. It prefers a higher pH level rather than a lower one, however. Kura, like other clovers and other legumes, must be inoculated. The correct Rhizobium strain Trifolium Spec 3 is used for Kura.

When planting Kura make sure to get good seed-to-soil contact. It should be planted no deeper than ¼ to ½ inch deep in a well-prepared seed bed. When you plant Kura by itself, broadcast 8 to 12 pounds per acre.

Kura can be planted in early spring, April or May, or it can be planted in late July or early August. Kura is much like alfalfa regarding growth, production, and

Kura is one of the best of the extremely ▶ tolerant winter-hardy clovers. It has survived in the most severe of northern winters when bird's-foot trefoil and other extreme plantings were killed by similar conditions.

quality but it is a lot easier to grow and manage than alfalfa. It is also a sturdier plant than alfafa once it gets established.

Kura is a top choice when it comes to planting a pure stand of extremely winter-hardy clover. I also use Kura in many nurse crop mixes. Used like this, Kura helps distract the deer from eating the primary crop.

Kura can also be mixed with bird's-foot trefoil, which is another extremely winter-hardy legume that is able to withstand severe winter temperatures. When planted alone or together, Kura and bird's-foot trefoil not only provide quality tonnage but also high levels of protein for your deer herd. They are top choices if you want to attract deer from November through January on your property.

RECAP

- **Seeding Rates:** Planted alone broadcast at 8 to 12 pounds per acre in a prepared seedbed.

- **Inoculate:** Use Rhizobium strain Trifolium Spec 3.
- **pH Level:** pH levels between 6.0 to 7.3.
- **Planting Time:** Early April to early May.
- **Depth of Seed:** Plant ¼ to ½ inch deep.
- **Fertilizer:** Use 300 pounds per acre of 19-19-19.
- **Companion Mixes:** Does very well planted alone. Even better plant with small grains rye, triticale, wheat, and oats, grasses, and other legumes.
- **Overgrazing:** Once established resistant to heavy grazing pressure.
- **Extends Grazing Season:** From October to late December.
- **Caution:** Slow to establish.
- **Avoid:** Planting later than early August.
- **Note:** Kura will outlast other extremely winter hardy clovers, including bird's-foot trefoil, alfalfa, etc.

EXTREME WINTER-HARDY CLOVERS AND LEGUMES

KOPU II CLOVER

Kopu II clover is a coated white clover that was bred for improved stolon production, persistence under heavy grazing, high yield, and large leaf size. Like most white clovers, they are preferred by deer, turkey, and other game birds. Kopu II has excellent long season growth and high energy levels. Kopu II has exhibited improved yield and persistence over other white clover varieties that were known as favorite white clover plantings.

Kopu II is often used to overseed existing pastures. It does best when seeded with a no-till drill or culti-packer. Kopu II can be planted in the spring or the fall. If planted in the fall, allow at least eight weeks before killing frosts begin to occur. Frost seeding also works.

Kopu II grows best on well-drained, fertile, loamy, or clay soils of a pH from 6.0 to 7.0 that are well supplied with minerals and moisture. A good mix would be with a grass like timothy at a 75 percent to 25 percent rate; 75 percent timothy and 25 percent Kopu II. Kopu II is a perfect companion with perennial ryegrass and also works well with orchard-grass and tall fescue.

Kopu II does well with adequate levels of calcium, phosphorus, and potash. Some managers worry about the fact that if ruminants eat too much white clover they could get bloat. However, whitetail deer are non-bloating concentrate selectors.

I have found Kopu II white clover to be a winter-hardy selection on our farm. It can produce until October and provide forage into early December. I buy my Kopu II coated or non-coated seed from Welter Seed and Honey Company (www.welterseed.com).

RECAP

- **Seeding Rates:** Planted alone broadcast 2 to 4 lbs per acre in a prepared seedbed. When planted in mix use 1 to 3 pounds per acre.

- **Inoculation:** Available pre-inoculated from Welter Seed Company.

- **pH Level:** Prefers a pH level of 6.0 to 7.0.

- **Planting Time:** Spring or fall.

- **Depth of Seed:** Plant ¼ inch deep.

- **Fertilizer:** When planted in a mix use 300 pounds per acre of 19-19-19.

- **Companion Mixes:** Can be planted alone, but does better when mixed with timothy grass or small grains rye, triticale, wheat, and oats.

- **Overgrazing:** Once established resistant to heavy grazing pressure.

- **Extends Grazing Season:** From September to November.

- **Caution:** At planting, make sure to get good seed-to-soil contact.

- **Avoid:** Avoid planting Kopu II as a mix—it does better when planted alone and will have a longer stand-life as well.

◀ This buck was killed eating in a Kopu clover food plot in late November. Kopu makes an ideal late-season planting that will extend grazing into December. Photo courtesy: www.wildlifeperfect.com.

MARATHON RED CLOVER

Marathon red clover was developed by the University of Wisconsin. It is disease-resistant and a long-lasting perennial red clover producing for three to four years. Marathon is very winter-hardy and it is superior to other red clovers in total long-lasting performance. It is best adapted to the northern half of the United States, making it another top-choice as a cold season planting.

As a red clover, it is often used in grass mixtures like timothy. Marathon should be purchased pre-inoculated. Planting depth should be ¼ inch deep in a well-prepared seedbed or thin stand of grass.

Seed production is dependent largely on insect activity. Plants do not self-pollinate. Bumblebees are particularly effective in helping with successful pollination.

RECAP

- **Seeding Rates:** Planted alone broadcast 10 to 12 lbs per acre in a prepared seedbed. When planted in mix use 2 to 6 pounds per acre.
- **Inoculation:** Available pre-inoculated from www.welterseed.com.
- **pH Level:** Prefers a pH level of 6.0 to 7.0.
- **Planting Time:** Spring.
- **Depth of Seed:** Plant ¼ inch deep.
- **Fertilizer:** Use 300 pounds per acre of 19-19-19.
- **Companion Mixes:** Can be planted alone, but does better when mixed with timothy grass, other winter-hardy clovers and legumes and or small grains rye, triticale, wheat, and oats.

- **Overgrazing:** Once established resistant to heavy grazing pressure.
- **Extends Grazing Season:** From November and December.
- **Caution:** Make sure to get good seed-to-soil contact.
- **Avoid:** Don't purchase Marathon red unless it is pre-inoculated.

SUMMARY

The bottom line about planting cold-season and extremely winter-hardy clovers and other legumes, is that a majority of plants you include in your program should be available and edible for deer from October to January. They will contribute significantly in consistently attracting deer to your land during the hunting season. If that is your end goal, then the above cold-season species profiles will help you substantially in achieving it.

OTHER EXTREME WINTER-HARDY CLOVERS AND LEGUMES

- Fixation Balansa Clover – 0 to 5 degrees Fahrenheit
- Alice White Clover – 0 to 5 degrees Fahrenheit
- Frosty Berseem Clover – 0 to 10 degrees Fahrenheit
- Ameristand 419LH Alfalfa – 0 to 10 degrees Fahrenheit
- Jumbo II Ladino Clover – 5 to 10 degrees Fahrenheit
- Vernal Alfalfa – 5 to 10 degrees Fahrenheit

12. Shrub and Other Wildlife Plant Choices

To round out a wildlife management program, special attention should be given to including a variety of wildlife plants that consist of a wide selection of different types of shrubs and other plants. Deer and other wildlife utilize many of the shrub and other plant choices listed on the following pages first and foremost as food and shelter. Does use the protection of these shrubs and plants to have and hide their fawns in and other wildlife tend to nest and rear their young here, too. Shrubs and other wildlife plantings also provide runways for an assortment of wildlife. When planting shrubs, they should be placed about 6 to 7 feet apart for best growth potential.

American Holly: The American Holly's fruit is used by game birds and songbirds as well as big game and other animals. This plant makes very good deer protective shelter. It typically grows as an understory tree in forests. It is rare in the north of its range in southern Connecticut, southeastern New York, and isolated areas of Cape Cod. The branches are short and slender. The roots are thick and fleshy. It will grow in both dry and swampy soil, but grows slowly. The flowers are pollinated by bees and other insects including wasp, ants, and night-flying moths. The berries are reported to be poisonous to humans, but are important as a survival food for game birds and songbirds that eat the berries after other food sources are exhausted. The

▼ American Holly forms a thick canopy that provides excellent cover from inclement weather and as protection from predators for deer and other wildlife.

tree also forms a thick canopy that offers protection for birds from predators and storms.

Bayberry: The mature height of the bayberry is 6 to 9 feet. Very aromatic, it will grow in a wide variety of site conditions from sandy, poor soils to heavy clay soils. These are plants that enjoy extremes, as they also prefer bogs, marshland, and wet woodlands. They grow in areas along roadsides, on sand dunes near mid-Atlantic beaches, and in old, abandoned fields. The fruit will persist through the winter, providing food for deer and game birds. Bayberry bushes are tough, hardy plants that have pleasantly scented foliage and berries. They are native to the continental United States and grow vigorously along the eastern coast and throughout the south. Bayberry shrubs are also known as candleberry, tallow shrub, waxberry, and tallow berry.

Beach Plum: A native shrub of the Atlantic coastal region, the beach plum is a round, dense bush that grows 4 to 10 feet tall. It prefers sandy, well-drained soils and full sun and has edible fruit that grows 1 to 1½ inches long. It is a good cover plant. Beautiful white blossoms cover the branches of this shrub-like tree in the spring. The blossoms develop into colorful fruits that all wildlife will eat, including deer, bear, turkey, and game birds. The fruit is popular among people who gather it to make delicious jams and jellies. It may be bluish purple, red, or even yellow when it ripens in September. It actually flourishes in the poorest soils imaginable. It is so hardy that it tolerates long droughts, sub-zero cold, and most diseases. It's a plant that will work well in any management program. Usually it bears its fruit the year following its planting.

Blackberry and Raspberry: These shrubs should be planted in and along edges, fence rows, and old fields. The fruits they provide are highly sought out by deer and other wildlife, including deer, bear, turkey, grouse, and song birds. Large, thick stands of these shrubs make excellent deer cover. Deer will use blackberry and raspberry bushes to bed in. They make excellent places for game birds to build nests and rear their young. They can be planted in some wooded areas as long as they can get at least half day of sunlight.

▲ Bayberry is aromatic and used to make scented candles. It's an excellent wildlife shrub as it tolerates a wide variety of soils, making it easy to grow.

Both blackberry and raspberry are top choices to plant as food for ▶ deer and other wildlife. Their thick stands also provide cover and nesting for wildlife.

Bristly Locust: Wow, this one is a top choice for wildlife managers and land stewards. It is a medium-sized, fast-growing, woody legume that grows to between 10 and 12 feet tall. It has a high drought tolerance and prefers well-drained sites in full sun. Bristly locust is excellent for erosion control, mine reclamation, or roadside banks; it spreads rapidly via suckers. Bristly locust's seed pods are 2 to 5 feet long and it has a purplish-colored flower. The bristly branches and pods make great cover that is hard to penetrate and creates an excellent barrier, preventing prying eyes seeing into areas along roads, etc.

Common Buttonbush: This is a large, woody shrub, 6 to 12 feet tall, that has a flower that forms a ball-like seed cluster that is approximately 1 inch in diameter.

▲ Don't prune elderberry or other shrubs. Pruning prevents shrubs from growing wild and gnarly, making thick cover deer seek out as security.

Eastern Dogwood: This is a valuable shrub for wildlife because its high calcium and fat contents make it palatable. In May, the copious white flowers are stunningly attractive. Eastern dogwood is an extremely hardy species. It can succeed in any soil of good or moderate fertility and can withstand temperatures down to –13° F (–25°C). The wood is heavy, strong, and extremely shock-resistant. The fruits, seeds, flowers, and twigs of this tree are an extremely valuable food source to many species of wildlife, including deer, black bear, turkey, grouse, pheasants, rabbits, beavers, squirrels, and many other non-hunted species of birds and other wildlife. However, the seeds of this tree are poisonous to humans. Dogwood provides excellent shelter and habitat for deer and other game.

Eastern Red Cedar: This is a columnar-shaped tree that, when grown in groups, can reach heights of 30 to 50 feet. Eastern Red Cedar prefers open, well-drained sites. Its twigs and foliage are readily eaten by all species of deer. The tree bears a small blue berry on females, providing food for all types of game and non-hunted animals. Male trees bear a tiny cone.

Cedar provides important nesting and security coverage for deer and other wildlife, particularly in winter when their dense foliage protects deer and other game from foul weather and cold temperatures and helps to escape detection from predators, especially in large stands of cedar. Deer often use cedar to rub their antlers on.

Elderberry: Native shrub of North America that grows up to 15 feet in height. Elderberry prefers moist, organic soils. The fruit is dark purple to black and about ⅛" in size. Elderberries are relished by many game birds, deer, bear, and other mammals. Deer also eat the twigs and leaves.

Elderberry is a fast grower and aggressive competitor with weeds and herbaceous species. Individual plants don't live very long; however, root masses produce new shoots quickly. Elderberry as a wildlife plant should not be pruned or cut. Pruning will prevent it from growing wild and gnarly, which creates the type of coverage deer and other wildlife use as security. This forest species will grow in full sun if the soil is well-tilled and watered. It can be planted as a hedge or alone. Elderberry provides effective erosion control on moist sites. The berries grow in clusters and its large, flat-topped, white flowers are edible to humans and used for making jams, pies, or wine. Deer and other wildlife seek this plant out for both food and cover.

WARNING: Elderberry plant parts are toxic to humans and animals; they are especially dangerous for children. Whistles made from the stems have been implicated in poisonings. Sensitivity to a toxin varies with a person's age, weight, physical condition, and individual susceptibility. Children are most vulnerable because of their curiosity and small size. Toxicity can vary in a plant according to season, the plant's different parts, and its stage of growth; and plants can absorb toxic substances, such as herbicides, pesticides, and pollutants from the water, air, and soil.

Highbush Cranberry: This is one of my favorite plants to grow to create food, bedding, and cover areas to keep deer on your property. It is a spreading, upright shrub, 10 to 15 feet tall. It makes large flower clusters in spring (4 to 5 inches) and bears a bright red, edible fruit in the fall that lasts well into winter. The fruit is eaten by all species of deer, bear, turkey, rabbits, grouse, pheasants, squirrels, and many other non-hunted animals. Highbush cranberry prefers moist, well-drained, open sites.

Prairie Willow: Although this plant does not grow tall, it does grow thick. It is a medium-sized shrub, 3 to 9

▼ Highbush cranberry is a spreading shrub that can grow to 15 feet high, creating thick, impenetrable cover for deer to seek shelter.

feet tall. It will grow well on dryer sites in full sun. It prefers sandy, well-drained, open sites, but will tolerate partial shade fairly well. The best aspect of this plant is that it grows in thick clusters and makes very good visual barriers from the neighbors' place or along roads. It is also an excellent choice to plant to create bedding areas for deer and other wildlife.

Pussy Willow: This thin-branched, medium-sized shrub will grow up to 20 feet tall. Pussy Willows like wetter areas—marshes, stream banks, flooded ditches, or wet bottomlands—and are good for erosion control. Grown in thick, heavy stands, deer will use it for cover.

Red-Osier Dogwood: This is a medium-sized shrub with numerous stems that can grows between 3 and 19 feet tall. The fruit is preferred mostly by Ruffed Grouse, but turkey will eat it as well. It is well-suited for wetter, open areas. It is good for erosion control, stream shade, and windbreaks. Deer will seek out dense stands of this plant for food and cover.

Rhododendron: This plant likes to be near streams and moist woods. It is a favorite for deer to browse in winter. Thick stands of rhododendron make very good cover for deer.

Sandbar Willow: This is a medium-sized shrub that offers terrific height, as it grows to 20 feet. It is often used for stream bank stabilization and riparian area restoration. While most hunters shy away from my advice to plant this willow for obvious reasons, it is a terrific plant for both food and cover for deer. The fruits of the Sandbar Willow provide important winter sustenance and shelter for deer, small game, and other wildlife. It can be planted almost anywhere and in any type of soil. The Sandbar Willow's red fruit is mostly eaten by wildlife throughout winter when they remain on the shrub. The fruit provides a needed food source when more desirable foods are scarce or dormant. Deer and rabbits eat the bark, fruits, and stems. Game birds, such as grouse and turkey, rely heavily on the fruits, as do many winter songbirds.

Sumac: This is a shrub commonly found in old fields and forest openings and can grow to 20 feet high.

▲ Deer eat sumac's fruit, twigs, and stems mostly as a late-fall and early-winter food source when other foliage is limited or completely dormant.

Sumac has heavy, stiff, brown twigs and branches. The leaves are 12 to 16 inches long. They exude a white, sticky sap. In fall, sumac leaves turn bright red. The bark of the sumac is grayish brown and has rough and raised pores. Sumac flowers from May to July. The male and female flowers are found in dense bunches among branched clusters, mostly at the end of new growth. Sumac's fruit usually ripens in August or September. As young shrubs, many types of birds and small mammals use sumac to nest in or to hide their young. Sumac fruit is eaten by songbirds as well as game birds. Deer and cottontail rabbits also eat the bark and twigs. Deer use dense patches of sumac to seek shelter from inclement weather and to hide from predators.

Wild grape: While they prefer to be planted in rich woods and along stream banks, wild grape will grow almost anywhere it can get decent soil and half-day sunlight. The more sun, the better. I like to make thick stands of this plant in overgrown fields and second growth stands of woods. The fruit is favored by most wildlife including deer, wild turkey, bear, grouse, etc. Thickets of wild grape are used regularly by deer for cover, fawning, bedding, and as browse.

By including these shrub plantings in your management program, you will increase the number of deer and other wildlife you attract on your property. These plants also encourage deer to use the cover, food, and protection from predators that they provide throughout the entire year, which increases the chances of housing deer on your land tenfold.

13. Fertilizing Oak Trees!

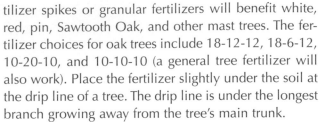

During the fall, acorn mast crop is about 40 percent of a deer's diet. Acorns are an important component of the fall and winter food sources. To help provide a good crop of acorns, I began to consider fertilizing oak trees and wrote an article in 1983 about doing so. Until that time, no one else had approached this overlooked subject. Today, more hunters and deer managers understand the importance of improving the nutrition of natural vegetation.

There are a few different mixes of fertilizers that can be used on different types of oak trees. Generally, fer-

tilizer spikes or granular fertilizers will benefit white, red, pin, Sawtooth Oak, and other mast trees. The fertilizer choices for oak trees include 18-12-12, 18-6-12, 10-20-10, and 10-10-10 (a general tree fertilizer will also work). Place the fertilizer slightly under the soil at the drip line of a tree. The drip line is under the longest branch growing away from the tree's main trunk.

The best trees to fertilize have a trunk diameter of about 20 inches or larger. The fertilizer will cause the tree to produce larger, sweeter, and more abundant acorns even when other trees aren't producing any acorns at all. Additionally, during good mast producing years, fertilized oak trees will even produce a *better* mast crop than the surrounding oak trees. By undertaking a yearly program to enhance the production of a few of the oak trees on the lands you hunt, you will not only provide a higher quality of forage for deer, but you will also create deer hunting hot spots.

Fertilizing oak trees on the lands you hunt serves three functions. It will not only improve the production of your oak trees, but also improve the overall health of the deer. It also acts as a highly effective decoy hunting tactic. Most hunters are totally surprised by the significant results they get from fertilizing oak trees. I'm often told the outcome was totally unexpected. The tactic of fertilizing oak trees will work on private, leased, or public hunting lands.

One of the key elements is not to get too greedy with the number of oak trees you fertilize if you use this strategy on public land. Then it is crucial to keep the trees you fertilize a total secret. That means you don't even share what trees you fertilize with your closest hunting partner. Trust me on this point. On land that is a shared lease with several hunting partners, you should keep the location of at least one fertilized tree to yourself. If you own the land, then you can let guests know where you want them to hunt so you don't have to be secretive about fertilizing your oaks. (Unless you give some friends permission to hunt when you're not there. If that's the case you may want to rethink telling them were your fertilized oaks are.)

Basically, you want to select two mature white or other oak trees to fertilize per 25 acres. The trees should be located as far apart from one another as possible within that amount of acreage. If you don't have

Use a pinch bar to make holes for fertilizer. ▶
Each hole should be made at the drip line (at ends of the longest branches from the main tree trunk).

white oaks on your land, any other oak tree will work just a well. The only reason I suggest trying to use white oaks first is that deer prefer white oak acorns over all other types of acorns. For this strategy to work to its maximum potential, select a few mature oak trees that have at least a main trunk diameter of 20 inches or more.

On our 192-acre property, I selected eight oak trees as far apart from each other as practical. If you have less or more land, adjust the numbers accordingly. Basically 1 tree per 25 acres is a good formula to work within. On smaller pieces of land from 5 to 45 acres, fertilize one or two oak trees. Use common sense on larger tracts of land, keeping in mind that the more trees you fertilize, the less effective the tactic will be, even through it provides good nutrition for game. This tactic will work best on public land when you select a single oak tree that is not part of a dense group of oak trees, but rather a tree that is among many oaks spread out within a much larger area.

By selecting an oak within a group or even near other oaks on public lands, eventually your tree will be discovered *accidentally* by others hunting the area. It won't take long for them to figure out deer are frequenting a particular tree more than they visit the others and there goes your hot spot. It is more unlikely that they will discover your single fertilized tree that is part of a much larger group of trees in a larger area. Most hunters will be looking for a patch of acorn-bearing trees growing closely together, thinking the more acorns that fall from the group of trees, the better it will attract deer. That is true only when they don't have a single tree that provides them with more abundant, sweeter, and larger acorns.

If you are more concerned about improving the overall woodlot management of your trees, then by all means you should fertilize as many oaks as you see fit.

problem of having too many trees for them to feed on prime-tasting acorns, which will make it much more difficult for you to predict exactly what oak tree they visit on any particular outing. Knowing where deer and other game will dependably show up puts you in an *optimum* position to have more sightings and shooting opportunities.

Once you have selected the tree or trees you want to fertilize, begin by making 12 to 18 holes deep enough to fit a fertilizer spike comfortably around the entire tree trunk. Make the holes directly under where the furthest branches are from the trunk of the tree with a pinch bar or similar type of tool. Remember, the holes *must* to be made directly below the drip line of the tree's longest branches for the fertilizer to work quickly and effectively. The drip line is found *directly* under the ends of the longest branches extending off the main trunk of the tree. Beneath the soil of the drip line is where the tree's feeding root system is located. If you fertilize too closely to the main trunk of the tree, the benefits of the fertilizer reduce substantially. Poke the holes deep enough to cover the entire length of the fertilizer spike and then some. *Before* placing the spike in the hole, break it in half, and then place both halves in each hole. Once the spike is in the hole, cover it with a few inches of soil, but don't pack the soil too tightly over the spikes. If you do this on public ground, throw some leaves over the area to disguise the newly made holes. I suggest fertilizing the trees once in the spring and then again in the fall. I put my fertilizer spikes in when there is rain predicted within a few days.

If you would rather use granulated fertilizer, simply fill the hole to within an inch or two of the top with the granulated mix and cover it with some of the remaining soil. Pat the soil down gently and smooth it with a leaf rake. Then cover it with leaves, twigs, and other forest debris to disguise what you have just done.

Fertilizing oak trees is a tactic that will produce acorns that are not only bigger, sweeter, and more abundant—the acorn crop of fertilized oaks will also drop later than surrounding acorns. This happens

However, if you fertilize oaks as a hunting tactic, then *don't* fertilize too many trees. If you do, it will provide the deer, bears, and turkeys with too many options to visit a wide number of trees. Instead of having a few to several locations where you *know* the deer and other game will be feeding at certain trees, you'll create the

In the unlikely event you can't locate the oak tree ▶
fertilizer with the recommended NPK, use a general
tree fertilizer instead. Photo courtesy: Ted Rose.

because the fertilizer makes the general health of the tree better and encourages the acorn stems to become stronger (healthier), resulting in the acorns remaining on the branches longer. The end effect is when most of the unfertilized acorns have fallen and been consumed by deer, bears, and turkeys. *Your* fertilized tree will drop its mast later in the fall. Usually during that time, you will be bow or firearm hunting from mid-October to mid-November.

The first year you employ this strategy, the tree will respond by providing a better acorn crop. There will be a noticeable increase in the tree's production in the second year, which the deer and other game will quickly zone in on. The acorns will begin to look bigger to you as well. They will also be noticeably more abundant.

By the *third* year, however, your fertilized trees will be producing bumper crops of acorns that will be bigger, sweeter, and more abundant and that will drop later than the trees that weren't fertilized. More importantly, the acorns will taste much sweeter to deer than the acorns from non-fertilized trees do. The "sweetness" of the acorns is a key factor that deer will zone in on and record to memory.

Here's how to *prove* how effective this tactic really is. At the end of the third year, select a fallen acorn from your fertilized tree. After biting the fruit of the acorn, you will notice it has a slight bitter taste, as all acorns do. Wait until the bitter flavor is gone and then bite into another acorn that has fallen from a tree that wasn't fertilized. You will instantly notice the acorn has a stronger bitter flavor. Its bitter flavor will be excessive compared to your fertilized acorn. Deer and other game interpret the less bitter acorn as being *sweeter* than the acorns they find and eat from other trees. Again, they will record the experience to memory and visit that tree over and over again for years to enjoy its better-tasting fruit.

If you share the location of the trees you fertilize with hunting companions other than your immediate family, you will discover what I did. Without a doubt, they will hunt the area when you're not there. If that is OK with you, then by all means let them know where it is. If you want to take a buck year in and year out at these secret locations, then keep as *tight-lipped* about the location of the oaks you fertilize with everyone except the hunters in your immediate family.

This fertilizing strategy also works on other natural vegetation, including wild grape vines, all types of berry-bearing bushes, and other types of plants that deer consume throughout the summer and fall. Find out what the deer prefer, then ask your local farm agency what the best mix of fertilizer is and apply it to the plant. It will increase production, nutrition, and volume of the plant and its fruit, bringing the deer to it on a reliable basis. Again, don't over-fertilize too many plants or you limit the success of the tactic.

It probably goes without saying by now how effective this fertilizing tactic will be on any wild fruit tree on your hunting lands. By choosing a few choice trees and fertilizing them, you will increase the amount, size, flavor, and abundance of the crop the tree makes.

We have well over 100 wild apple trees on our farm and a few pear trees. I prune and fertilize the pear trees and some key apple trees near some of our better hunting blinds and tree stands. Over time, the deer have learned exactly which trees bear larger, more abundant, and better-tasting fruit each season. They actually visit the trees during early fall every day. Sometimes they stand there as if they are waiting for the fruit to drop (which is always later than the fruit trees I don't fertilize). *It is such a simple plan, one that consistently provides success.*

Pruning wild fruit trees, vines, shrubs, and bushes helps, too. Pruning should only be done when trees are asleep (dormant). It can be done soon after the leaves drop and there has been a hard frost. Usually I begin my pruning in late October. It can also be done in the winter from November to January, but pruning trees early allows more time for the tree to heal and recover from the pruning process. If you prune any later than January, you could send the tree or plant into shock and it will take a year or two to recover. During that time, it will not produce fruit, mast, grapes, or berries.

Give the oakand other vegetation-fertilizing strategy a try. It should be an important part of your food plot and wildlife management program. I promise you will see immediate results during the first fall. In each subsequent year, the acorn production will get better and better, as will any other vegetation or fruit tree you fertilize. It is a simple strategy to employ and one that reaps huge benefits. Don't hesitate another season without trying it.

For the record, to my knowledge—and I have researched this—I was the first outdoor communicator to write a magazine article about the hunting strategy of fertilizing oak trees in 1979. I have never found any evidence that any other outdoor writer wrote about fertilizing oak trees as a hunting tactic prior to 1979. Thankfully, that is not the case today. There are countless articles on this subject now and many others are writing about how successful a tactic fertilizing oak trees really is.

14. Minerals, Vitamins, and Proteins for Larger Antlers

*J*ust how does one go about improving the antlers of the bucks on your land? The simple answer is through a multi-tined program that provides deer with the right type of minerals, vitamins, and proteins—and in the right quantities. Whether we like to admit it, most deer hunters are obsessed with the antlers of whitetail bucks—so much so that many deer hunters go to extraordinary lengths to educate themselves about every aspect concerning deer antlers.

Several years ago, on one of my television shows, I coined a term meant to be complimentary to describe whitetail deer hunters, including *myself*, who are totally passionate (some might even say to the point of being obsessed) with anything concerning a whitetail buck's antlers. The phase I used was "bonehead." Since *bonehead* generally is used to describe someone who is missing a card or two from the deck, I want to be sure that when I use the term *bonehead* here, you understand it is meant in a positive manner related to the bone on top of a buck's head. I hereby claim that I am an unabashed bonehead and speculate most of you reading this book are, too.

For most land and deer managers, the entire basis of creating a food plot and deer management program is to produce bucks that grow larger antlers. Unfortunately, not all managers live in areas where the soil contains the combination of minerals in the substantial quantities like it does in Wisconsin, Illinois, Michigan, Iowa, Kansas, and similar states and provinces. The minerals found in the soils in these areas are chiefly responsible in helping bucks grow very impres-

sive sets of antlers. On the other opposite side of the coin, throughout most of the states in the northeast and New England, the soil simply doesn't have the necessary primary minerals of calcium and phosphorous nor the number of other elements (trace minerals) that are *required* by bucks for them to grow large sets of antlers. For a buck to grow a set of antlers like they do in the areas I just mentioned, there are three basic essential factors a buck needs to achieve. These elements

► This buck had everything he needed to grow a set of antlers like this—age, genetics, and access to quality nutrition including primary, trace, and micronutrients.

include age, genetics, and prime nutrition, which include taking in all the necessary minerals needed to develop superior antlers.

AGE

For a buck to achieve his best set of antlers, he must reach adulthood, which biologists generally agree is from three and a half and four and a half years old. (Some biologists feel a buck reaches maturity from four and a half to five and a half years old.) Therein lies one of the most crucial aspects of creating a deer management program. Managers must abide by the common-sense concept not to shoot yearling bucks (immature male deer) for them to get old enough to grow their best set of antlers. I'm paraphrasing here, but the phase used by the Quality Deer Management Association, "Let him go to let him grow," should be the call-to-action statement for any dedicated deer manager who wants to see and harvest larger-antlered bucks. For that matter, it should be the call-to-action for any buck hunter who wants to see and kill bigger-antlered bucks.

▼ The antlers on this mature buck are impressive. He had to be cagey enough to survive several hunting seasons. Photo courtesy: Ted Rose.

Even though a buck reaches his best set of "head bones" between the ages of three and a half and five and a half years old, managers can still improve the size of a younger buck's antlers starting from when they are yearlings or two-and-a-half-year-olds by providing them with the type of complete nutritional needs they require at that early age.

GENETICS

The genes a buck inherits are inescapably linked to many factors of the buck's body size, hair color, weight, behavior, and the size and shape of his antlers. The bottom line is that if a buck isn't born with the type of genes he needs to achieve very large antlers, he simply won't grow huge sets of antlers. There simply isn't much that can change that fact even if the buck is provided high-quality nutrition and is allowed to reach a mature age.

With that said, however, nutrition *does* play a key role in allowing a buck to reach his maximum genetic potential size no matter what that size ends up being. In other words, if a buck ends up with genes to produce a set of antlers that falls within a specific size range, improved nutrition will almost always help to *increase* the average set of antlers.

This is why it is so important for those who manage their land and deer herd to always establish the very best buck-to-doe ratio as they can, so Mother Nature can take care of the natural selection process. The more bucks for a given number of does, the more they compete for the chance to breed. Little bucks get pushed out and the older bucks have more offspring to pass on their genes. This is why it is so important to harvest as many does as is practical on your land. That's why game department's doe management permits are "golden" to dedicated deer managers.

NUTRITION

Nutrition, which includes quality food stuffs and sufficient intake of a variety of quality minerals, is as important as age and genetics. In fact, there are some biologists who believe nutrition is even more essential than age and genetics. Quality nutrition, and, more importantly, premium mineral supplements often produce bigger antlers within the shortest period of time— in some cases, as quickly as the first year. Nutrition,

therefore, is the easiest of the three factors to improve.

By providing quality mineral supplements to your deer herd, you will help increase the size of your 4- and 6-point bucks to 6- and 8-pointers who have noticeably wider antlers. The formula is quite simple; to produce better-antlered bucks, you must provide high-quality nutrition and reduce the numbers of female deer on your land. Trophy-type habitats have the right amount of deer within the land-carrying capacity.

MINERAL SUPPLEMENTS

For most food plot managers, providing nutrition for their deer and other wildlife through a variety of food plots, forest management, and enhancement of the natural vegetation is a primary part of their program. However, the one component that can't be as easily controlled is the available mineral contents within the soil. Minerals are the main restrictive factor in antler development.

It isn't groundbreaking news that antlers are comprised approximately of half protein and half minerals. Because antlers are bone, the mineral content is made of calcium and phosphorous. Vitamins A and D are therefore essential to the ingestion and utilization of calcium and phosphorous. Bone also contains small amounts of other elements of various mineral compounds commonly called trace elements. While the trace element amounts are tiny, they are also vital to antler growth. Trace elements or micronutrients include copper, zinc, iron, manganese, boron, sulfur, calcium, cobalt, molybdenum, and chlorine.

Female deer require liberal amounts of calcium and phosphorous during pregnancy. They require even

◀ A buck like this is what developing a management program can do. Including minerals and vitamins in a program could put this buck in your scope. Photo courtesy: Ted Rose.

◀ When does have access to quality minerals and vitamins, they produce stronger, healthier fawns because their milk is more nutritious.

more substantial amounts of calcium and phosphorous for milk production to their fawns. Bucks must ingest calcium to grow their antlers. As I mentioned earlier, not all areas provide enough of the primary or trace minerals naturally. Therefore, land managers have two options.

In states and provinces where it is legal to do so, land managers should plan to add huge, yearly doses of minerals into the soil, which is an expensive and time-consuming practice. On mid-size to large management areas, the best plan to add minerals directly into the soil is to contact a farm feed and grain store and have them deliver several tons or more with a spreader or dump truck to the land. The truck can dispense the minerals over the desired plots that the land manager can then till or disk the minerals under the soil.

This practice kills two birds with one stone: The minerals will considerably help the plants to grow healthier and allow them to transfer the mineral benefits to the deer.

Many feed and grain places that mix their minerals can also include vitamins expressly intended for white-tailed deer in the order. Including the vitamins with the minerals will cost more, but will be well worth the investment. This two-sided plan helps support better antler growth for bucks and provides does with a

more complete nutritional offering than they would otherwise get from natural sources or from plantings in areas that lack natural minerals. However, as I mentioned, this is a time-consuming and expensive method.

On small tracts of land, an entirely different mineral application might be more practical and much less expensive. On small, established food plots, using commercially prepared mineral supplements is a more affordable and realistic plan. As with the previously mentioned plan, minerals must be applied during the year for several years to be most beneficial to deer. In either case, if a year is skipped, the deer will end up negating any benefits they have previously gained.

The most practical method for a majority of deer managers to provide the necessary minerals needed to develop better antler growth is to include a more controlled, long-term mineral supplement program in their management plan—but only where it is legal to do so. The easiest way to provide minerals to deer is by using the granulated form. Mineral blocks are helpful, but only when enough of them are provided. One or two mineral blocks simply aren't enough to provide the quantity and quality of minerals needed by deer. If you use mineral blocks, you must buy them in sufficient numbers.

▲ Deer Cane Mix+ is an excellent brand of minerals. Most companies make quality minerals. However, check the label to be sure it includes all the minerals bucks require to grow larger antlers.

When you use granulated minerals, you can also mix them with other types of supplemental foods. Although most granulated minerals provide heavy does of the primary minerals calcium and phosphorous, some don't include the trace minerals in enough quantity. Although trace minerals aren't the overriding elements to grow antlers, they are needed in enough quantities for various biological processes in deer. Check the label of the granulated minerals you buy. If you need to add some trace minerals, you can purchase them at most feed and grain stores.

You can also custom-order granular minerals to your specifications. Usually the mix of minerals will include large amounts of potassium, phosphorus, and calcium. You can ask the feed and grain store to mix in the other trace or macronutrients including sodium, manganese sulfate, ammonium sulfate, cobalt, selenium, iodine, magnesium, copper, and zinc. Research has confirmed that large antlers often contain much higher amounts of sodium, zinc, and manganese than smaller antlers do. Additionally, if you plan to include vitamins in your minerals, make sure to add vitamin

A, D, and E and add any other nutrients designed to enhance skeletal development, general health, and overall body growth. Quality mineral feedings encourage larger antler growth in the buck populations over short periods of time.

When purchasing minerals, don't be tempted to buy them at a feed store; their minerals are designed for livestock and therefore contain more salt than other more expensive designer-granulated mineral mixes. Therefore, always read the ingredients on the label of the mineral supplement products you intend to purchase. Look for brands high in sodium, selenium, iodine, magnesium, cobalt, zinc, manganese, phosphorus, calcium, copper, vitamins, and other nutrients intended to enhance antler development and overall health and body growth.

The intake of the right amount of quality minerals will help a buck achieve larger antlers and increased weight and assist does with better fertility and reproduction, better fawn survival, and increased general growth and body development. However, it usually takes a couple of years before a noticeable increase

◀ Minerals can be purchased custom-made. Or they are available in most sporting goods catalogs or stores in large or small quantities.

occurs in antler size among bucks. With that said, other than button bucks, an overwhelming number of our yearling bucks sport at least a set of 6-point antlers as their first proper set of headgear. Our two-and-a-half-year-old bucks generally have 8-point racks.

To substantially elevate and enhance the mineral content in high enough quantities to benefit antler growth, general body condition, and general health, this type of mineral undertaking must be a long-term endeavor and may last up to several years. The amount of acreage to which the minerals and/or vitamins are provided to the deer will determine how much of them should be used.

Deer need minerals during the spring "green up." That is when mineral powders, blocks, or licks should be placed on the ground throughout the property for deer to locate them quickly and for easier access. To apply powdered or granulated minerals, simply go by the exact instruction label provided with the product by the manufacturer. Some powders must be mixed

▲ When using minerals and vitamins, always use them exactly as the directions suggest. Photo courtesy: Hunter's Specialties.

▲ A deer's body needs minerals most in spring just before "green up." Deer are much more inclined to visit mineral sites at this time than any other time of the year. Photo courtesy: LuckyBuck.

with water and others simply dumped on the ground. I have better success with mixes that did not have to be mixed with water. They are also much easier to apply.

Over twenty years ago, when it was legal to do, I used minerals to help increase antler size on the bucks I hunted. I established several mineral holes on a 750-acre piece of land I leased. I created each mineral site off the well-beaten walking trails I used. I made them next to—but not on or along—the most *active* deer trails that led to and from bedding areas to take maximum advantage of the comings and goings of the deer using the trails. As the directions suggested, each site was close to a thicket or other type of cover so deer would feel more secure visiting the site even during daylight hours.

I created the sites in mid-April just before "green up." As the directions suggested, I checked each site about six to eight weeks later to determine the activity level of use by deer and to refresh each site if need be. I was taken aback at what I found. While I expected to see some sites had been used, each and every site demonstrated "high traffic" use by deer. Even more

impressive, each site's dimensions were noticeably increased and the amount and different sizes of tracks suggested that all age groups of deer were using the sites as well. The deer continued to visit the mineral sites throughout the year with varying highs and lows of activity. It became apparent to me that deer have an instinct and need to ingest the various minerals that were available at each of the sites. I have no doubt creating small mineral multi-sites to provide additional supplement vitamins and minerals for deer is a beneficial practice for land managers, but *only* if it is a legal practice in your state or province.

PROTEIN SUPPLEMENTS

Protein is also an important building block for antler growth. It helps establish the cartilage-like framework and the blood-rich velvet to distribute the elements needed to form antler makeup to the structure.

To help bucks develop bigger antlers, protein should be made available as early as February in the south and March in the north—or at least before bucks begin to develop the first sign of their new antler growth. Protein supplements will help to quickly kick off the process of antler development and provide bucks with a vigorous start to growing their new set of antlers.

Protein supplements are mostly available in pellet form. They can be specifically prepared by feed and grain stores to your exact specifications. Or they can be purchased already prepared in bags from a variety of sources that also make minerals.

A supplemental mineral, vitamin, and protein feeding program, particularly in regions where the soil lacks the amount of minerals bucks need to grow larger antlers, is a good and useful management tool and addition to any deer management program. By providing minerals, vitamins, and protein supplements, deer will receive a more complete nutritional diet than their natural range can provide them. A long-term supplement plan will help not only in larger antlers for the bucks, but also in an increase to the overall health of the deer herd (where such programs are legal).

15. Managing to Grow Adult Bucks

ertainly hunters who start a management plan on their land or on long-term leases should strive to be better land and wildlife stewards by supporting all the concepts that create improved landscapes and healthier wildlife. By developing a policy to enhance the habitat and for all wildlife, hunted and non-hunted species alike, managers morph from just being hunters to land and wildlife caretakers of a cherished and irreplaceable bounty. This is a virtuous goal that will benefit not only the current custodians, but also their children and their children to come.

Unquestionably, encouraging landowners and hunters to become better stewards of their lands and the game that inhabit their lands was the genesis of the primary concept undertaken by the Quality Deer Management Association decades ago. As I mentioned earlier, the Quality Deer Management Association has played a *momentous* role in educating and assisting hunters throughout North America in the virtues of creating more wholesome landscapes and healthier wildlife for millions of hunters and non-hunters alike.

I consider their book, *Quality Food Plots—Your Guide to Better Deer and Better Deer Hunting,* the Holy Grail of food plot and deer management. It is *the* keynote book in my library. Anyone who is serious about creating a woodlot and deer management plan should include it within their collection of important writings. I guarantee you will refer to it over and over again.

▼ The author proudly admires his son's buck. The dandy 8-point was walking to a food plot. Pajsa is a high-yielding variety forage hybrid brassica with sweet leaves bred to withstand heavy grazing.

Although the end goal of many hunters is to become better land and wildlife stewards, it is more likely their main motivation for creating a management plan was to see and take more deer and, more specifically, larger antlered bucks. Frankly, this goal was *my* primary reason for beginning my plan. However, to manage for bucks so they grow bigger antlers, and eventually, hopefully, large enough antlers to be called trophy-class animals, it takes a long-term commitment that requires several components be consistently observed without deviation. The first and foremost element to seeing bigger bucks on your property revolves around a very basic fundamental point. Unfortunately, this one practice is difficult for many hunters to follow. This is particularly true if the time they have to deer hunt is limited.

Spike and Other Small Antlered Yearling Bucks

For those managers who want to improve the antler size of the bucks on their land, the primary method to realize that goal is to implement a plan to protect all yearling bucks. This is a crucial part of any program that intends to enhance the antler size of the bucks hunted on the land. As I mentioned, this isn't as easy an agenda to execute because for decades hunters have been brainwashed into believing that spike and other small antlered yearling bucks are inferior and should be eliminated from the herd. For instance, it wasn't many years ago that hunters read and heard that harvesting every spike buck was a necessary deer management control tool. There was a long-held belief that a spike buck wouldn't or couldn't ever develop a quality set of antlers because the buck's genetics were substandard. It was also believed that eliminating spike and other small antlered yearling bucks stopped them from passing on their alleged substandard genes. Over the years, however, countless long-term biological and scientific studies have absolutely disproven this long-held, erroneous conviction.

The research is well-defined, and it has shown that the majority of spike bucks within the many studies that have been done over the last decade can go on to develop larger antlers—as long as they had access to quality nutrition and lived to two and a half years old. These bucks often developed 6-point or better antlers in their second year and subsequent years.

Many of them that were allowed to reach three and a half years old went on to develop even larger 8-point sets of antlers. While a notable percentage of the bucks involved in the studies never achieved a set of trophy-class antlers, the study did prove that spike and other small antlered yearling bucks could indeed grow respectable larger antlers if they were allowed to live past their first year.

The evaluation of such studies throughout the years should be sound enough evidence for any reasonable hunter to agree that protecting yearling bucks from being killed is all that is required for hunters to improve the antler size of the bucks on the lands they hunt. Therefore, killing spike or other small antlered yearling bucks simply isn't a wise management practice for hunters who undertake a deer and land management program—or for any hunter, for that matter, who is interested in seeing and bagging larger antlered bucks. Consequently, the Quality Deer Management slogan took hold within the deer hunting fraternity: "Let him go to let him grow." This phrase has become the call to action for millions of hunters throughout North America.

Thankfully, protecting yearling bucks today is a more accepted practice by deer hunters throughout North America than any other time in the past. They are beginning to understand and embrace the critical importance of yearling buck protection programs that are more commonly called Antler Restriction Programs (ARP). Some hunters have come to realize it is more beneficial to allow spike bucks and other small-antlered yearling male deer to reach their second and third years of age before they consider shooting it as a yearling.

I want to be clear that while most spike bucks will grow larger antlers within a few years, not all spikes and other small antlered yearling bucks end up developing impressive 8- to 10-point sets of antlers. If they have a poor genetic makeup that simply doesn't allow them to grow large antlers, even if they grow 8-point antlers, they will always be small and spindly compared to bucks who have a better genetic makeup. However, enough yearling bucks do go on to grow better antlers—the type of antlers many hunters would be absolutely pleased to shoot and proudly display as mounts in their trophy room.

Through our record keeping of our own personal hunting experiences on our farm, Kate, Cody (our son), and I have been able to confirm that spike bucks and other small-antlered bucks (3- or 4-pointers) that are given the chance to reach two and a half years old often develop small sets of 6- to 8-point sets of antlers. If they survive to be three and a half years old, we have noticed their antlers will develop into larger 8-point racks. Through both scientific documentation and personal observations, the study information on yearling spike and other small-antlered bucks has helped to encouraged hunters to more strongly support the concept of protecting yearling bucks and allow them to "walk by." In the end, ARP programs have provided hunters with a chance to see more bucks on each hunting outing and have allowed hunters more opportunities to bag larger-antlered bucks on the lands they hunt.

Even after all the evidence provided by studies and research, however, some hunters and novice deer managers still cling to the hard-held belief they should remove all spike or other small-antlered yearlings to prevent them from passing on inferior genes. Another commonly used excuse to shoot yearling bucks by some hunters is "If I don't kill them, someone else will." These hunters are *never* going to improve their chances of taking larger-antlered bucks on the lands they hunt. When they decide to kill yearling bucks without regard to the deer's age or antler size, the only thing they accomplish is to severely limit their chances to take larger-antlered bucks in future seasons.

With that said, I want to be emphatic that I'm not suggesting that every hunter should not shoot a yearling buck with small antlers. First-time hunters should be able to take any buck they feel comfortable

▼ By protecting yearling bucks, hunters assure themselves of seeing and bagging bucks with larger antlers. Photo courtesy: Ted Rose.

◄ Most hunters start a deer and food plot program to get adult bucks on their land with antlers like this buck. Photo courtesy: Ted Rose.

shooting. Hunters who have never killed a buck during their hunting lifetimes should also not be held to not shooting a spike or other small-antlered buck (yearling or otherwise). I also exempt hunters who only get a day or two a deer season to hunt. However, for those hunters who want to see larger bucks or who gripe about not seeing enough adult bucks, or for the deer managers who simply want to improve the antler size of the bucks on their land—they must commit to allow-

ing yearling bucks to live another year to realize their goals. That's the undeniable truth to buck management.

Female Deer

Another long-held deer management misconception held particularly by old-time hunters is not to kill any female deer. They strongly feel that the more female deer, the more buck fawns they are born. The fact is that to accomplish a healthy buck-to-doe ratio, as well

▲ Kate with an old, "dry" doe shot on our farm. We try to avoid taking nursing does and/or does in prime breeding age.

as a normal social structure within a given deer herd, female deer within all age classes should be taken in the right amount of numbers to balance the overall herd. By keeping the buck-to-doe numbers to a healthy carrying capacity, they also eliminate deer that overbrowse food sources.

When there are too many deer on a piece of property, the overpopulation numbers begin to put heavy pressure on the habitat's ability to produce quality forage since the habitat can only support a certain number of deer within its boundaries. When the available forage can't produce enough nutritious foods for the deer living on land, it eventually leads to a critical mass overpopulation problem that most often ends with a heavy winter kill of the deer herd within that habitat.

An overpopulation of does eventually leads to breeding complications by not having enough mature bucks to breed the ever increasing numbers of female deer. This phenomenon often ends with does being bred by inferior bucks that pass on less than desirable genes. There will always be more female deer than male deer on the land. Therefore the deer manager is never able to achieve the ultimate goal of creating a 1-to-1 buck to doe ratio. Even a more practical number like 3-to-1 or 5-to-1 (does to bucks) will become impossible to achieve. If a deer manager is eventually able to accomplish three or four female deer to one male deer, they have achieved a noteworthy deer management plan on their land.

Therefore, any dedicated deer manager who develops a long-term management plan *must* understand some female deer must be harvested, particularly if they want to see bigger-antlered bucks on their land. If does are protected, it will only lead to the complete and utter failure of any long-term deer management program. Any qualified biologist will support the fact that female deer *must* be harvested in the correct numbers to have a healthy deer herd and habitat and a successful deer program. *You can take this advice to the deer hunting bank.*

To discover how many does should be shot on a given piece of land, it is highly recommended managers hire a deer biologist to do a survey to advise how many does should be removed from the herd each season. The ultimate goal is getting your deer herd numbers to a 1-to-1 figure (one doe to one buck).

The hunters who own or lease small properties often question whether they can develop a realistic deer and land management plan that includes the opportunity for them to manage for bigger-antlered bucks. This is always a very complicated question to answer because there are so many unknown factors that are involved to provide an educated reply on small pieces of land. For instance, if a small piece of property is surrounded by much larger lands (all of which are under a deer management program), the chances are much higher that a successful deer management plan can certainly work on small pieces of property, even as small as 25- to 50-acre tracts.

On the other hand, if a small 25- to 50-acre managed tract of land is surrounded by neighbors that are killing yearling bucks or any buck that passes by their stand without regard to the deer's age or antler size, then generally it will be difficult to manage for larger-antlered bucks on these small parcels—but not totally impossible. When managing for larger-antlered bucks with small acreage, it is tremendously helpful to enlist the cooperation of the neighbors or employ some other unique deer management tactic. With that said, however, I can personally vouch for the fact that even without neighbor cooperation, it is possible to achieve a buck management program on small lands with 50 to 100 acres. Practically speaking, however, the larger the parcel is, the easier it is to grow and bag larger-antlered deer.

▲ Keeping the numbers of does in check is crucial for a successful management program. It's a good idea to hire a wildlife biologist for professional advice. Photo courtesy: Ted Rose.

This was the first buck taken on our land in 2001. ▶
The antlers measured about 110 inches. Antlers of the adult
bucks on our property now average 140 inches or more.

We began our deer management plan in 2001. At that time, taking a 110-class buck on our property was considered a good buck. Our ultimate goal, however, was to consistently be able to shoot bucks that measured 130 to 140 Boone and Crocket (B&C) inches. The buck management priority was to establish a portion of our land as a sanctuary. The area we chose turned out to be a 26-acre parcel in the center of the 192 acres we have. We planted dozens of food plots to provide higher-quality forage for the deer and for us to see and take more deer and larger bucks. We developed rules to help bucks achieve an older age class, too. One of the first rules was to make an effort to only shoot bucks that were at least two and a half years old and had 8 points or better. We have stuck to the 8-point rule for twelve years despite the fact that all our connecting neighbors continue to kill any buck that passes their stands. We established other buck management rules and guidelines as well.

▲ Cody holds a 9-point set of antlers from a buck killed on our farm. The rack measured about 134 inches.

By 2004, we started to see 8-point bucks with antlers measuring about 120 to 125 inches (and still the neighbors killed any buck they saw). In 2005, all the veteran hunters on our land were only allowed to take 8-point bucks that appeared to be three and a half years old or older. Occasionally, a younger buck was taken by a first-time hunter or someone who couldn't absolutely identify the buck's age. But, for the most part, we have kept the three-and-a-half-year age-class rule. In 2007, the average 8-point buck on our property was sporting a set of antlers that measured about 130 inches. Interestingly, at that time, several neighbors began telling us they had never seen "as many big-racked bucks since we owned the land." However, *they* continued to take spikes and small-antlered bucks.

In 2009, some 8-point bucks on our property had antlers measuring 130 to 140 inches, which confirmed to us that our buck management program was working. Over the last two deer seasons (2010 and 2011), two mature bucks that aged at four and a half and five and a half years old and had antlers that scored 142 and 147 inches respectively were taken by Cody and me. And, yes, you guessed it—the neighbors *still* continue to shoot yearling bucks or any other buck they see. The point I'm making is, even if your neighbors don't support a complete deer management program that also includes protecting yearling bucks, don't let that stop you from doing so. You can manage for bigger-antlered bucks despite the fact that your neighbors are taking spikes and other small-antlered immature bucks.

To accomplish a productive buck management plan requires the implementation of many of the elements I discussed throughout this book. All of these allow the opportunity to see more deer each and every time you go afield and the opportunity to bag mature bucks with bigger antlers in a few short years. All you have to do is be creative and stick to your own overall management plan and your particular buck management goals despite what some of your potentially "brain-dead" neighbors say or do.

Of course it should be remembered that any complete management program must include another important management practice that is worth repeating: It has to include shooting female deer in appropriate numbers to get as close to a 1-to-1 buck-to-doe ratio as possible. Other elements include a secure sanctuary; planting nutritious food plots, fruit, oaks, and other trees; creating lots of thick or impenetrable cover; and using other deer management tactics to make your overall buck and doe management program succeed. You just have to be tenacious and stubborn about the goals you set and not worry about what the neighbors think or do regarding their buck hunting practices.

A Few More Thoughts about Antler Protection Programs

With each new deer season, millions of deer hunters prepare to gather in deer camps across North America. Each and every one of them has daydreamed with adrenaline-charged anticipation that this year is *their* year to place their crosshairs on a buck with a notable set of antlers—or perhaps even a mature, trophy-class antlered buck of a lifetime. For most deer stalkers, this is an age-old fantasy fueled by years of disappointment in not having opportunities of seeing and harvesting an adult buck. (This is particularly true throughout the northeast and New England states but also in many other states and provinces.) It lends emphasis to the old adage that all hope springs eternal—no matter how misguided the hope is. Sadly, daydreaming won't achieve the ultimate goal of bagging a mature whitetail buck for an overwhelming majority of stump-sitters. Only a well-thought-out, responsible, and realistic buck management policy instituted across the country and Canada can make their vision a more common-place occurrence and reality. Nothing short of such a plan will protect young whitetail bucks and provide them the time they require to grow into mature animals that sport impressive sets of antlers.

Organizations like the Quality Deer Management Association (QDMA) have brought to light the magnitude of the necessity to protect yearling bucks from being harvested. Their national efforts on this front have spurred other dedicated state organizations and countless hunters nationwide to embrace the yearling buck protection philosophy. In my home state, an organization striving toward protecting yearling bucks from being harvested is New York State Whitetail Management Coalition (NYSWMC). They are headed unswervingly and competently by President David Hartman.

The research and statistics support a majority of New York State hunters who want to see and bag mature bucks. However, the topic of antler restrictions (or yearling buck conservation, or yearling buck protection, or whatever you prefer to call it), remains inexplicably controversial within the very small percentage of the New York deer hunting fraternity. A 2010 survey done by Cornell University documented that state-wide only 16.3 percent of hunters opposed a yearling buck protection and/or Mandatory Antler Restriction Program (MARP). It went on to say that 57.4 percent of hunters support the programs and 8.1 percent of hunters were neutral. Basically, an overwhelming majority (65.5 percent) of New York State's deer hunters are supportive of having the New York State Department

of Environmental Conservation (NYSDEC) institute an antler restriction program to help protect yearling bucks from being harvested.

Still, in New York deer camps, and anywhere else hunters gather throughout North America, the subject of antler restriction to protect yearling bucks from being shot indeed remains a subject more volatile than an exploding supernova star. I have seen this topic stir passionate conversations of differences of opinions between brothers, friends, and even fathers and sons.

I meet thousands of deer hunters each year online at my deer seminars across the country, at hunting lodges, and at hunting clubs. Interestingly, it almost always turns out the same: Hunters who complain to me about their state or province's inability to produce larger-antlered bucks inevitably turn out to be the same minority of people who are against antler restriction programs (ARP) to help protect yearling bucks. They are obviously dealing with a conundrum within themselves. If hunters want to see and bag more mature bucks with larger antlers, they must decide to issue a "Free-Pass Card" to all yearling bucks they see. They have to do so without using a million and a half excuses why a yearling buck should be shot.

Protecting yearling bucks through antler buck restrictions remains as confounding as it is contentious. In my home state, research clearly documents New York deer hunters want to see and kill mature bucks. Yet the confusion and misunderstandings stubbornly surrounding the policy of protecting yearling bucks remains perplexing and the burr under the saddle that prevents achieving the end goal—better buck hunting for bigger-antlered bucks.

The objective to achieve bigger-antlered bucks in New York is to have every wildlife management unit within the state undertake an antler restriction program. It is a simple reality, whether you refer to it as antler restrictions, yearling buck conservation, or yearling buck protection, it trickles down to a finite point: allowing immature yearling bucks the time they require to grow into harvestable, mature deer that sport larger antlers. It isn't rocket science and it has been proven to be highly successful in areas where it is practiced for years, in twenty-two states across the nation.

One of the problems in New York, however, is unfortunately the New York State Department of

Environmental Conservation (NYSDEC) started to refer to antler restriction as "*mandatory* antler restrictions." I surmise the NYSDEC has unknowingly associated a negative connotation to ARP. The terminology has resulted in the small percentage of hunters against protecting yearling bucks becoming more vocal and politically active. They have sent their message to politicians and the NYSDEC. In turn, the politicians have become reluctant in their support to institute a sound and practical yearling buck protection program that will surely better the state's overall buck hunting. The old adage, "The bearing that squeaks the loudest gets the grease" is without question currently limiting the overwhelming majority of deer hunters in New York to experience better buck hunting. Hunters, no matter where they live, who support AR programs have to counter the antis by organizing and sending letters to their politicians and game departments.

They should also join coalitions that support ARPs. For instance, in New York, any hunter who supports protecting yearling bucks should join the New York State Whitetail Management Coalition. There is no charge to become a member and the newsletters and updates will keep hunters who support ARP in the know. Through the determined and unswerving efforts of David Hartman, the president of NYSWMC, an ARP launched in several counties and regions in New York in 2005 and 2006. More recently, NYSWMC expanded the program into other areas of the state, bringing the total wildlife management units embracing an ARP to eleven.

If the minuscule percentages of hunters throughout North America who don't support protecting yearling bucks through antler restrictions actually want rock-solid evidence of how successful ARPs can be, they don't have to look far. In New York's Sullivan and Ulster Counties (the areas that have been practicing ARPs since 2005 and 2006), 85 percent of the bucks now harvested are between two and a half and three and a half years old. The three-and-a-half-year-old buck harvest is 36 percent of the harvest in the ARP zones, yet it is only 12 percent statewide. Yearling bucks make up only 15 percent of the harvest—a vast improvement over the rest of New York State that is using the 3-inch antler size limit law. New York's deer hunters are now seeing and taking the biggest bucks since the 1920s within these protected areas. No wonder the Cornell surveys found that continuing the ARP is overwhelmingly supported by 77 percent. More interestingly, for the last several years, ARPs have been endorsed by 90.5 percent of hunters in the antler restriction areas.

For the naysayers who steadfastly refuse to look at ARPs with an open mind, here are some other pertinent points.

- When the adult buck population numbers are low, normal breeding and socializing behaviors become severely reduced.

- When adult buck numbers are *within the right capacity* of the deer population, behaviors such as scraping, rubbing, vocalizing, and fighting increase dramatically, adding enjoyment and excitement to the overall hunting experience.

- When there are sufficient three-and-a-half-year and older bucks within the deer herd, hunters will be able to use strategies such as rattling, deer calling, decoying, creating mock scrapes and rubs, and other proactive tactics much more effectively.

- There is no cost to implement an ARP.

- ARPs have proven track records of success nationwide. Pennsylvania is a classic example of a highly successful ARP even though it initially was an extremely controversial subject.

- Hunters whose primary goals include putting deer meat in the freezer benefit from harvesting heavier bucks, providing more meat for their table.

- Hunters both young and old benefit from seeing more deer and, in particular, observing more adult bucks, which increases the overall enjoyment of being afield. This also allows hunters to observe the natural behaviors within a healthy, well-balanced deer herd.

- ARPs to protect yearling bucks are not designed to impose on the rights of other hunters to freely choose the types of bucks they want to take. That has never been the mantra. Indeed, NYSWMC and those hunters who support ARPs are dedicated to the betterment of deer and deer hunting for all deer hunters throughout New York State.

According to Dick Henry, who is a veteran deer hunter and highly accomplished biologist, "I have

▼ When a property has a balanced buck-to-doe ratio, hunters see more natural behavior and sign. The buck on the right is showing aggressive body language as well as vocalizing his displeasure to the buck on the left. Photo courtesy: Ted Rose.

▲ By setting sound buck and doe management practices and abiding to them, bucks will mature and grow antlers like this buck. Photo courtesy: Ted Rose.

never seen a single whitetail deer management program that has invigorated and excited hunters more. Hunters in the current ARP areas in New York are hunting a deer herd that many generations of New York hunters have *never* experienced."

I have known Dick Henry for nearly thirty years and respect his skills and knowledge regarding whitetail deer. He is a true professional. All the folks who work within the NYSDEC are professionals. They work hard to do the best they can within their guidelines. Like all game departments, they have a delicate balancing act that must please hunters and non-hunters alike, which is never an easy row to hoe.

Within three short years of initiating our yearling buck protection program on our land, we began to notice dramatic increases in the antler development of our adult bucks. This is exactly what would happen anywhere yearling bucks are given a "free pass" in ARP areas. From the experience we have gained in our ARP, we have come to the conclusion the longer an ARP goes forward, the higher the guarantee there is for hunters to see and bag bucks with antlers that dreams are made of.

Hunters who believe that simply developing food plot management programs will help them bag larger-antlered bucks are in for a rude awakening. To have a complete management program, you *must* implement protecting yearling bucks along with antler restrictions. For those who hunt public lands, but still want to see better-quality bucks, it is crucial to organize and become more politically active to support ARPs in your state or province. It doesn't take too much effort to write a letter to your representative and to your game department and voice your frustration in their lack of support to introduce a law to protect yearling male deer. If all the hunters who support protecting yearling bucks wrote a letter after reading this, more states and provinces would have ARPs in place. Politicians will react positively to such a mass response, knowing if they didn't take action, they could very well lose votes in an upcoming election.

Consider this last point: Those hunters who *don't* take the time to voice their opinion in support of ARPs to their politicians and game departments can count on the fact that they will have to continue to deer hunt under the current status quo. For healthier and better balanced deer herds, and to enjoy the overall hunting experience, make your voice heard. By doing so, you'll not only improve your deer hunting, but you'll also ensure better deer hunting for your children and future generations to come. In life, if you want something badly enough, you must be willing to work and fight hard to achieve it.

16. Create a Refuge

*I*f you intend to establish a management program, you should also seriously consider planning to include a refuge (often referred to by hunters as a "sanctuary"). However, a refuge must be established as the word "refuge" is defined in dictionaries. The definitions include:

- a condition of being sheltered from pursuit,
- an area of safety, free of danger, or trouble,
- a place where no harm can come to its occupants,
- anyplace providing safe accommodations,
- a place of total immunity.

Merely setting aside a portion of acreage and calling it a refuge, but not treating it as such, is not worth the effort of doing in the first place.

The prerequisite of making a section of land into a refuge is to create a secure area for deer that remains absolutely undisturbed during the entire year and totally free from any type of human trespass. It must also never be entered by anyone after it is established. This is the only way a refuge, sanctuary, safe haven (however word you choose to refer to it) will allow deer to feel categorically comfortable and secure enough to seek shelter in the refuge to protect themselves from predation.

I can't stress enough that whether it is a small 50-acre or a large tract of 1,000 acres, a refuge must be exactly as the word is delineated and referenced in dictionaries. I hope I made that point extremely clear. If not, what I'm saying is: if you set aside a portion of land as a refuge, then stay the hell out of it. This rule is the number one component required to create a sanctuary that will actually attract and keep deer, including mature bucks, using your land and calling it "home."

A sanctuary should only take up a small percentage of ground, perhaps 5 to 10 percent of your total acreage to establish an utterly secure refuge. For these areas to be even more attractive safe havens to deer, their creation must be planned carefully. A place of total safety must also include good cover, overgrown patches of thorn thickets, and similar type heavy cover. It should also include a small natural water source or even a tiny manmade pothole will do. It should have some natural forage growing within it; a few old apple trees would be a bonus. If more abundant and nutritious food sources including food plots, chestnut and other mast trees, or fruit trees can be provided close to it, but outside of its borders, all the better.

Before selecting a site for a refuge, try to pick a location that includes some or most of these elements. If only a few of these elements are present in the spot you choose, but the location is prime to make a sanctuary (like the center of your property), then postpone creating it for a year. During that time, you can plan to put in cover-type plants, a pothole for water, and plant an apple tree or two. Plant plenty of thick and fast-

growing shrubs like bayberry that grow to 6 to 9 feet; high brush cranberry that grows between 10 and 15 feet; sandbar willow, a shrub that can grow to 20 feet tall and is excellent forage for deer; sumac; and dogwood. Deer will eat and bed in all these plantings. You can also make hinge cuts to existing trees over the year to provide more reachable natural food while creating even higher and more secure-looking cover. In other words, if the site is a first-rate location for a refuge, but lacks some important elements, create them before

dedicating the area as a sanctuary. It will be too late to do it after you have established it as such. The end goal is to create abundant cover and browse that is hard to see and walk through.

When a refuge is created properly, deer quickly learn to feel completely secure within its boundaries. Once that happens, they seldom need or want to leave the sanctuary to seek security on other properties. The only time does or bucks will forsake the security of a sanctuary is during the rut, but even then only for short periods of time.

◄ This is a 10-acre refuge on our land. It includes a large wet, swamp-like area with evergreens, thick cover, and beaver ponds.

Creating a refuge and including the elements I've mentioned has helped us tremendously in increasing the total numbers of deer considerably that call our land "home." In fact, creating a total *non-hunting, no-trespass zone* has been the single most effective strategy we employed on our land to better our deer sightings and buck kills. We were fortunate that the area we chose to create our sanctuary happened to have good cover and almost all of the other elements within it. More beneficially, it was located smack-dab in the middle of the land. The 26 acres includes overgrown vegetation, thickets of second growth, a small section of pines that I planted prior to making it a refuge, lots of second growth, and an abundance of other natural cover. Three sides of our sanctuary lie adjacent to our planted fields. The other side borders an area of dozens of apple trees and thick second growth. After posting the sanctuary in 2001, we never entered it again for any reason. While I am certainly curious about what the interior area looks like, the benefits of creating a complete

▲ There is no reason to ever enter a refuge other than to recover a wounded or dead deer.

for shed antlers." Another explanation to enter the refuge given to me is to "check out the number of scrapes and rubs" within the refuge. Still other excuses range from curiosity, to look for "tracks and other deer sign," to log the area, or to plant food plots or fruit trees. Some people told me that they entered their sanctuary in order to, "count the number of deer they see while walking through it." This is the most ridiculous of all reasons to enter a sanctuary.

The only rational reason for anyone to enter into a refuge is to retrieve a wounded deer. However, even then there must be specific rules about how to recover a wounded deer from within a refuge that must be followed without exception. To keep our sanctuary totally pressure-free, we have a rule that doesn't allow anyone to enter the sanctuary even to look for a wounded deer within. If a wounded deer enters the area (fortunately, none have since it was created), the only time we are allowed to look for it is at night. By not allowing anyone to chase after a wounded deer in the refuge during daylight hours, it accomplishes two goals. First, it prevents spooking the wounded deer out of the sanctuary and perhaps onto the neighbor's property. Secondly, it doesn't disturb the deer within the refuge and force them out and onto the neighbor's lands. It only takes one time to disturb a mature buck living in a sanctuary for him not to return to it again.

The best time to enter a refuge to either retrieve a dead or wounded deer is during total darkness. Wait an hour or so after it gets dark to enter a refuge to find a dead or wounded deer. By then, the does, fawns, and yearlings will have left the sanctuary to feed. Bucks will have left to look for receptive does or to eat. If this practice is followed, it will go a long way toward helping to keep the meaning of a sanctuary intact.

year-round safe haven far outweigh satisfying my own inquisitiveness.

In my talks with hunters and deer managers they often tell me about their "sanctuaries." The conversation inevitably gets to a point where they mention a variety of reasons why they "had to" enter their "sanctuary." One of the prime justifications is to "look

Develop specific guidelines on how to go about this. First make a rule that states that before entering the refuge to recover a dead or wounded deer, you must first firmly establish the deer is actually *in* the sanctuary. This can be accomplished soon after the wounded deer is suspected of entering the sanctuary. First set up other hunters in stands that are near the refuge and let things settle down for an hour (if enough daylight is still available). Then the hunter who wounded the deer must *slowly*—and I mean at *a snail's pace*—walk along all four borders of sanctuary looking for blood. If blood is not found, the odds are that the deer is still in the refuge. However, if blood is found, the deer most likely only ran through the sanctuary and has headed someplace else. Obviously, once blood is located,

the hunter should follow the blood-trail. What this prevents is an unnecessary entry into the sanctuary—a useless trespass has been avoided. If it is determined the deer is in the refuge, then the only ethical option left is to enter the refuge. If that is the case, no more than two hunters should be allowed in to the sanctuary to look and/or recover the animal. Once again, that should only take place well after it gets dark.

Our refuge has developed into a high-traffic deer area. There are countless deer trails leading in and out of our refuge. Deer can often be seen bedding or standing in the area as we work nearby fields. They have learned over years that no matter what is happening outside of the protected area, they are completely safe as they are left *totally* undisturbed while they remain

▼ When does use a refuge regularly, they become live decoys to resident bucks. During the rut, they lure transient bucks to your land too. Photo courtesy: Ted Rose.

▲ This type of thick cover makes an excellent refuge.

inside the sanctuary. It only took our deer one season to figure out where the safest place was when the pressure starts on the neighboring farms. As soon as hunting season begins, the number of deer on our land rises instead of declines, all thanks to our totally secure refuge that we never trespass on. To our surprise, not only do the deer use the area to find security, but so do the turkey. Since the establishment of the sanctuary, we learned a lot about how important a completely undisturbed refuge is in attracting and holding deer and other wildlife.

Throughout the years, we learned to plant food plots that are strategically located near or bordering the refuge. Some of the plots close to the sanctuary are non-hunting zones. Others are bow-hunting-only plots and some are firearm-hunting-only. During the spring and summer, we maintain as low a profile as possible while planting plots along or close to the sanctuary.

We also only walk or ride ATVs (at the slowest speed possible) on trails made along all our borders to keep from disturbing the deer that bed in the sanctuary and other places on our property as well.

When a refuge is created, it will offer a haven to several groups of does that quickly learn it is a place of year-round safety. Year after year, we see more does using the sanctuary. Many times, it is not unusual for us to sit in a deer blind in late summer or early fall, and even throughout the entire firearm season, and watch ten to thirty or more deer exiting the sanctuary from different points to feed in the food plots. Once you attract and keep these does on your land, you will inherently attract bucks, particularly throughout all the phases of the rut. We have documented over the years that harvested bucks are often those we have never seen either while sitting in blinds or on our trail cameras. Our refuge takes up slightly more than 10 percent of our 192 acres. The key for our safe-haven success program is that we absolutely enforce our strict off-limits policies to us and to all our hunting guests.

I assure you that you can take everything I mentioned in this chapter to the *deer-hunting bank* for immediate success. Create a refuge on your land and you will see the difference in the numbers of deer in just one season. Another trick to a successful refuge program is not to put excess pressure on the land or fields that surround your sanctuary either. Stick to the absolute no-trespassing rules of your safe haven. Don't ever give in to the pressure of your hunting companions or your own temptations to walk through your sanctuary. Remind them and yourself that when deer sightings and kill numbers are what you seek on land surrounding the refuge, it means your sanctuary is doing its job.

The excitement and the anticipation is that you may be in the right stand at the right time one morning or evening when a doe in estrus unknowingly coerces a buck to leave your sanctuary and she walks the buck past your stand. Then, and only then, will you realize the importance and practicality of creating a place of safety that never disturbs your deer.

One final thought on this subject. Our sanctuary signs read: STAY OUT … SANCTUARY. I bought them not only to warn others as much as to remind Kate, Cody, and myself about the absolute importance of never penetrating our refuge.

17. Other Wildlife Plantings

All too often, managers get caught up developing food plots designed mostly to benefit deer. Managers should also consider specific plantings that target specific species of wildlife groups such as waterfowl, upland birds, turkey, and small game. The following suggested plantings are particularly favored by turkey, waterfowl, upland birds, and/or small game.

WILD TURKEY

Chufa Seed for Wild Turkey

One particular beneficial planting to consider is chufa. Chufa is a perennial sedge plant that produces a nut-like seed on its root system that is similar to peanuts. Chufa is among the most preferred forage foods of wild turkeys and wild hogs. Chufa plants have underground tubers, which are the part of the plant that turkeys eat. A single chufa tuber will produce a plant that can grow fifteen to seventy-five additional underground tubers when mature. Once chufa matures, turkeys locate the underground tubers by scratching the surface to get at the tuber that lies just under the surface of the ground. Tubers provide high amounts of protein and fat, making them particularly nutritious for wild turkeys. So, this plant is a prime choice for wildlife managers. Chufa plants also benefit other wildlife, including ducks and deer. Sometimes it takes turkey, ducks, and particularly deer a season or more to learn about chufa. The quickest way to get wildlife familiar with this planting is to turn the soil over lightly, exposing the tubers. This helps considerably to "teach" wildlife the benefits of eating this beneficial plant.

Chufa can be planted from late April to mid-August. Some say the plant will sometimes reseed, making it a potentially a biennial planting. The best experience I have had with planting chufa, however, has been to

▼ The goal of a chufa food plot is to attract wild turkeys in the spring. Turkeys, deer, and other wildlife dig or scratch the tubers from the ground once the plant matures. Photo courtesy: Ted Rose.

replant each spring. For best success, plan to plant at least at least a half-acre plot of chufa.

Chufa plants will grow in a variety of soils. Chufa performs best, though, when planted in well-drained, sandy, or loamy soils. Clay soils can support chufa but only when they are not *pure heavy* clay soil. Usually, chufa will grow anywhere that corn or grain sorghum can be successfully grown. Chufa can be difficult to find. I located and purchased it from www.seedland.com. Other places to locate chufa and other turkey seed sources are included in Chapter 12, along with more detailed planting information about chufa.

Other plantings that are highly sought after and preferred by turkey include both short and tall varieties of sunflowers, small grains, particularly cereal rye (*Secale cereale*), which is not to be confused with annual or perennial ryegrass. They are completely different plants. Other good choices for turkey plantings include winter wheat, spring oats, bird's-foot trefoil, red and crimson clover, alfalfa, and other legumes. Other plantings sought out by turkey include all types of wild berries. In fall, turkey actively seek out corn, forage sorghum, and cut soybean fields to peck up all the leftover kernels, seeds, or beans left on the ground after harvesting occurs. Turkey will remain close by harvested grain fields and remain in the fields or near them until they have consumed every last kernel of corn, sorghum seed head, sunflower seed, or soybean.

However, while these plants are highly preferred by turkey, one of the most sought after of all food stuffs by turkey are berries. Any land and wildlife manager looking for a plant that is highly nutritious and will attract turkey from all points of

the compass should include planting several types of berry plants. Berries are also a favorite food source to all other game birds, deer, bear, and other non-hunted wildlife. They are an important planting that will help to complete even the most inclusive food plot program. An excellent source to purchase berry plants

▼ Chufa is a perennial plant that attracts wild turkeys. It is high in fat and protein. Chufa is very hardy and can last for years. Deer, boar, and pigs also eat it. Photo courtesy: NWTF.

▲ Two plantings that are a favorite of pheasants are tall sunflowers and grain sorghum. Photo courtesy: Ted Rose.

is the Willis Orchard Company (www.willisorchards.com). Their friendly, knowledgeable staff will answer any questions and help in suggesting the right berry plants to buy for your region.

PHEASANTS AND OTHER UPLAND GAME BIRDS

Ringneck Pheasant

Ringneck pheasants—as well as all other species of game birds including types of quail, grouse, partridge, chucker, doves, pigeons, woodcock, snipe, and ptarmigan—are attracted to most of the same plantings that turkey also find appealing. Each species does have a favorite plant that it finds more attractive than the other plants. For instance, the Ringneck pheasant's two most highly favored foods are the tall or short varieties of sunflowers and corn, followed closely by grain sorghum. Other plants include most of the small grains like buckwheat, cereal rye, triticale, and, of course, wheat.

Grouse

The drummer of the woodlands is the ruffed grouse, the *U.S.S. Enterprise* of all game birds, as grouse are capable of reaching warp speed. All grouse forage their environment for an extensive diversity of food items. They will eat new tree buds, berries, flowers, mast, fruit, and the seeds of many grain crops as well.

When I hunt grouse in the fall, the first place I check is my wild apple orchards. I have countless older apple trees that produce excellent crops of wild apples. Inevitably, as my dog Kira and I push through the thickets of apple branches, we almost always put up several grouse who instantly explode, rocket, tear, rip, launch, thunder, blot, or otherwise fly away at warp speed 9.9. Have you ever heard a grouse described as it simply flew away?

Grouse wander far and wide in search of different foods, so they are rarely seen frequenting food plots. But that doesn't mean they don't eat in food plots—they do. If you want to attract and hold grouse on your land, plant a variety of different types of clovers along the wooded edges and in small strips within the woods because grouse, like all game birds, like to feed close to thick cover.

Quail

I envy the game manager who is fortunate enough to have bobwhite or other type of quail on their land. These little buggers are real homebodies. Therefore, if you provide them cover, water, and their favorite foods, you'll have some excellent quail hunting in your future.

While quail will eat much of the same types of food other game birds eat, they prefer the large seed heads of both tall and short varieties of sorghum. Another favorite food source of quail is millet. They will also seek out wheat, oats, and, of course, corn.

By now, you're getting the picture that the aforementioned specific food plot plantings will not only attract other types of game to your land, but will also encourage self-sustaining breeding and nesting by game birds and other small game. To further enhance a complete upland bird, small game, and waterfowl program you must also incorporate other management elements to round out this type of program.

Potholes

If possible and affordable, it will be highly beneficial for you to create a small pond when developing a wildlife management plan for other types of wildlife. If that is not in your budget, however, an alternate plan would be to build several tiny potholes in different areas on your property. The most cost effective way to do this is to hire an experienced backhoe operator for a day. You will be amazed how many potholes a skilled backhoe operator can dig in that amount of time. Another option is to rent a tiny backhoe and dig

▲ Quail are homebodies and will remain on lands that provide them with food, water, and cover. Photo courtesy: Ted Rose.

your own small pothole-sized watering holes. Keep in mind if you don't know how to operate a small backhoe, it will be more practical to hire a skilled operator so you'll get much more value for the money you spend.

A small watering pothole doesn't have to be large to supply a water source for upland birds, small game, waterfowl, and even deer. Potholes are nothing more than depressions in the ground with the sides draining to a slightly deeper center area. They fill from rainwater, water that is just below the surface, and from springs. A wildlife pothole that is about 3 feet in diameter and 6 to 12 inches deep will attract different types of wildlife. Of course, if you can double the size of the diameter and the depth, your potholes will be even more attractive to all sorts of amphibious wildlife, too. Small potholes attract also attract waterfowl, particularly wood ducks.

The best locations to place tiny watering potholes are in areas where the soil will tend to hold water more effectively. To prevent potholes from filling with soil or getting too many nutrients in them, it is important to build them in places where they won't receive direct runoff from surrounding areas. This is particularly true for larger-sized potholes than mentioned above. By simply planting grass around the edges of the pothole and letting it grow, it will act as a filter and will remove sediment and unwanted nutrients, helping to keep the pothole water clean and clear.

By creating specialized upland game food plots, hinge-cuts, watering holes, nesting areas, blow-down type cover, fruit and berry plantings, and by removing "junk" trees to encourage sunlight to reach the understory, managers will enhance their upland game bird habitat exponentially along with their bird game hunting opportunities.

▲ During the peak of the rut, bucks chase does all day and often get overheated. They take advantage of any secluded pond or pothole, like this one, to cool down.

Create Cover

Create thick, low cover throughout your property by planting a variety of shrubs. Some choices include Highbush cranberry, which is valued by all game and non-game birds alike. Another good choice is elderberry, which not only provides an excellent food source, but also grows in thick clusters and up to 15 feet tall. Bristly locust is a fast-growing shrub that reaches heights of 10 to 12 feet. Its bristly branches and pods make excellent cover. Lespedeza bicolor is a large, leguminous shrub that grows to about 10 feet high. It will provide food and shelter for pheasant, grouse, quail, and other bird game species as well as deer and small game. There are many more types of shrubs to choose from as well.

Hinge-Cutting

Another way to create structure or "living" cover for game birds (in addition to deer and other wildlife) is to use a wood-cutting procedure called hinge-cutting. Hinge-cutting is a management tool that creates living cover and allows the tree, shrub, or other vegetation to continue to provide ongoing browse.

This practice also creates a thick, sprawling mat of vegetation that upland, small game, and deer can use for cover. It also provides excellent escape cover for turkey poults, chicks of game birds, fawns, and the young of small game from predators like fox, coyote, hawks, and the like. It also creates outstanding cover for nesting areas.

It can be used to half-cut trees of all sizes and brush, saplings, and shrubs. Creating an area where trees are leaning and brush is piled on top of natural vegetation ends up looking like hell to the human eye, but wildlife instinctively see this snarled pile of vegetation as a haven from danger, a secure bedding area, a hidden barrier or screen, and a secure place to eat.

To cut small saplings, brush, or shrubs, begin by making the first cut about 3 feet off the ground or just about belt-high. Hold whatever you intend to cut tightly in one hand, then hack them with a machete-type cutting tool. Make a few cuts to allow the vegetation to bend over further. For larger vegetation, saplings, and shrubs, use a small handsaw or a small chainsaw. Sometimes after making the cut or cuts, it will still be

▲ This apple tree was hinge-cut. It still provides wild apples that yearlings and fawns can reach.

necessary to push the sapling or vegetation further down until it lies parallel to the ground.

When hinge-cutting large trees, make the cut parallel or level to the ground, then saw through the tree until it begins to slowly lean over and eventually have the upper part of the cut lay on the ground. The objective is to keep as much of the tree attached as possible. Therefore, once the tree begins to slowly lean, don't cut too much further. The cambium layer is the portion of the trunk lying directly under the bark. The cambium layer feeds the tree. It is necessary to protect this layer on one side of the tree for the tree, shrub, or other vegetation to continue to live for years.

Two great tips to cutting as little into the tree as possible is by pounding a 1-inch plastic wedge into the cut, forcing the top of the tree over significantly and allowing gravity to take over. The other tip is to use a long pole with a hook on the end to pull the tree down when it needs a little encouragement.

Another option when making hinge-cuts is to cut some smaller trees first and then cut the larger trees. The larger trees wind up falling on top of the smaller trees. These smaller trees support the larger trees when they fall. Often even when a large tree is hinge-cut correctly, the momentum of the trunk hitting the ground often causes it to break off at the site where the hinge-cut was made.

When making hinge-cuts with small, medium, or large trees or other vegetation, remember it is crucial to keep safety in mind. Accidents when making hinge-cuts can happen quickly and unexpectedly if you're not paying full attention to the job at hand.

I particularly like to hinge-cut old apple trees for grouse and other wildlife. Once they lean over, they continue to provide fruit for many years that is in reach of all wildlife. When the apples fall from the branches, game birds, small game, and fawns are more able to crawl under the thick branches to get to the fruit than full-grown deer are.

I also include felling large and small "junk"-type trees that are of no nutritional value to wildlife or are trees that have outlived their harvest value. I had a for-

ester mark the "junk" trees on my land, and Cody and I began cutting them down shortly after. The plan was to cut the trees so they fell as close to one another as possible to create what looks like a section of woods with blow downs. All types of game birds as well as deer and other wildlife instinctively use blow-downs as secure bedding areas as well as for protection from foul weather.

By including the recommendations in this chapter, you will not only enhance your upland game bird, small game, waterfowl habitat, and natural propagation exponentially, but you'll also ensure yourself top-quality hunting opportunities for these game animals for many years to come.

18. Food Plot Hunting Tactics

he next sentence could serve as an entire chapter and be the smallest section ever written in a book about hunting over food plots. The shortest thought on the subject of how to hunt over food plots is: *Don't hunt them at all.*

That statement, however, at least for me and many other deer and food plot managers, is highly unrealistic. It is too broad and very uncompromising. Many respected experts *categorically insist* that hunting deer over food plots will cause deer, particularly mature bucks, to go into temporary hiding at best or cause them to go *"totally nocturnal"* in the worst case scenario. I respectfully disagree with both analyses by these qualified and well-meaning authorities, but I do so within certain limitations.

Anytime and anywhere deer, particularly mature bucks, undergo unusual hunting pressure, their reaction is quick, effective, and predictable. When they are made nervous by human presence or hunting pressure, they tend to become "spooky," and as a result, they have a habit of quickly changing their travel patterns, making them seem invisible to hunters. Please note I did *not* say that once they get edgy, they immediately visit food plots only in the darkness of night. Or, worse yet, they quickly leave the area entirely and head for parts unknown. Nor did I say they will become totally *nocturnal.*

Veteran outdoor professional opinions on this subject are more realistic and credible. They contend that deer—and again, mostly the mature bucks and does—will only *lessen* their daylight use of feeding in food plots. They visit the plots during the last fragments of light or moments before dawn. This is a much more real-world statement and it's an accurate declaration *most* times. However, it is still too much of a categorical statement regarding why food plots should not be hunted.

What causes hunting over food plots to become problematic? There are many issues, and they hinge on an equally large number of factors. The first dynamic is the size of the management program. For instance, if the property being managed is 50 acres or less and only has a few tiny food plots whose total acreage amounts to an acre or two, it won't take long for the deer to learn to avoid the food plots and feed instead in other areas on natural foods. This is mainly true if the plot or plots are hunted over and over again. This

▲ To kill a mature buck in a food plot during daylight hours, the plot must not get excessive hunting pressure. Photo courtesy: Whitetail Institute.

scenario has a very limited outcome. Inevitably, it will end supporting the claim that deer will drastically reduce or totally stop all daylight use of food plots that are hunted due to the potential danger.

According to statistics, the average management program encompasses more total land acreage than previously believed by researchers (about 135 acres). However, the average land owner actually only plants 3 to 10 percent of the total acreage owned in food plots. But even on properties that range from 100 to 1,000 acres or more, successful food plot hunting requires careful planning and even more cautious hunting tactics. Additionally, you must take special consideration when deciding what types of seeds to plant in the plots that will be hunted, the wind direc-

▲ A buck casually feeds at midday in a "no-hunting" food plot planted in Whitetail Institute clover. Half of all food plots should be in non-hunted areas.

tions of each plot, the heights and locations of the stands or blinds, and much more.

While some plots can be created from the start to be hunted successfully, other food plots have to be set aside as no-hunting-zone areas. If strict guidelines are developed for the hunted plots and the rules are followed consistently, the plots will provide daylight sightings of mature bucks and does. Unfortunately, when the rules are ignored, even occasionally, it will quickly lead to adult bucks and does using the plots much less often during daylight hours.

I didn't say they would avoid it totally because I don't believe bucks go totally nocturnal, even when they undergo heavy hunting pressure. The key word in that sentence is "totally." The one primary factor that simply doesn't allow this to happen is Mother Nature. She provides an overwhelming instinct to all creatures to pass on their genes, even if it means risking their lives to do so. In other words, sex overrides vigilance, even by the most cautious, secretive of bucks. All bets are off during the rut, including male deer becoming completely nocturnal. Anything can happen during the breeding period, including a dandy mature buck blindly following an estrus doe that is hungry into a food

plot, even if that plot has undergone hunting pressure. With all that said, outside of the rut a food plot that is hunted too hard can end up curtailing its daylight use by deer, but not entirely eliminating it.

During the buildup and decline of each of the three phases of the rut (pre-rut, primary, and post-rut), the odds of shooting a mature buck in a plot hunted too often can vary from unrealistic to very possible. Although the unrealistic comment may sound contradictory to what I just mentioned in the previous paragraph, keep in mind the key words are "a plot that is hunted *too often.*" Trust me when I tell you that when the rules to hunt food plots are followed diligently, and the plots are hunted sporadically, the chances of killing a good buck dramatically increases as long as the proper tactics are used without fail. *You can take that statement to the deer-hunting bank.*

Remember that each phase of the rut occurs during different times during hunting season. The seeking phase of the pre-rut, when many young bucks knock themselves out trying to locate a doe in heat, takes place during the archery season in many states. These young bucks expend a lot of energy with little return. I liken it to teenage boys who can't help themselves from checking out every skirt they encounter. Rarely do they end up achieving their end game.

Each rut phase presents particular hunting opportunities when it comes to hunting over the food plots. During the chasing stage, there will be good opportunities to take a mature buck in a food plot on any type of hunting terrain as long as you don't apply too much hunting pressure over the area. During the primary rut, however, deer begin to transition from chasing does to actually breeding them. This timeframe usually occurs in late November and it provides some excellent hunting as long as you are hunting food plots (or general hunting areas) that have modest to mild hunting pressure.

The behavior of adult bucks in the rut compared to immature bucks greatly differs. As I said, young bucks get so enthusiastic in the rut and unfocused during the pre-rut that they cause themselves to run low on gas by the time the primary rut kicks in. Their proliferation activity is spent long before does are willing to stand for bucks. Adult bucks, on the other hand, treat the rut much like the old joke of the two bulls on the hill. The young bull spots a herd of female cows below him and

▲ The behavior of mature bucks during the breeding season differs greatly from the demeanor of immature bucks. Photo courtesy: Ted Rose.

pletely disciplined about it. They don't chase every skirt they see; instead, they have learned over the years to quickly recognize which does are ready to stand for them and immediately "hook up" with them. As I have said about the peak of the rut in print and on television for many years, it usually occurs around November 10 through November 15, give or take a few days throughout certain latitudes from east to west. This can be somewhat problematic for hunters because, many times, bucks force the does into secure thickets and keep them there, while keeping themselves out of sight from hunters and other predators.

Luckily for hunters, mature bucks become more active and visible *after* the peak of the primary rut when they are then seeking any remaining does that have not been successfully bred. Because the young bucks have exhausted most if not all of their energy chasing after every doe they see, now they are basically out of steam. This leaves the remaining does in estrus to the adult bucks that have been savvy enough to have saved their energy and are still able to service any receptive doe they find.

As with all species of deer, including moose, elk, caribou, mule-deer, and whitetails, after the peak of primary rut has waned or is near its end, mature bucks go into what is known by season hunters and outfitters as a "lock-down pattern," or lull. The lull period usually takes place in very late November. It happens a few weeks or so before the last phase of the rut kicks in, known as the post or late rut. I have long claimed that the late rut is the best time to kill a mature buck. This rut phase usually happens from about December 10 to December 17—again, give or take a few days on either end. This is when fawn does come into their first estrus cycle and yearlings that were not successfully bred also come into another estrus cycle. This is prime time to kill a mature buck, particularly over a secluded food plot that hasn't been hunted hard. Young does, even when they are in estrus, really can't figure out what is happening to them, and they continue to keep food as a high priority. They are responsible for unknowingly leading a savvy old buck into a food plot.

In 2010, during the late rut, I killed a terrific 13-point buck on our farm. It was December 20, the last day of the New York muzzle-loader season. I was on the way to work when I saw a small herd of does in one of my

says to the old bull, "Come on, let's run down there and sniff out all those ladies." The old bull looks at him and smiles sarcastically and replies, "Go ahead and run down there. I'll walk down and take care of the few who aren't running away from you."

Mature bucks that have been fortunate to live through a few hunting seasons have one crucial thought process: survival. Their end goal is to stay alive and make it through another season. The old veterans take on the rut as experienced survivors of seasons past and treat it accordingly, which is to say they are com-

fields. One doe that was no more than a yearling was eating while flagging her tail from side to side. She was obviously in heat. Despite seeing this, I continued to drive to my office. Once there, I could not stop thinking of what I had just witnessed and quickly returned home to go hunting.

I changed and took a stand in a field planted with turnips, Swede, and sugar beets. It was 10 AM and the weather was clear, but extremely frigid, with the temperature hovering in the single digits, despite the sunshine. I sat in a blind we call Little View, anticipating that the small herd of does I saw earlier would visit it sometime over the next couple of hours. I didn't have to wait that long. Within an hour, a lone yearling doe emerged from the woods between the field I was watching and the field I had seen the does in on the way to work.

The doe ran into the field and began to chow down on the turnip bulbs. As I watched her, I could see her tail flagging. My anticipation began to get out of control and I was getting edgy. I had to stop myself from turning my head in all directions, trying to locate a mature buck that might be lurking in the nearby woods watching the young doe. Moments later, a terrific buck, at least for our farm, trotted from the woods into the food plot. He didn't waste a second; as he reached the doe, he tried to mount her and slipped off. When the smoke from my muzzle-loader cleared, the buck lay dead in the middle of the food plot. It was just past 11 AM. The food plot was only hunted a half-dozen times during the entire several weeks of deer season.

One key factor to killing a mature buck in a food plot during legal shooting hours, particularly outside of the

primary rut, is not to hunt over the same plot more than one day in a row. To keep the hunting pressure to a minimum, only hunt over a food plot every few days. I know this can be a hard rule to follow, but if it is practiced faithfully, it will pay off in big dividends year after year. Over my forty-eight years of hunting whitetail deer, I, too, have been guilty of over-hunting a particular blind now and then. But I have never over-hunted a food plot.

To ensure deer will visit the plot in daylight, try not to set up a tree stand at the very edge of the food plot.

By hunting this turnip plot only a few times during ▶ the deer season, the light pressure made this buck feel safe enough to follow a doe into the plot at 11 AM.

Although deer will get used to seeing the stand, hunter movement usually alerts deer to their presence. You can eliminate deer seeing movement of a tree stand along the edge of a food plot by simply setting the tree stand up a few dozen yards into the wood line. If you want to set up a stand at the edge of a food plot or along a field's edge, use a deer blind. It helps to reduce movement tremendously. Many of my food plot blinds are intentionally set up 100 yards or more

▼ Deer quickly abandon a food plot once apples, acorns, or other mast, like chestnuts, ripen and fall.

from the actual food or plots that I'm watching. But it should be noted that as soon as a deer is shot from a tree stand or blind, deer will immediately become more cautious of the blind the next time they enter the food plot. Therefore, once a deer is taken over a food plot, we don't hunt from that blind for at least a week and sometimes for the remainder of the deer season.

While it is a commonly known tactic to avoid using the same approach and departure to and from a stand, when it comes to hunting over food plots, this tactic is an absolute "must-do" to preserve the deer's comfort zone in using the plot to feed in during daylight hours. Going to and from a hunted food plot stand the same way each time will eventually allow deer to sense your approach. A savvy method to avoid this is to go to the stand using different directions, at different times of the day, while always keeping the wind in your favor. I often mow several narrow trails that lead to a single blind so I can take different directions when approaching the same blind. It also helps to leave the stand from different areas at different times as well.

Keep in mind food plots that deer are currently using heavily will be abandoned by them as soon as more seasonal and appealing food sources become available. You'll waste a lot of your valuable hunting time hunting over most food plots when an ample crop of acorn, chestnut, or apple become available. Those hunters who refuse to abandon hunting over food plots when different natural food items ripen are destined to spend many long hours watching tweety-birds and squirrels instead of seeing deer, particularly mature bucks.

The "Dos"

To benefit the most from the plots you intend to hunt, create many different size food plots in as many different types of locations as possible. The plots can range from tiny, 20-feet-by-200-feet plots

▲ This winter-hardy Swede crop drew deer all times of the day during the gun season in late November. Plant unusual crops that aren't found on neighboring lands and you'll assure yourself of maximum deer traffic.

attractive, especially to a crafty old buck who during the summer and into October likes to feel more comfortable eating in the small, less visible plots before entering a larger, more visible food plot. This is particularly true prior to the rut.

I hunt "buck staging" plots almost exclusively during the archery season. Often a group of does, yearlings, and fawns will march by the stand, heading to the larger plots in the fields. When the bucks show up, they will hang back to eat in the small, hidden plot before entering the larger, more open plots at dusk. During this time of fall, the rut hasn't encouraged them to ignore being cautious yet. The "buck staging" plots provide prime bow-hunting opportunities in early fall.

Another good idea is to set up some hunting plots as bowhunting areas only and others in areas that are more adapted to using a firearm. Use common-sense hunting tactics like entering the areas as quietly as possible. As I mentioned earlier, change directions regarding the way you get to the stands each time you enter and leave them. Go to different stand locations that will be downwind based on prevailing wind directions. Enter and exit stands as silently as possible and without disturbing bedding areas or heavily traveled trails. Avoid leaving a stand if you think your departure will spook nearby deer. A word of caution here: If you must remain in a stand after legal hunting hours to watch deer and want to avoid spooking them, unload your firearm and slowly and carefully lower it to the ground while you remain in the stand. When a deer is shot while it is in food plot, place the entrails in a heavy plastic bag and bring the bag back to camp in the ATV. This practice goes a long way to reducing your coyote problems.

to ¼ acre or larger. Create different-shaped hunting plots, including some that are typically shaped (square and rectangle), but most that are irregularly shaped like letters (C, F, J, L, P, S, T, U, V, X, and Z). Place them in a variety of terrains including woodlots, open fields, at the edge of thickets, or near a pond or lake. Plan to place them in more secluded, less visible areas for them to regularly attract deer during daylight hours.

I also create small food plots planted with legumes in more concealed places that I refer to as "buck staging areas." I put these plots about 50 or more yards in the woods and away from primary food plots that are planted in fields or that border the edge of woods. These small, hidden "buck staging" plots are very

Our management plan includes a multi-food plot program on our farm. Each year we plant more than twenty food plots in a variety of sizes and letter shapes. They are located in different types of terrain from open fields to more concealed areas. Each plot has a different type plant or mixture of plants so our deer have a wide variety of food choices to explore. About 50 percent of the plots are seeded with plants that can't be found on neighboring lands.

By following this plan, we have killed several mature deer during daylight hours; most were taken between 10 AM and 1:30 PM. All the deer, including bucks, were in our cold-weather food plots. One was taken in a sorghum field, another in a plot of chicory, the third in a sugar beet field, the fourth buck in a turnip plot. A buck taken by my son, Cody, in 2011 was shot from my favorite stand, Porcupine Blind. Cody saw two mature bucks walking into the woods. He guessed they had just come from a food plot about 100 yards above his blind in a small field. One buck had 8 points and a high rack. The second buck's antlers also had 8 points, but they were noticeably heavier and wider.

They slowly picked their way through the woods, heading toward our refuge, which is about 250 yards below Porcupine Blind. An hour and a half later, as Cody was getting ready to leave the blind, he spied the larger buck casually walking through a thick patch of second growth about 60 yards in front of the blind. As he passed the west window of the blind, Cody noted he was walking directly toward a food plot of Pasja. (Pasja is a Forage Hybrid Brassica, which is a cross between a forage turnip and forage rape.) Pasja is a multi-graze forage brassica that has excellent extended grazing potential as it is very winter-hardy.

Cody stopped the buck by making a soft, estrus-blat. When the buck heard the enticing vocalization, Cody said, "The buck instantly turned 180 degrees and froze in his tracks." The buck was obviously trying to locate what he thought was a doe in estrus. According to Cody, "Ten long minutes passed before the buck decided to move again." The heavy-antlered 8-point finally took several steps and stopped again in the

▼ Cody and his hunting buddies a.k.a. "The Ultimate Nerd Hunting Gang" (L to R): P. Cody Fiduccia ((MBA Binghamton University; MPA Cornell University; PhD-student, Cornell University); Brandt Kayser (MSES, UNC Charlotte); Eric Schultz (Fulbright Scholar, MPA Cornell University, CIA Analyst), and Victor Schultz (PhD, Rensselaer Polytechnic Institute).

small opening of the second growth. Cody placed the crosshairs on the buck's shoulder and squeezed the trigger. The Winchester 150 grain XP-3 slammed into the buck and it fell in its tracks.

As we do with all the deer (bucks and mature does) killed on our land, we send their teeth to a lab in Texas to be properly aged. The only way to accurately age a deer, or any mammal, for that matter, is by taking the root of a tooth, preparing a very thin stained slice of the root, and counting the rings of cementum under a microscope. We sent the two center front teeth of Cody's buck to Henry Chidgey, the co-founder of Wildlife Analytical Labs, LLC in Burnet, Texas (www. DeerAge.com). After the teeth were analyzed, we received a full report, including the buck's exact age, which was five and a half years old. Anyone who is serious about managing their deer herd or simply interested in knowing the age of deer harvested on their lands should keep accurate records of how old each deer was when it was taken. Using a service like DeerAge.com is both a smart and beneficial strategy.

Over the last dozen years, four adult bucks were taken as they stood in our food plots either eating or standing by a doe during the middle of the day. One buck was first seen and then killed as he was coming from and heading back to a food plot at 10:30 in the morning. For us, this is hardcore proof that it is very possible to successfully hunt bucks (and does) in food plots during daylight hours, as long as the rules I mentioned earlier are adhered to. The old adage that all bucks "go nocturnal" and avoid food plots during daylight hours during hunting season is simply not true.

If you create some food plots to hunt over and some as non-hunting plots, you, too, can have the same type of success. But I can't emphasize this enough—your success will totally depend on if you take the aforementioned advice seriously and use it without ever straying from the rules. Don't be shy about using at least some of your food plots as hunting plots. It will provide you with a lot of fun and excitement— that's a promise.

◀ This is the same Swede plot on page 79. Note how much taller and lush it is in September. The deer didn't begin eating it until late November.

19. Tips to Attract Bucks During Hunting Season

here is a good chance that you turned to this chapter first. If you did, it is perfectly understandable, as the endgame for a majority of deer managers is to draw bucks into their lands during the archery, firearm, and muzzle-loading deer seasons. Each year, I talk to countless deer hunters who attend my deer hunting clinics at sport shows. The most commonly asked question is: "How can I increase the number of mature bucks I see during hunting season?" Without a doubt, the question that inevitably arises even more than the question above is: "How can I *hold* mature bucks on my land?"

The short answer to that particular question is that you absolutely can't hold a buck on a piece of land, especially if it is a very small property. My most frustrating problem with some professional outdoor communicators is that sometimes they use improper deer hunting jargon or terminology to make a point. Few professional writers or outdoor television hosts realize what they say or write is often taken as verbatim by their audiences. (Please understand that I'm not criticizing other outdoor professionals; I have also been guilty on occasion of misusing hunting tactic terms that can be much better described.)

I'm sure many experienced deer hunters realize the odds of *holding* a mature buck on a given piece of property is as farfetched of a theory as it would be

for addicted gamblers to hold on to their money in Las Vegas. Therein lies the quandary; the word "hold" when referring to holding a buck on a particular piece of land is just not a practical term to use. Well-meaning outdoor professionals who use such emphatic phrases only end up confusing the people they are trying to share their legitimate deer hunting experiences with.

For instance, the most often misused statement by some outdoor professionals is: "Bucks go totally nocturnal." It is the single most classic example of the misuse of a hunting term. There isn't a buck in North America who becomes a totally nocturnal deer, even after it may undergo heavy hunting pressure. There are simply too many hunting variables to make such a categorical statement.

Think about it: Isn't it possible that a mature buck can get jumped from its bedding area by some other deer hunters in broad daylight? Basically, the answer is that it is not only possible; it happens often. Bucks also move about small distances during daylight hours to check nearby scrapes or to refresh a rub. Another reality preventing bucks from becoming totally nocturnal is the breeding season. A doe in estrus could easily lure a buck into following her right past a hunter on stand during daylight hours. During extremely cold weather, mature bucks instinctively move about, albeit in short distances, to feed and generate enough energy from the forage to keep their body temperature up. A buck could be chased out of its hiding spot by a coyote in daylight. Or a buck may be enticed to leave its bed during the day to follow the trail of fresh estrus scent. And of course there is daylight natural movement by male deer that occurs even under heavy hunting pressure.

Therefore, to unconditionally suggest bucks go totally nocturnal because of hunting pressure and that they will not move about at all during daylight is a far-reaching overstatement that can and does mislead many deer hunters. There are simply too many random circumstances that can come into play that could end up placing a buck in your scope during daylight hours. Therefore, these unpredictable circumstances that occur could certainly end with a dandy buck in your scope during daylight hours.

◀ It is virtually impossible to "hold" a buck, particularly a mature buck, on any given piece of "fair-chase" property. This is especially true during the rut.

When a few well-meaning outdoor communicators continually spread the misnomer that bucks are totally nocturnal, it often leads other hunters to firmly believe they absolutely have no chance of killing any size antlered buck, never mind a trophy buck during daylight hours. This is especially true of young, inexperienced deer hunters. If you still don't believe that the odds are against bucks becoming totally nocturnal, please consider this: The New York State buck harvest records show that from 1978 to 2011, an average of 3,380,169 adult bucks were killed in New York State (some of which undoubtedly included adult bucks as well as trophy-class-sized animals).

I ask you, if all bucks go totally nocturnal because of hunting pressure, how then were the three million plus bucks killed in New York State? If they were only moving during the night, the only logical answer to how they were shot is that hunters poached them at night. This comment is a hypothetical statement. The 3,380,169 bucks taken in New York State were all taken during legal daylight hunting hours and none of them were taken illegally at night. However, it does

make the case for poking holes in the statement that bucks go "totally nocturnal" when undergoing heavy hunting pressure.

What really happens is bucks become more secretive and instinctively realize it is far safer to remain hidden in cover than it is to reveal themselves by running off, even when a hunter (predator to a deer) passes within feet of where they are concealed. They also change their movement patterns, moving less at dawn and dusk and more from 10 AM to 1 PM, even if the movement is limited.

The point I'm urgently trying to convey to you here is that many hunting terms are inadvertently used vaguely. Although the imprecise phrases shared by well-meaning outdoor professionals are *valid* guidance, they end up misrepresenting tactic information. When I refer to attracting and *holding* mature bucks on your land, I'm really suggesting it is possible to attract and lure mature bucks *more frequently* to your land, **not** actually holding them permanently on your land. I can't even suggest that a buck can be enticed to stay on a piece of property by planting food plots. It simply just isn't so.

◀ With hunting pressure, adult bucks change their daylight movement patterns. They often move from 10 AM to 1 PM. Rarely do bucks go "totally nocturnal."

▲ A balanced buck-to-doe ratio will lure adult bucks to your land and encourage them to remain there for longer periods of time.

▲ To attract bucks regularly, a management plan must include key components like water, food, natural cover, refuge, and does. Photo courtesy: Ted Rose.

So setting aside all the fine distinctions of terms and phrases for now, just how does a deer manager attract and increase the numbers of mature bucks into *repeatedly* visiting their land? Actually, it isn't all that complicated to achieve as long as you don't try to over-complicate how to get it done. While it *isn't* practical to believe mature bucks can be kept or held on a particular piece of land, it is *definitely realistic* to believe that mature bucks can be lured into spending a lot of their time on *your* place rather than the *neighbor's* lands.

The short answer to this dilemma is to make sure your land is attractive during the entire year to female deer. Although having does on your land is a crucial factor in attracting mature bucks, it isn't the only piece of the puzzle. There are several chief factors that will enable you to achieve the goal of attracting mature bucks to your land more regularly and to even have one or two of mature bucks call your land "home." In no real order of importance, the essential elements include:

- fresh water sources
- high-quality natural and planted foods
- a *totally secure and never* penetrated refuge
- a healthy buck-to-doe ratio
- low hunting pressure
- a variety of secure cover for the deer.

These factors will help greatly in making your piece of ground home base to mature bucks and does.

I mention this because I want to be absolutely clear that just planting food plots isn't enough to draw adult bucks into your land consistently. You must develop a management plan that will provide all the elements needed to attract the general population of deer and to lure in older bucks, as well. Think of your deer management and food plot program as many parts of an overall puzzle. While they are important single puzzle pieces, alone they cannot complete the entire puzzle. But when all factors of a well-thought-out and-implemented management program come together, they will work rather smoothly to achieve your overall directorial goals. Always keep the puzzle analogy in mind while developing your program. Leave any one element out of the strategy and it remains an unfinished task.

www.skyhorsepub

WATER

Let's begin with the most important of the five elements of developing a complete management program: fresh water sources. As any biologist will tell you, deer that live in areas other than arid regions get most of their daily intake of water by extracting it from the plants they eat. However, with that said, a deer that has access to fresh water via ponds, streams, and even manmade pot holes that collect fresh water from rain-runoff or underground springs will readily visit the pot holes to drink from. This is especially true during the rut when mature bucks dehydrate themselves by constantly chasing estrus scent trails and running does hard. They use ponds, streams, and pot holes not only to drink water, but also to cool down their body temperature. I have seen mature bucks immerse themselves to their chest in a pond or other water source in an attempt to cool down. When a mature buck seeks out a core area, he will almost always make sure it includes at least one reliable fresh water source within his home range.

FOOD SOURCES

As I have said in previous books and on our television show for many years, plant it *right* and they *will* come. Remember that food plots are valuable hunting tools. But to consistently attract all age classes of bucks, food plots must be combined with the other four bits and pieces of the puzzle. I can't emphasize this enough: Food plots are not the hunter's silver bullet some people believe them to be. Anyone who has hunted on lands planted with food plots quickly learns that they are not always a deer's *first* choice.

Deer will quickly forsake all varieties of plants in food plots to seek out ripe, natural offerings such as apples, pears, other wild fruits, acorns, and chestnuts and will remain eating them until they are totally consumed. Deer will even abandon agricultural crops including corn, soybean, alfalfa, butternut squash, or pumpkin.

It always amazes me how hunters who don't grow food plots are quick to point out that the reason fellow hunters kill bigger bucks than they do is because they hunt over their food plots. These are the same hunters who set up deer stands in apple orchards, at the edges of alfalfa, corn, soybean, and other crop fields. A curious set of values, isn't it? The point is food plots and agricultural crops definitely have their "dry" time when deer totally abandon them in favor of more naturally available vegetation. Once again, food plots are not a magic bullet.

A deer manager's end goal when planning and developing a food plot program should be to entice multiple mature bucks into using their property as much as possible. This is often achieved by planting a few warm-weather plantings, and by including a higher percentage of winter-hardy plantings that are more attractive to deer during the firearm seasons from November through January.

Adult bucks will be instinctively drawn to choose their core areas in places offering reliable, naturally available food sources. In farm areas, they will also look for core zones that include staple agricultural farm foods. Ideally, if a mature buck's core area also

◄ Cody with an 8-point buck shot at 12 noon in a food plot of Imperial Chicory PLUS. A mix of Imperial Clover and Chicory. An ideal warm/cold season forage that attracts deer.

includes some warm-season plantings along with winter-hardy food plot plantings that are *unavailable* elsewhere, deer managers can significantly raise the bar to attract mature bucks to their land on a more dependable basis, particularly during hunting seasons.

While it is important to include nutritious year-round plantings, it is even more practical and crucial to provide plantings that are more palatable and nutritious from October through January. The longer the food plots are available, the more accustomed, dependent, and comfortable an adult buck becomes feeding in them. That is why we plant at least 50 percent, and most times more, of our food plots with winter-hardy plantings.

REFUGES

To make my point *yet again* about creating *bona fide* refuges, I will compare it to a particular episode of *Seinfeld*. In that show, Jerry is at the counter of a rental car company to pick up a vehicle that he reserved. The woman at the counter tells Jerry she doesn't have a single car to rent him. Jerry tells her, "But I made a reservation." Once again, the woman states there aren't any vehicles to rent him. Jerry then tells the woman, "Anyone can just *take* a reservation, but you have to know how to *hold* the reservation."

The same point applies to creating a refuge on your hunting property. Anyone can just make a refuge, however, you have to know how to *treat* it like a refuge. As I have mentioned before, a genuine sanctuary provides the occupants within it total refuge or safe haven. A refuge for deer is a place where they can find asylum; it's meant to provide your deer with shelter from human danger, a zone of complete safety from hunting pressure. Excess hunting pressure, and in some circumstances even light hunting pressure, is the number one element that ruins every hunter's chance of tagging a mature buck. When you create a sanctuary, you absolutely must treat it as such or it will never truly be a place of absolute refuge for your deer and especially for your mature bucks. Once you establish an authentic refuge, remember to never enter it for any reason whatsoever, except to recover a dead or wounded deer.

Any sanctuary treated as a total no-trespassing area will quickly become a secure refuge for deer on your land and from your neighbor's property, including mature bucks. Our sanctuary is 26 acres, or about 15 percent of the total land we own. Creating a totally secure refuge on our land has been one of the most crucial steps we used to attract both bucks and does to our farm and to have them think of it as "home." Creating a refuge that is treated as such will vastly improve your deer sightings and mature buck hunting opportunities. *You can take that statement to the deer-hunting bank.*

◄ Savvy deer managers carefully monitor and control the number of female deer on their land.

THE DOE DYNAMIC

On one hand, it is advisable to encourage does through a variety of management techniques to call your piece of property "home." There are, on the other hand, two theories regarding having too many breeding does on a particular piece of land. One camp thinks having a sizeable population of propagating does will be beneficial in attracting and seeing more mature bucks chasing does during the rut. The second camp believes having too many does can actually be less advantageous. They feel a property that has too many female deer results in bucks not having to work hard to find a doe in heat. The end result is that bucks arrive on the land where a lot of does are in heat and thus significantly reduce their wanderings looking for does.

I feel both speculations are correct to some degree. The fact is too many does on our land is better than not having enough does living on the property. The key issue about how many does you have on your land directly relates to the buck rutting activity levels. With a healthy buck-to-doe ratio (a 1-to-1 ratio to a maximum of two to three does per buck) will create a dynamic, if not vigorous, breeding throughout all three phases of the rut.

REDUCE YOUR HUNTING FOOTPRINT

No matter where you hunt or what tactics you use to pursue whitetail deer, your hunting activity creates excess human presence. Deer relate to excess human intrusion as predator pressure. Trespass into a mature buck's core bedding area more than once or twice during the hunting season and the buck will undoubtedly adjust his movements and habits to your presence by moving to a more secluded, undisturbed area or holding tight to cover as you pass him by.

The quick fix to this dilemma is to reduce your footprint within your property during deer season. The first step to keeping your deer feeling secure is to create trails that literally run alongside your property boarders. Once you establish these trails, set up tree stands and blinds or use portable climbers to hunt along the fringes of your land.

Another tactic to reduce your intrusion during hunting season is to enter and exit your deer stands as carefully and as quietly as possible. If you are spooking deer each time you enter your woods, it is definitely time to make an adjustment in your approach. If you bump them on the way out in the evening, the same advice holds true.

On our 192 acres, we have a combination of 51 wood and metal tree stands, enclosed plastic hunting houses, and tent blinds. Some stands are intentionally close to one another. Others are only used during the archery or firearm seasons. Other stands are used to capitalize on wind changes, or to take advantage of a drive put on by the surrounding neighbors. Having that many stands on 192 acres gives us almost unlimited flexibility and options.

By having 51 blinds, we can quickly adjust to hunt from a blind that offers better wind currents than another location might offer. More importantly, it pro-

◀ This blind is one of eleven on our land. We have 51 stands to provide a myriad of ways to enter and leave the property and to take advantage of wind directions.

vides a lot of opportunity for us to change stands at least every other day, if not more. All in all, 51 stands help us to significantly reduce our human presence. I'm not suggesting everyone needs 51 stands on their land, but having a dozen or more stand options from which to choose will help keep your presence down which, in turn, helps to keep your mature bucks from looking for a safer home.

CREATE COVER, COVER, AND MORE COVER

Creating cover is a crucial piece of the puzzle. One way to figure out if the cover on your land isn't appealing to deer is to use stealth cameras. If your cameras are only capturing buck images at night, you can be absolutely assured that your property is lacking in the type of cover that bucks feel is secure enough to bed in.

If your land does not have a variety of secure cover for deer to use as protection and bedding, you have to take the necessary steps to change it. That may mean planting different types of shrubs and other plants to create secure cover. To keep bucks on your land, you must pay attention to this very important piece of the puzzle. It may require hiring a professional to come in and provide you with the type of advice you need to add the element of secure cover to your land.

The aforementioned suggestions will help you make your land a center of attention to mature bucks in your area. Remember, it is not realistic for deer managers to think they can actually *keep* or *hold* mature bucks on their land, despite how large or small the piece of ground is. A mature buck is genetically designed to cruise the local area, and even some far-flung outskirts if need be, in search of finding food, water, or mostly to locate receptive does. By using the above advice as practical common-sense tactics, you will increase the number of adult bucks that frequent your land. Perhaps even a couple of them will end up calling your land "home."

20. How Old Was That Deer?

The astute wildlife manager understands the importance of keeping accurate, long-term records detailing certain criteria of the deer killed on their lands. For those developing a quality deer and land management program, documenting each buck and doe harvested is imperative. When kept unfailingly, year after year, these records will form a comprehensive log detailing the *overall success or shortcomings* of the deer killed within the wildlife management program.

GATHERING DATA

The compiled statistics provide a valuable ongoing record to show at a glance if your program is working as planned. The key pieces of data are the accurate age of each buck or doe taken during the season, and their live and dressed weights. For instance, each deer killed on our farm is brought back to the barn where it is first weighed to register its "live weight"; then the entrails are removed and the deer is weighed again to record its "field-dressed" weight. By field-dressing the deer in the barn, we prevent coyotes from finding free grub on our land.

More importantly, we are able to record the exact live weights of the deer we harvest. This helps us to know if our plantings are providing sufficient nutrition, carbohydrates, and other elements to help the deer gain weight from year to year. To record accurate weights it is important to own a high-quality scale to weigh your deer with. Knowing the accurate live- and field-dressed weights of the deer you shoot will help you to harvest more mature bucks and does.

THE GUESSWORK AGING TECHNIQUE

To me, it is more, or at least equally, important to also accurately record the age of each deer taken within a quality deer management program. The key

element of this type of record-keeping is determining the *exact* age of deer through proven scientific methods. Unfortunately, even today, with all the detailed biological information we have about deer, there are far too many old wives' tales about how to accurately age a deer. The methods used run the gambit from aging a buck by the number of tines on the antlers, to the color of hair on the deer's muzzle, the gait of

▼ Eric Schultz with his first whitetail buck. Although our deer management rules allow first time buck hunters to take any buck they choose, Eric opted to abide by our 8-point or better rule. The incisor teeth were sent to Wildlife Analytical Labs, LLC for an exact age analysis to include in our records.

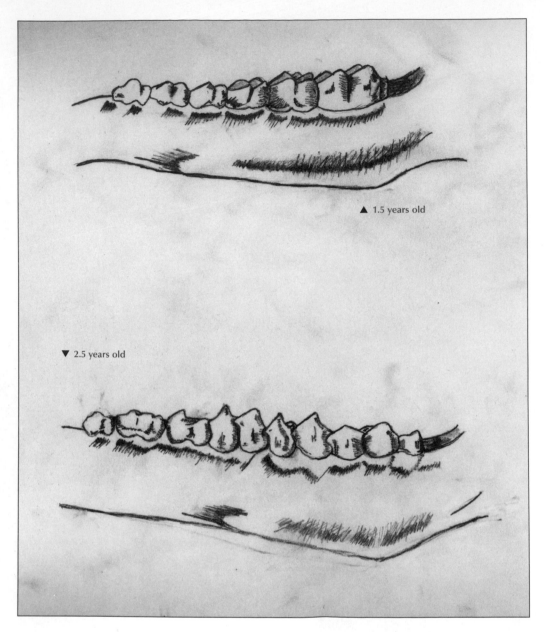

▲ 1.5 years old

▼ 2.5 years old

◀ Aging deer using the "eruption aging" method (by counting the exact number of teeth) is reliable on deer up to 2.5 years of age. (Drawing by my 13-year-old nephew Max Dawson)

its walk and sway in its back, the droop of its belly, and on and on. While some of these can be methods to determine the *approximate* age of a deer, they are nothing more than guesswork and therefore none of them prove to be reliable ways to determine the exact age of a deer.

AGING BY TOOTHWEAR

There are better ways than those mentioned above to determine the age of a deer. One process includes examining and counting the exact number of teeth in the deer's mouth. This is referred to as the "eruption aging" process. This method of counting the deer's teeth works best when the deer is between two and a half and three and a half years old. But once a deer reaches three and a half years of age, there is no longer an absolute way to determine its precise age by counting its teeth or examining its jaw.

Another method is to analyze the deer's lower jaw and determine the age by the wear of the teeth, the replacement and the loss of teeth, along with the amount of dentine that appears on them. However, most wildlife biologists acknowledge these two methods are less than reliable for getting an exact age and should only be used as general guidelines for estimating a deer's age.

I don't recommend either method for deer managers who need to know the exact age of the deer they harvest. It is crucial for any dedicated deer manager to get accurate readings of a deer's age in order to determine if their deer management program is working as planned.

SCIENTIFIC ANALYSIS SYSTEM

There is only one absolutely reliable way to age a deer accurately. That is by removing the deer's two center incisors from the lower jaw and sending them to a specialized forensic laboratory that uses a process known as Cementum Annuli Tooth Analysis to precisely determine the age of the deer.

A certified laboratory technician cuts thin slices of the root of the tooth at the micron level, then stains the roots, places them on a slide, and, using a microscope, counts the layers of the cementum. The number of rings is equal to the number of years the tooth has been in the deer's jawbone.

As any qualified biologist will confirm, deer and all other mammals deposit cementum on the surface of the tooth below the gum line. Cementum forms annuli, or aging rings, similar to the oval bands found inside the trunk of a tree. When the analysis takes place at a specialized histological laboratory, it provides *the* most accurate method used to precisely determine the age of a deer. No other aging method can provide this type of exactness.

The laboratory I use to age the deer we kill on our land is reliable and affordable. Whitetail Analytical Labs, LLC, is located in Burnet, Texas, and specializes in aging deer.

You can visit their website (www.deerage.com) to find out more detailed information on how to get your deer aged accurately and dependably. You can also call Henry Chidgey, the co-founder of Wildlife Analytical Labs, LLC, and talk to him or one of his qualified lab technicians at 512-756-1989.

If you are ready to take the guessing game out of aging your deer, you can order Wildlife Analytical Lab's prepaid Forensic Lab Test and Deer Aging Kit. The kit includes a durable DVD-style hard plastic case, prepaid laboratory cementum annuli order card, tooth

▲ To get a reliable and accurate age of a deer, remove the front two center incisors seen here and send to a lab for analysis.

removal instruction card with 11 high-quality photographs, envelope and protective insert for both incisors Certificate Order Form, and addressed envelope to mail your specimen and order to. The cost of the kit is $25 each, plus $6.95 shipping and handling for one to three kits.

Teeth sent to Wildlife Analytical Labs take about 120 days or less (they guarantee it) to be analyzed by the lab and sent back to you with the accurate age of your deer. You can get the process done faster by an optional upgrade, which costs slightly more money.

You can order a prepaid forensic lab test and deer aging kit to accurately age your deer at www.deerage. com.

Believe me, it is a worthwhile investment. All hunters should keep track of the age of every deer, buck or doe, they kill on their land. Remember, while it is possible to age a deer by counting its teeth, the accuracy of counting teeth only extends to a deer that is no more than two and a half years of age. To precisely know the age of deer beyond that, the deer's lower two front incisors must be properly removed and sent to a lab to perform a Cementum Annuli Tooth Analysis.

21. The Importance of Weighing Your Deer!

Another task deer managers should perform is to record the weight of the deer *before* field-dressing it and its weight *after* the deer innards have been removed. This information should be entered regularly into a management journal and logged with both the live and dressed weights of the deer harvested each year.

If you can't easily get your deer back to camp before field-dressing it, there is still a way to record its "live" weight without hanging it on an accurate scale. You can buy a commercially made, flexible cloth measuring tape called Vital Records Tape Measure from a company called Do-All Outdoors (www.do-alltraps.com) and click on the Nav-Bar that reads "Dead Deer Line." This unique tape measure provides approximate live weights *and* field-dressed weights of the deer. It also estimates the amount of weight of the edible meat after processing based on size measurements.

Tape also includes age determination illustrations based on teeth in the deer's jawline, as well as a sex and age chart based on track size. The Vital Records Tape Measure is small and lightweight and can easily be carried in a daypack. Before field-dressing the deer, place the tape around the entire chest of the deer right behind the forelegs and read the measurement.

By keeping an accurate and detailed log of the age and weight of all animals harvested on your hunting ground, in just a few short years you will have a more accurate picture of what type of antlers to expect from the different age and weight groups of the bucks within the herd you hunt. You will also be able to pattern the typical weights of the deer that inhabit the land. Wide variations from the average weights should send up a red flag and alert you that something in the management plan is off-kilter. With this information, you can quickly take whatever steps are necessary to improve your food plots, deer management practices, or what-

▼ If it isn't practical to weigh the live weight of deer at camp, use a tape measure in the field to record live and field dressed weights, etc. Photo courtesy: Do-All-Outdoors.

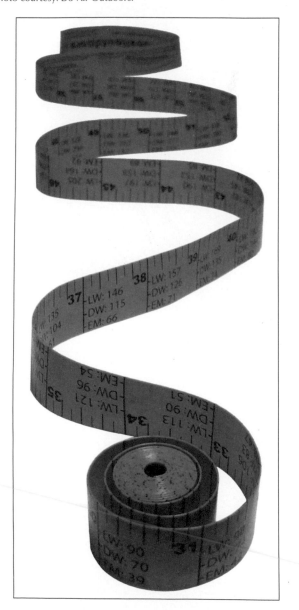

▼ Cody and I took these two bucks in Quebec, Canada. We brought them back to camp to field-dress them and to get accurate live and dressed weights.

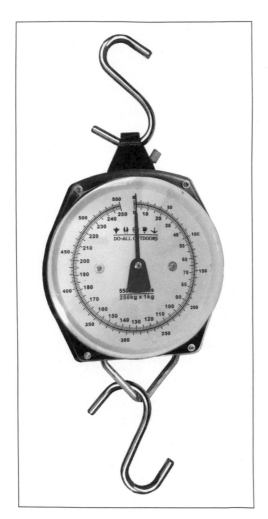

ever environmental factors may be changing the herd's pattern and size.

I am an absolute believer in aging and weighing (both live and dressed weights) all the deer taken on our farm. I feel this information is an integral part of both my management program and my deer hunting skills. Begin aging and weighing your deer this season if for no other reason than to win some bets from your hunting companions who guess the age of the deer harvested through less reliable methods. Knowing how to accurately determine the age and weight of your deer will make your hunting more interesting, your venison more tasty, and will provide you with crucial management information about the deer you hunt. Most importantly, you'll be able to leave the guesswork up to less serious or less dedicated hunters.

The chart below will help you to determine the live weight, field-dressed weight, and the amount of edible lean meat of the next deer you shoot. A quality scale (www.doalloutdoors.com) will provide a more accurate reading, however.

◄ Do-All Outdoors Dead Deer Line of products is useful and reliable. Their scale weighs game to 550 pounds, and it's the most accurate scale I have used. Photo courtesy: Do-All-Outdoors.

CHART #1

FIELD METHOD FOR ESTIMATING A DEER'S WEIGHT			
Chest Circumference	Live Weight	Field-Dressed Weight	Weight of Edible Meat
20"	49 lbs.	36 lbs.	23 lbs.
21"	53	39	24
22"	56	42	26
23"	60	45	28
24"	65	49	30
25"	69	53	31
26"	74	57	34
27"	79	62	36
28"	85	67	38
29"	91	72	41
30	97	77	44
31"	104	83	47
32"	111	90	50
33"	119	97	53
34"	127	104	57
35	136	112	61
36"	145	120	65
37"	156	129	69
38"	166	139	74
39"	178	149	79
40	191	160	85
41"	204	172	90
42"	218	184	97
43"	234	198	103
44"	250	212	110
45	267	228	118
46"	286	244	126

Note: All weights approximate. (Source: Vital Records Measuring Tape)

22. Dead Deer Really Do Talk!

As I have mentioned in previous articles and books, I have kept *detailed* records on all aspects of my deer hunting for more than fifty years. I record any pertinent information I feel will aid me in future hunts. The categories include the usual information hunters should record, such as weather conditions, barometric levels, air temperature, wind direction, mast crop conditions, etc. However, I also believe it is equally important to record *atypical* information.

I record what I feel is some of the most important information after I take a buck. I carefully examine its entire body and enter all pertinent information about the buck (or doe) into the log records. For instance, I look for bodily injuries, oddities in the hooves, broken, chipped, or cracked antlers. I look for the presence of cysts, the condition of the organs (like flukes on the liver), injuries to the penis or testicles, eye injuries, and even the number of the ticks on the deer (not by the actual number, but rather a note saying ticks were light, medium, heavy, or infested). I also look for fresh cuts, healed scars, rips in the ears, torn or partly missing tails, bruised areas, swelling around the eyes, recent archery or firearm wounds, broad-head or bullet fragments, missing teeth, and much more.

Gathering and recording all this information has helped me decipher many of the reasons and even some of the mysteries of my kills. It has also helped me to absolutely identify bucks through an oddity on the hooves, or by an unusual body marking, or a healed injury. Often, the things I find help me deduce some of the less obvious reasons why the buck was killed. In other words, my forensic inspection actually allows the dead deer to talk to me. This is not a new tactic for me. I first wrote about this in 1979 in a magazine article and included a chapter on it in my first book, *Whitetail Strategies—A No-Nonsense Guide to Common Sense Deer Hunting,* in 1990. I mention this so you don't think I copied the "forensic" phrase from one of the many crime shows on television. When a hunter takes the time to vigilantly examine their deer, almost each and every time he or she will gather some piece of previously unseen information. This data may indeed prove useful on future hunts.

I always begin by closely examining the deer's hide. Many years ago, I shot a buck whose hide was almost totally covered with briars. From this I determined that the only place on the farm where the buck could have collected that many burdocks on his hide was in a lone swale filled with an excessively thick patch of burdock. A few days later, I spotted a buck whose

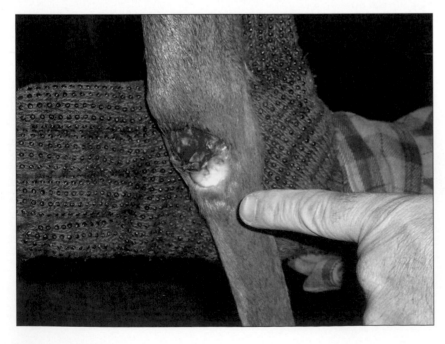

◄ I found a tiny piece of bullet fragment in this wound. It satisfied my curiosity about what caused the injury. It aided me in identifying the buck as one that limped by my stand several days before.

hide was also covered in a lot of burdock. And so, two days later, I shot a big 8-pointer as he emerged from his burdock bedding area in the swale. Back then, it was legal to take a second buck in New York on a deer management permit. The unusual amount of burdock on the back of the first buck revealed the second buck's hiding spot.

Examining a deer internally and externally usually provides important clues, including the current social status of a buck. I was once able to determine that a buck I shot was a dandy 8-point I had seen in a down-and-out fight with another buck. Because their antlers were locked together tightly and they were 100 or more yards from my stand, I couldn't tell what type of antlers either buck had. I did notice that one buck had a tine that looked like it was digging into the skull of the other buck. However, the buck with the antler digging into his head ended up winning the fight. Several days later, I rattled in a buck and shot him. When I examined the buck I found an ugly hole that penetrated deep into the head of the buck at the base of his pedestal. (See the accompanying photo.) This wound absolutely and unquestionably identified the buck as the winner of the fight and the buck I thought had had an antler gouged into his head.

Rack color sometimes indicates where a buck spends the majority of his time. A bleached-out white rack usually suggests that a buck spent a lot of time rubbing off the dry blood after shedding his velvet. It can imply he was living in an area with an excessive amount of sunlight that helped to lighten the color of the antlers. If you happen to scout a buck with a completely white set of antlers, a good place to look for his core bedding area won't include dark cedar swamps or dark patches of evergreens. Bucks that inhabit these types of areas traditionally have racks that are much darker in color than normal. However, like all deer hunting, nothing is written in stone. The exception to a buck's antlers being light or dark also results from the rubbing phenomenon. When a buck rubs excessively, he removes the dark, dried blood from the antlers no matter where he is living. However, most times, he won't rub long or hard enough to give the rack a highly polished, bleached-white look.

An important indicator of where your buck was bedding and feeding comes from the contents of his stom-

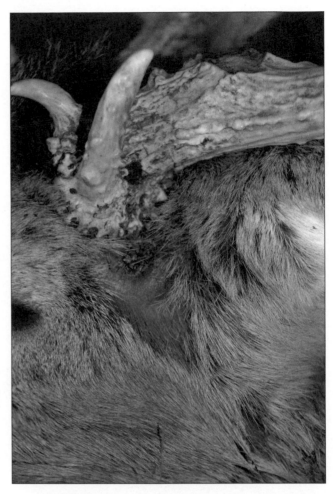

▲ Look closely, and you'll see where the tip of a tine penetrated deeply into this buck's head. I saw the other buck that won the fight just a week before I shot this one.

ach. This is where you separate the men from the boys. After shooting a deer, open the stomach, and examine the contents meticulously. I look at the most digested food particles as well as the mostly undigested food stuffs. Knowing what the buck has recently eaten and what he ate first accurately determines his travel route prior to his demise. Each of the deer's four stomach compartments must be observed when doing this. By examining the stomach contents of killed deer, you will begin a process of learning what routes deer travel during fall and winter and what natural or planted foods they prefer eating during those times of year.

Next, I keenly inspect the deer's hooves. Deer hooves often help to confidently identify a buck I have killed through the uniqueness in his front right hoof. I once chased after one buck nicknamed Mr. Big for the entire 2009 deer season. The buck mesmerized me, and, as a result, I knowingly committed several novice mistakes like hunting the same blind over and over again. A big buck can even make a seasoned veteran like me look like a novice.

Chasing Mr. Big in the 2009 deer season ended with the reality that he had outwitted me. I planned to set my sights on another buck for the 2010 season. On the last day of the muzzle-loading season of 2010, I killed a terrific 13-point buck. His rack looked oddly similar to Mr. Big's, but it was different enough that I didn't give it much thought.

It wasn't until I was examining the 13-pointer's hooves in the barn that I came to realize the buck might very well be Mr. Big. Mr. Big's tracks always left a very unique print from his right front hoof. One toe turned in sharply to the right and the other toe on the hoof had a piece of it missing. In the spring and summer of 2009, I had seen Mr. Big in our fields a few times and because his front print was so odd I took several pictures of it in mud, dirt, and sand. One evening in January 2010, I was driving down my road at 11 PM to plow a friend's driveway. On the way I was shocked to see Mr. Big standing defiantly in the road. We stood staring at each other for several seconds as the huge snowflakes silently fell. Then, without much

▼ We never remove the entrails of a deer in the field. They are hung on the "deer-pole" or in the barn to examine the stomach contents, and the entire body for injuries or anomalies, and record all noteworthy information.

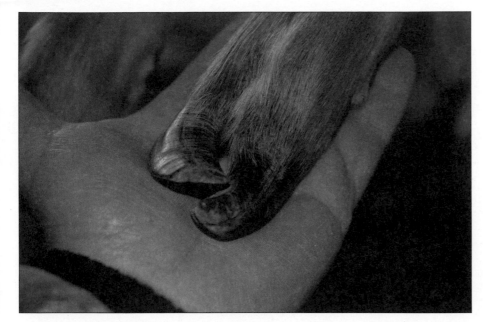

◄ This photo shows the 13-point buck's one toe turned inward and the other with a sizeable chip in it. The same identical characteristics were left by Mr. Big's tracks.

fanfare, Mr. Big walked indifferently into the woods. When I looked at his tracks in the snow, I went back home to get a camera to take some photos of them.

As I looked at the front right hoof of the 13-point buck I killed, I confirmed it had the exact type of peculiarity on his front right hoof that Mr. Big's hoof had. I suspected it would leave an identical print in the ground. I cut off the right leg, took it outside, and with my best effort to imitate a buck placing his hoof into the snow, I pressed the hoof firmly down into the newly fallen snow.

The track looked identical to Mr. Big's prints, so I took a picture of it. I went back into the house and compared the new image to the picture I had taken on that frigidly cold and snowy night ten months earlier. As I carefully compared them, there was no denying that they looked precisely the same.

Then and there, I realized the buck hanging in the barn was Mr. Big. I had finally taken him, albeit by some odd turn of fate. Had I not inspected the 13-point

buck carefully, I would never have imagined it was Mr. Big. Therein lies solid proof of how important and interesting it is to closely examine a taken deer.

Over the forty-eight years I have been studying dead deer, I have had many similar situations where I have garnered information that has led me to kill a buck or discover some other element that has helped my deer hunting tactics. I could have included at least a couple dozen anecdotes. Rather than running on, allow me to assure you that for either dedicated deer managers or regular hunters who want to take their deer hunting skills to the next level, examining dead deer will pay off in big dividends. Make this type of forensic inspection of all deer killed on your land an important part of your management program. It will enhance your overall deer management agenda and the information will be "golden." Plan to start thoroughly examining the deer you kill next season and you will discover for yourself that "dead deer do indeed talk." *You can take that to the deer-hunting bank.*

Seed Company Sources

Companies that include an asterisk before them are those I have had personal experience with buying and planting their seeds. I can vouch for the reliability of their products.

Agassiz Seed Company
1-701-282-8118
www.agassizseed.com

Antler King
1-888-268-5371
www.antlerking.com

BioLogic
662-495-9292
661-494-8859
www.mossyoakbiologic.com
www.plantbiologic.com

*BuckLunch
888-373-0667
www.BuckLunch.com

Cooper Seed Co.
877-463-6697
www.cooperseeds.com

Edward Fort Nurseries (Trees)
866-295-8733
info@edwardfortnurseries.com

Elk Mound Seed Company
800-401-SEED
www.elkmoundseed.com

Ferry-Morse Seed Company
800-626-3392
www.ferry-morse.com
sales@ferry-morse.com

Frigid Forage
218-759-4656
sales@sunrichfarm.com
www.sunrichfarm.com

*Hunter's Specialties
319-395-0321
website@hunterspec.com
www.hunterspec.com

National Wild Turkey Federation (NWTF)
800-THE-NWTF
www.nwtf.com

Pennington Seeds
800-285-7333
www.penningtonseed.com

*Preferred Seed Company
716-895-7333
Info@preferredseed.com
www.preferredseed.com

Purina Mills
800-227-8941
877-454-7094 x5167
robert.echele@purinamills.com
www.deerchow.com

Quail Unlimited
803-637-5732
www.qu.org

▼ To round out any food plot plan, managers should always include a percentage of the overall food plots to warm-season clovers, particularly if the program is based in the south.

Record Rack TM
800-392-5757
www.record-rack.com

Ruffed Grouse Society
412-262-4044
www.ruffedgrousesociety.org

Seedland, Inc.
888-820-2080
sales@seedland.com
www.seedland.com

Tecomate
800-332-4054
888-440-9108
brentmcaliley@bellsouth.net
www.tecomate.com

*Welter Seed & Honey Company
800-470-3325
www.welterseed.com

*Whitetail Management System–Quaker Boy
800-544-1600
www.quakerboygamecalls.com

*Whitetail Institute of North America
800-688-3030
info@whitetailinstitute.com
www.whitetailinstitute.com

The Wildlife Group
800-221-9703
wildlifegroup@mindspring.com
www.wildlifegroup.com

Wildlife Nurseries, Inc.
920-231-3780

*Wildlife Perfect Seed
541-928-1651
www.wildlifeperfect.com

Glossary of Terms

Acidic: Soil with a pH level below 7 is considered acidic. A pH scale measures soil chemistry from a range of 0 to 14. The optimum pH range for most plants is between 6 and 7.5.

Alkaline: On a pH scale of soil chemistry ranging from 0 to 14, soil that has a pH level above 7.0 is considered alkaline.

Annual: An annual plant usually germinates flowers, and dies within a year or season. Annuals generally live longer if they are prevented from setting seed.

▲ Arrowleaf clover is an annual legume that partners well with small grains. Photo courtesy: Cooper Seeds.

Bole: Another word used to describe the trunk of a tree.

Bonehead: A term of endearment coined by Peter Fiduccia, a.k.a. the Deer Doctor, to describe any big game hunter who is passionately preoccupied with deer antlers to the point of being zealous or fanatical. Boneheads are completely unashamed of their obsession, and often will constantly express their views. Sometimes they are insufferable.

▲ The author's cousin Leo Somma with a dandy 10-point Canadian buck.

Broadcast Spreader: Any spreader or seeder, mechanical or used by hand, to dispense seed, fertilizer, or lime by spreading it indiscriminately onto a prepared food plot bed or ground.

▲ Here, a push-broadcast spreader is used to plant an acre with sunflower seeds. Photo courtesy: Chapin Intl.

Brush Hog: A brand name used to describe a rotary cutter pulled behind a tractor or ATV to cut 1- to 3-inch saplings, brush, bushes, weeds, and other natural undergrowth.

▲ The author uses a brush-hog to mow a clover field.

Carrying Capacity: The number of animals a particular habitat can realistically support without harm to either the species or the habitat.

▲ This corn field improved the overall habitat, keeping deer numbers healthy. Photo courtesy: T. Rose.

Chisel Plow: An implement used for the shallow plowing of soil.

Create the Entire Illusion: A slogan originated by Peter Fiduccia, a.k.a. the Deer Doctor. By applying this hypothesis to any or all strategies, hunters will increase their deer hunting success tenfold.

▲ The author with a terrific NY buck shot in a food plot along an "inside corner."

Cultipacker: An implement used after disking to press small seeds tightly into the soil's surface in order to create better seed-to-soil contact.

▲ The author's son (Cody) compacting a plot of sugar beets.

Cultivator: A piece of equipment designed to disturb the surface soil. Most often used for weed control between row crops such as sorghum, corn, and other grains.

Dibble: Also called a "planting bar." A shovel-like hand tool with a beveled arrow pointed head, used to open narrow slots in the ground in the planting of conifers and other small 5" to 18" trees and shrubs.

Disk Harrow: An implement used to loosen or break up furrows of plowed ground using several round, thin, steel-plated wheels with sharp or serrated edges.

▲ Cody disking a 2-acre field to plant forage rape in.

Dormancy: A period when a plant's growth, development, and activity are temporarily stopped. This minimizes metabolic activity and helps plant life, as resting and not actively growing will conserve energy.

Dwarf Species: A smaller size description of a plant or tree. Most often used in reference to fruit trees, some hardwoods, and plants like sunflower, corn, and sorghum.

Fertilizer: Three elements (nitrogen, phosphorus, and potassium, most often referred to as NPK) blended together in different percentages in accordance with the needs of different plantings.

▲ Push broadcast spreaders can be used to spread seed, fertilizer, or lime.

Fixation: The ability of clovers and other legume plants to extract nitrogen from the air and attach it to the root nodules for the plant's use eliminates the need for fertilizers with high nitrogen content.

Forage Brassicas: An annual plant usually germinates flowers, and dies within a year or season. Annuals

generally live longer if they are prevented from setting seed.

▲ Swede is my favorite plant of all the different of brassicas. Deer start to eat the leaves and bulbs usually by mid-November, making Swede a perfect plot to hunt over. The photo was taken in late September.

Forb: An herb other than grass.

Grains: A cereal crop including wheat, triticale, oats, barley, rye, sorghum, and corn. Most grains have relatively small seeds and/or kernels.

▲ Rye (*Secale cereale*) is a nutritious small grain providing 10 to 25 percent levels of protein.

Gravity Spreader: A device pulled behind an ATV or tractor to scatter seed, fertilizer, or lime in consistent application depending on the width of the spreader.

Hand Spreader: A shoulder-bag or hand-held cloth and plastic device used to uniformly dispense small amounts of seed or fertilizer by using a hand-crank. Most often used in small food plots.

Herbicide: Chemical solutions used to kill unwanted vegetation. Some herbicides are specifically designed to target only grass or broadleaf plants and they do not affect other plantings. Other herbicides are designed as "non-selective" and they kill all plant growth, sometimes leaving the area barren for long periods of time. The emergent herbicides kill foliage by burning the tops that have emerged through the soil. Pre-emergent herbicides kill the seeds and prevent them from germinating. Some herbicides are systemic and pass through the stem and root of the plant, thereby killing it.

▲ Pronto Big N' Tuf is an affordable herbicide that kills both grass and weeds.

▲ Hand spreaders prevent damaging newly growing plants that tractor wheels often kill.

Herb: A seed-producing annual, biannual, or perennial that does not develop persistent woody tissue but dies down at the end of a growing season.

▲ Chicory provides 10 to about 30 percent levels of protein.

Herbivore: An animal that eats plant life almost exclusively.

▲ All ruminant mammals of the family of Cervidae (including moose, caribou, elk, and deer) are herbivores. Photo courtesy: T. Rose.

Idle Land: Sections of a dormant land that is currently uncultivated or used.

▲ This field was left idle for a year in order to raise its pH levels significantly higher.

Inoculants: The most commonly used soil inoculants are rhizobacteria that live symbiotically with clovers and other legumes like peas, beans, etc. The bacteria live within specialized nodules on the root systems of clovers and other legumes, where they process atmospheric nitrogen into a form available for the plants to use. Soil inoculants are mycorrhizal fungi that attach to the roots of plant species to help conduct water and nutrients for the plant's use.

▲ The author adds water to Rhizobium bacteria (strain H) to properly inoculate the lupine seed shown here.

Junk-wood Trees: Less desirable tree species that have little to no wildlife or commercial value.

▲ Professional forester Mark Decker sprayed the less desirable trees to identify which timber we should remove to improve our woods.

Legumes: Any legume of the genus Trifolium, composed of 300 or more annual and perennial species that have trifoliate leaves and flowers in dense heads. Clovers are highly palatable to deer and high in protein, phosphorus, and calcium, providing valuable nourishment.

▲ Red clover is a terrific companion with ladino, and/or arrowleaf clovers. I also plant it with my two favorite small grains, rye and triticale.

No-Till Planting: A technique of planting used when the ground is not plowed or tilled. A seeding machine, usually with a compactor attached, is pulled behind an ATV or tractor and dispenses seeds through slots that open at different measurements. It then compacts the seed to improve seed-to-soil contact.

NRCS (Natural Resource Conservation Service): A government department that provides helpful information and aerial and topographical maps to landowners.

Omnivore: An animal that eats both plant and animal life.

One-Point Hitch: A ball mounted on a bar extension at the rear of an ATV or tractor to make it possible to attach the receiver to a pull-behind planting or other type of implement.

Over-Seeding: A term more commonly referred to as top-seeding. Over-seeding is most often used to plant tiny seeds like turnips, clovers, and small grains, that are either broadcast by a hand-held, mechanical, or shoulder-mounted seeder. Over-seeding is also a technique used to place small seeds over the top of a thinning or existing crop, and sometimes on top of snow-covered ground in the winter.

Perennial: Plant life that continues to remain active, growing, and healthy from one year to the next.

▲ This is a plot of Kura clover on our land. Kura is extremely winter-hardy.

Pesticide: A chemical solution that is used to kill insects that are harmful to plants in either their larval or adult stages.

Plow: An implement used to turn over soil or sod to a depth of from 4 to 12 inches. Often used singly or as a one-bottom, two-bottom, or more plow.

PTO: A power-take-off device most often located on the rear of tractors. It is designed as a rotating gear shaft driven by the engine speed and used to transmit power via a driveshaft to a pull-behind implement such as a seed spreader, mower, or brush-hog.

QDM (Quality Deer Management): The knowledgeable practice of implementing wildlife and habitat management programs to promote healthier game and better land stewardship.

▲ As a sign of commitment to the Quality Deer Management Association (QDMA), this sign hangs prominently in my barn.

Rhizome: The lateral, underground roots extending from a plant that allow a plant species to reproduce.

Sanctuary: A sanctuary is more appropriately referred to as a *refuge* when related to deer and wildlife management. A sanctuary is a dedicated piece of ground created by the landowner to provide deer and other wildlife an absolute safe haven, or refuge. By extension, the term has come to be used for any place of total and unlimited safety—not to be entered into or trespassed on for any reason.

Scarification: Seeds with hard coats may need to be scarified, a process in which the seed coat is modified in some way so that moisture can enter and allow germination to begin.

Share-Cropping: A cooperative planting effort between a landowner and a farmer. The farmer provides the equipment, labor, and supplies to plant the agreed-upon crop or crops within a specific amount of acreage.

Sheet Water: Also referred to as standing water, sheet water is on the ground's surface and is permanent, such as a pond, lake, or stream.

Soil Test Sample: A small, representative amount of soil taken from several areas of an intended planting location. The sample is sent to a lab to determine the current pH readings in order to determine the type of fertilizer and lime required to raise or lower the pH levels to successfully grow a specified plant species within the tested plot.

▲ These are the tools the author uses to collect soil samples on his land.

Sprayer: A steel or plastic tank filled with herbicide or pesticide to apply to food plots or to eliminate unwanted brush and other growth. Tanks holding twenty-five to fifty gallons or more can be mounted at the rear of an ATV or tractor and used with a widespread "boom-arm" with several spray nozzles. Smaller tanks holding up to three gallons can be worn on the back to dispense chemical solutions via a handheld metal wand with a single spray nozzle.

▲ My wife, Kate, applying herbicide with a sprayer to kill grass and weeds in this plot.

▲ The author uses a three-point spreader to apply fertilizer to this clover plot.

SWCD (Soil & Water Conservation District): A government department that advises landowners and provides topographic maps and aerial photos of tracts of land in each county.

Take It to the Deer-Hunting Bank: A catchphrase coined by Peter Fiduccia, a.k.a. the Deer Doctor, to illustrate a particular piece of advice believed by him to be *exceptional;* therefore, it should be stored in a deer hunter's strategy *"vault"* for future success.

Three-Point Hitch: Generally found at the back of a tractor or an ATV. It is attached to a pull-behind planting or other implement via two side-arms, one to either side, to stabilize a heavier implement and prevent side-swaying.

Three-Point Spreader: A cone-shaped metal or plastic implement mounted on a tractor or ATV to uniformly spread seed, fertilizer, and lime on the ground via a spinning disk operated by a PTO.

Wetland: Any ground that remains totally or partially covered with water for much of the year and attracts wildlife, particularly waterfowl, turtles, amphibians, and the like.

Windbreak: Generally a straight planting of evergreen and other trees planted tightly next to one another to allow their branches or year-round leaves to block prevailing winds, usually from the north or west. The windbreak protects structures, food plot plantings, young trees, etc., from strong gusting wind, driving rain, sleet, or blowing snow.

A row of pines used as a windbreak to protect the plantings in the food plots below them.

Index